HEALTH CARE ISSUES, COSTS AND ACCESS

MEDICAL MALPRACTICE

CONSIDERATIONS AND PROPOSALS

HEALTH CARE ISSUES, COSTS AND ACCESS

Additional books in this series can be found on Nova's website
under the Series tab.

Additional E-books in this series can be found on Nova's website
under the E-book tab.

HEALTH CARE ISSUES, COSTS AND ACCESS

MEDICAL MALPRACTICE

CONSIDERATIONS AND PROPOSALS

VINCENT BRASWELL
AND
DON MCCLOUD
EDITORS

Nova Science Publishers, Inc.
New York

For permission to use material from this book please contact us:
Telephone 631-231-7269; Fax 631-231-8175
Web Site: http://www.novapublishers.com

Additional color graphics may be available in the e-book version of this book.

Library of Congress Cataloging-in-Publication Data

ISBN: 978-1-61942-141-7

Published by Nova Science Publishers, Inc. † New York

CONTENTS

PREFACE

This book presents background and an examination of the issues before Congress as it relates to medical malpractice with a focus on the economic issues and historical experience.

Chapter 1 - Medical malpractice presents challenges for policy makers, physician/provider purchasers of insurance, and companies offering professional liability insurance covering medical providers as it is buffeted by three distinct, uncoordinated, policy drivers: the health care system, the legal system, and the insurance system. While instances of medical malpractice arise within the health care system, determinations of fault and the assessment of monetary damages are made through the tort system, and damages are paid through the insurance system, which distributes costs across the pool of insured providers. Health care providers experience most of the cost through the insurance system. Because of the complexity of the interactions between these three systems, policy changes in one area may have unanticipated consequences in another area. For example, quality improvements in the health care system could result in fewer instances of medical malpractice, but if other circumstances change in the tort or insurance systems, the premiums paid by providers for medical malpractice liability insurance could still increase.

Chapter 2 - As a policy area, medical malpractice involves issues related to its prevalence in the health care system, the market for provider liability insurance, and the resolution of malpractice complaints through the tort system.

Medical malpractice has attracted congressional attention numerous times over the past decades, particularly in the midst of three "crisis" periods for the liability insurance market in the mid-1970s, the mid-1980s, and the early 2000s. These periods were marked by sharp increases in medical liability insurance premiums, difficulties in finding any insurance in some areas as insurers withdrew from providing coverage, reports of providers leaving areas or retiring following insurance difficulties, and a variety of public policy measures at both the state and federal levels to address these historic crises. Which public policy measures have been effective in addressing the difficulties in the medical malpractice liability market has been a matter of debate, in part because these difficulties have been at the intersection of the health care, tort, and insurance systems.

Chapter 3 - Insurance is a critical piece of a modern economic system, but it often goes unnoticed until it becomes prohibitively expensive or its availability is curtailed. Such problems occurred in the medical malpractice liability insurance market most recently in the early part of the 2000s. Many physicians experienced substantial increases in insurance premiums, and there were reports of problems with availability of physician services due to doctors retiring or relocating from areas that had seen high premium increases. This was not the first time such a crisis has been proclaimed; similar events occurred in the latter half of both the 1970s and 1980s. In the latter half of this decade, overall losses for medical malpractice insurance have dropped and premiums have moderated. Public discussion of medical malpractice has lessened as well.

Chapter 4 - Medical malpractice liability is governed by state law, but Congress has the power, under the Commerce Clause of the U.S. Constitution (Art. I, § 8, cl. 3), to enact tort reform laws that would affect actions for medical malpractice liability brought under state law. In the 112th Congress, H.R. 5, the Help Efficient, Accessible, Low-cost, Timely Healthcare (HEALTH) Act was introduced by Representative Phil Gingrey on January 24, 2011, and was marked up on February 9 and 16, 2011, by the House Committee on the Judiciary. This bill would preempt state law with respect to certain aspects of medical malpractice lawsuits. Past Congresses have considered similar measures.

In: Medical Malpractice: Considerations and Proposals
Editors: Vincent Braswell and Don Mccloud ISBN: 978-1-61942-141-7

Chapter 1

MEDICAL MALPRACTICE: BACKGROUND AND EXAMINATION OF THE ISSUES BEFORE CONGRESS

David Newman, Vivian S. Chu and Baird Webel

SUMMARY

Medical malpractice presents challenges for policy makers, physician/provider purchasers of insurance, and companies offering professional liability insurance covering medical providers as it is buffeted by three distinct, uncoordinated, policy drivers: the health care system, the legal system, and the insurance system. While instances of medical malpractice arise within the health care system, determinations of fault and the assessment of monetary damages are made through the tort system, and damages are paid through the insurance system, which distributes costs across the pool of insured providers. Health care providers experience most of the cost through the insurance system. Because of the complexity of the interactions between these three systems, policy changes in one area may have unanticipated consequences in another area. For example, quality improvements in the health care system could result in fewer instances of medical malpractice, but if other circumstances change in the tort or insurance systems, the premiums paid by providers for medical malpractice liability insurance could still increase.

From 1997 to 2006 nationwide direct premiums earned among medical professional liability insurers increased, and have fallen slightly since the 2006 peak. Losses and costs (direct defense and cost containment expenses) peaked in 2003 and have since fallen over 45%. The loss ratio for medical professional liability insurers (losses and costs divided by direct earned premiums) peaked in 2001 and has been declining since. The improving situation since the mid 2000s nationally, however, masks continuing problems in some states and among some specialties. For instance, in Pittsburgh, malpractice premiums for physicians have increased an average of 8.5% annually since 2000—exceeding medical and general price inflation.

The topic of medical malpractice is contentious, with many individuals holding strong views. The current system, which refers claims of medical malpractice to the judicial system, has both positive and negative attributes. Because medical errors do occur, the primary question for policy makers is how to deal with these errors.

While there are numerous tort reform proposals, summary studies, including one by the Medicare Payment Advisory Commission (MedPAC), have shown that many reform proposals are likely to have a limited impact on premiums, lawsuits, or awards, among other things. Other reform proposals, such as health courts, remain untested. One reform proposal that does have a track record in reducing malpractice payments, among other things, in some states is caps on noneconomic damages. Legislation that would implement such caps nationally, H.R. 5, has been reported by the House Judiciary Committee and the House Energy and Commerce Committee.

INTRODUCTION

Medical malpractice presents challenges for policy makers, physician/provider purchasers of insurance, and companies offering professional liability insurance covering medical providers.[1] Medical malpractice is buffeted by three distinct, uncoordinated, policy drivers: the health care system, the insurance system, and the legal system. While instances of medical malpractice arise within the health care system, determinations of fault and the assessment of monetary damages are made through the tort system;[2] most of the direct costs of the system to health care providers are experienced through the insurance system, which distributes costs across the pool of insured providers. Because of the complexity of the interactions between these three systems, policy changes in one area may have unanticipated consequences in another. For example, quality improvements in the health care system could result in fewer instances of medical malpractice, but if other circumstances change in the tort or insurance systems, such as an increase in the cost of capital for insurance companies or an increase in amounts awarded in the tort system for medical malpractice claims,[3] the premiums paid by providers for medical malpractice liability insurance still might increase.[4]

Depending on how one counts, the nation is perceived by some to be in the midst of its third modern medical malpractice crisis and at least the fourth in the past 225 years.[5] The first medical malpractice crisis occurred from 1835 through 1865, and that crisis confronted many of the same issues raised in the more recent crises, including but not limited to the number of lawsuits, the proper role of expert testimony, a lack of trust in lay juries, the perception that plaintiffs' attorneys can sway the emotions of jurors, the need for specialized judges knowledgeable in medicine, the size of jury awards, the tendency to sue those with "deep pockets," the appropriate standard of care, the relationship between malpractice suits and quality improvement, and the impact of malpractice suits on future access to care.[6] The three modern crises date from the 1970s, 1980s, and late 1990s.[7] Perhaps the most significant difference between the first crisis and modern crises was the historical absence of malpractice insurance.[8]

A malpractice crisis is often characterized as having several key components, of varying importance over time, but including [9]

- increasing medical liability premiums for providers;
- a lack of available or affordable insurance for some providers or specialties or in some locations;
- the cost of defensive medicine undertaken to avoid or minimize potential liability;
- excessive jury awards for legitimate medical malpractice claims and jury awards for questionable claims; and
- the impact of physicians and other providers leaving the field of medicine or moving to a more provider-friendly locality due to either malpractice costs or the perceived risks of malpractice liability.

These adverse characteristics, when evident, can be detrimental to the nation's health care system.

It is undisputed that medical errors occur. The Office of the Inspector General of the Department of Health and Human Services recently found that 13.5% of hospitalized Medicare beneficiaries experienced adverse events during their hospital stays, including 1% experiencing a hospital-acquired infection and 1.5% experiencing an event that contributed to their deaths.[10] Physician reviewers determined that 44% of these events were *clearly* or *likely* preventable.[11] In 2006, the Institute of Medicine (IOM) reported there were "1.5 million medication errors costing $3.5 billion a year in extra medical costs, including 400,000 preventable drug-related injuries in hospitals, 800,000 in long-term care settings, and roughly 530,000 among Medicare beneficiaries in outpatient clinics."[12] A 2000 IOM study estimated that between 44,000 and 98,000 Americans die each year from medical errors, and that preventable adverse events in hospitals were estimated to be the seventh most common cause of death.[13] While these errors occur, only some are likely to be preventable and only some of the preventable errors are due to negligence.

While the legal system is one environment in which liability for negligent acts may be resolved, it is not the only system that can deal with these sorts of errors. In addition, even if one concludes that the tort system is the appropriate place to resolve such claims, this does not necessarily imply that the current tort system cannot be improved. Both the current tort system, and any potential substitute, can be assessed on a variety of criteria, including the following:

- How well does it encourage safe behavior and improve quality of care?
- How well does it identify poor performers and create incentives, either market-based or regulatory (which can include professional peer review), for poor performers to improve their performance or to leave the market?
- How well does it identify truly injured parties, as contrasted to non-injured parties?
- How quickly and efficiently (low administrative costs) are injured parties properly compensated?

Unfortunately for those seeking simple answers to these complex questions, the evidence on key issues, such as the scope of the malpractice crisis and its causes, the extent and cost of defensive medicine, the impact of alternative reform proposals, and potential savings from reform, is, as discussed below, often contradictory or lacking.

A key question for policy makers going forward is how to deal with medical errors in an efficient manner that encourages safe behavior, maintains or improves quality of medical care, and appropriately compensates injured individuals without unduly burdening the health care system. This report is intended to provide a grounding in the various policy aspects of medical malpractice and develop a framework for evaluating alternative proposals. While potential liability for medical malpractice can affect all health care providers, including hospitals, non-physician providers such as nurses and physicians assistants, pharmacists, and pharmaceutical companies, among others, the focus of most of the academic literature has been on physicians. While one can make inferences from the academic literature on physicians to other providers, the primary focus of this report is on physicians.

LEGAL BASICS OF MEDICAL MALPRACTICE

Most claims for medical malpractice are torts brought under a theory of negligence. This section first provides some background on the basics of tort liability, with a particular focus on liability based on negligence. Second, it examines some common law concepts that are the basis for many tort reform initiatives. These are statutes of limitations, damages, the doctrine of joint and several liability, and the collateral source rule.

Generally, a tort is a private or civil wrong, other than breach of contract, for which a court may provide a remedy in the form of an action for damages.[14] In other words, the tort system acts as a mechanism through which an individual who has suffered an injury or incurred damages caused by an act or omission of another—a tortfeasor (the alleged wrongdoer)—can seek compensation in court from that tortfeasor. Tort law has its roots in the common law (i.e., judge-made law).[15]

States, over time, have passed statutes that codify the common law and sometimes change tort law. These changes may affect the availability and amount of remedies for a particular injury. Therefore, when a plaintiff brings an action against a tortfeasor, the laws or court decisions of a state will govern the action.

The aims of tort law can be generally identified as (1) the maintenance of a self-help mechanism that victims and their relatives and friends can avail themselves of, (2) retribution against wrongdoers, (3) deterrence of wrongdoers, and (4) compensation for the victims of wrongdoers.[16]

Over time, courts have come to recognize that in the realm of torts there "exists a spectrum of culpability."[17] Most plaintiffs seeking recovery bring their tort suits based on a theory of negligence, which is generally acknowledged as "conduct which falls below the standard established by law for the protection of others against unreasonable risk of harm."[18] Broadly speaking, in a tort action for negligence, a plaintiff needs to prove by the preponderance of the evidence that the defendant had a legal duty to the plaintiff, that the defendant breached this duty, and that such action or omission to act was the actual and/or proximate cause of the plaintiff's injuries.

A plaintiff must show negligent conduct, or the breach of duty, by establishing that the tortfeasor failed to use such care as a reasonably prudent and careful person would use under similar circumstances.[19] This standard is generally considered ordinary negligence, in contrast to gross negligence, which is defined as "the intentional failure to perform a manifest duty in reckless disregard of the consequences as affecting the life or property of another."[20] The prevailing view is that there are no "degrees" of care in negligence, only different amounts of care as a matter of fact; for purposes of this discussion, however, "ordinary" negligence is "based on the fact that one ought to have known [the] results of his act."[21] In contrast, gross negligence "rests on the assumption that one knew the results of his act, but was recklessly or wantonly indifferent to the results."[22] Furthermore, an action based on negligence is different than an action based on strict liability, in which the defendant is held liable without a finding of fault, so long as the plaintiff can establish that the tort occurred and that the defendant was responsible.[23]

Because the standard of care has come to include various concepts against which a defendant should be judged, such as whether the defendant exercised "ordinary care and skill" of a reasonable person, what the defendant "knew or should have known," and the foreseeability of the incident, Judge Learned Hand crafted a test in an algebraic formula to capture these various factors in a way that courts could use them in decision making. In *United States v. Carroll Towing Co.*,[24] Judge Hand wrote what has become known as the *Learned Hand test*:

> Since there are occasions when every vessel will break from her moorings, and since, if she does, she becomes a menace to those about her; the owner's duty, as in other similar situations, to provide against resulting injuries is a function of three variables: (1) The probability that she will break away; (2) the gravity of the resulting injury, if she does; (3) the burden of adequate precautions. Possibly it serves to bring this notion into relief to state it in algebraic terms: if the probability be called P; the injury, L; and the burden, B; liability depends upon whether B is less than L multiplied by P: i.e., whether B < PL.

Text Box 1. Ford Pinto Negligence Case

Well-known cases such as the Ford Pinto or McDonald's hot coffee incident provide examples of how these calculations are to be performed. In the Ford Pinto case,[28] Ford designed the Pinto with the gasoline tank behind the rear axle—a location that had a higher probability of resulting in a fire in the event of a rear-end accident.[29] At trial, there was testimony that Ford engaged in a cost-benefit calculation and concluded that a reengineered gasoline tank would cost roughly $11.00 per vehicle, or $137 million across all vehicles sold, while the benefit of a safer gasoline tank was just $49.5 million (assuming 180 deaths at $200,000 per death and 180 serious burns at $67,000 per serious burn case). Ford's estimate of the potential costs to include a reengineered gasoline tank exceeded its estimate of the potential benefit, and it opted not to incorporate a safer gasoline tank in the car.

At trial, evidence was entered into the record suggesting that the cost to "fix" the gasoline tank was actually less and the benefits higher, since the jury valued the claimant's life and injury higher than Ford. Therefore, Ford was found negligent for not engaging in adequate precautions. The jury's decision suggests that it believed Ford should have valued the prospect of loss of life higher than it did when making safety decisions, and its decision also signaled additional information on how society values injuries and deaths so others engaged in risky activities can avoid negligence claims in the future.[30]

Thus, a "reasonable person" would compare the costs of avoiding an accident with the costs of the accident. As long as the costs of avoiding the accident are lower than the potential costs of the accident, "the failure to take precaution that would avoid the injury is negligence, for the reasonable person will spend the money necessary to avoid the injury."[25] In other words, this formula directs individuals to engage in a cost-benefit calculation balancing the costs of avoiding a loss against the cost and probability of a loss.[26] Although critics may find the *Learned Hand test* distasteful since it forces one to place value on difficult-to-value attributes, such as life, loss of limbs, or loss of consortium, and ultimately reduces difficult discussions to dollars and cents, in the view of others, it simply formalizes "what has been negligence since negligence was first adopted."[27]

MEDICAL MALPRACTICE

Most medical malpractice claims are brought under a theory of negligence, which, as discussed above, has developed to "encompass a wide range of activities ... and it adjusts its standards to those varieties of conduct, including professional activities."[31] On a fundamental level, an action for medical malpractice is generally a claim against a provider of health care for injuries or loss incurred as a result of the provider's failure to adhere to the current and applicable standards of care. If a court determines that the health care provider's conduct did not meet the applicable standard of care, then the health care provider will be held legally responsible. Accordingly, to hold a provider legally liable and to recover damages, the plaintiff must prove the four elements of a negligence case: (1) a duty of care, (2) violation of the standard of care, (3) causation (that the injury was caused by the substandard conduct), and (4) compensable injuries.[32]

In medical malpractice, the duty of care generally arises out of contract law, express or implied,[33] where the medical provider agrees to treat the patient with proper professional skill. Second, for negligence to arise, the plaintiff must establish that the provider breached the duty of care or did not provide a professional standard of care.[34] Courts had struggled with whether a physician would be held to a "national" or "local" standard of care with respect to their conduct.[35] With the standardization of medical training and advances in communication and technologies, among other things, a majority of states use some form of a national standard while adopting some "locality" features concerning the use of expert testimony.[36] Thus, a physician will generally be under a duty "to use that degree of care and skill which is expected of a reasonably competent practitioner in the same class to which he belongs, acting in the same or similar circumstances."[37]

It is important to note that not all injuries necessarily give rise to successful negligence claims.[38] A cause of action for negligence also requires the plaintiff to demonstrate that a provider's negligent conduct was an actual or proximate cause of his injuries in order to maintain an action for malpractice. For example, in *Paige v. Manuzak*,[39] the court refused to hold a hospital liable for negligently administering penicillin post-operatively to an allergic patient because there was no evidence that the plaintiff's subsequent complications were proximately caused by the negligent use of the drug.

Text Box 2. Key Legal Concepts

Statutes of Limitation—historically, absent a statute, a lawsuit could be brought at any time by one party against another. Today, for various causes of action, state legislatures have enacted statutes of limitation, which generally "limit the time within which an action must be brought."[40] Statutes of limitation are generally viewed as necessary to avoid stale or dated claims and, more importantly in the present context, to allow "prospective defendants to better estimate their legal obligations and cap their liability."[41] Generally, a shorter statute of limitations would allow insurers to limit their potential losses due to claims and "more accurately account and reserve for any potential claims," whereas a longer statute of limitation would favor claimants.

Damages—are defined as the compensation the law will allow for an injury.[42] Usually, the term *damages* is modified to better characterize the loss being compensated for and can include *economic damages*, *noneconomic damages*, and *punitive damages*. The term *compensatory damages* includes both economic and noneconomic damages, and *punitive damages* may also be called *exemplary damages*.

- **Economic damages**—relate to monetary losses that result from an injury, such as medical expenses, lost wages, and rehabilitation costs. Generally, these are awarded to replace the loss caused by the wrong or injury. Economic damages are relatively objective, easily monetarized, and calculable.
- **Noneconomic damages**—are often defined in statutes and are viewed as somewhat subjective, non-monetary, intangible losses that are not precisely calculable. These can include pain and suffering, mental and emotional anguish, inconvenience, lost of consortium or companionship, physical impairment, and disfigurement.[43] Determining the amount of noneconomic damages is traditionally subject to broad discretion on the part of juries, which must attempt to equate two variables—money and suffering. State efforts at malpractice reform have focused, in part, on capping noneconomic damage awards. The effect of these efforts are reviewed below.
- **Punitive damages**—(also called exemplary damages) while awarded to plaintiffs, are intended to punish and deter particularly egregious conduct on the part of the defendant. Although punitive damages are also noneconomic by nature, state statutes that impose caps on punitive damages usually treat them separately from caps on noneconomic damages.

Joint and several liability—a common-law rule that, if more than one defendant is found liable for a plaintiff's injuries, then each defendant may be held 100% liable. Any defendant who pays more than its share of the damages is entitled to seek contribution from other liable defendants. The historical argument in favor of the rule is one of fairness—"Who should suffer, the innocent victim or one of the wrongdoers who can afford to pay?"[44] Alternatively, under comparative negligence, a defendant is only responsible for the damages caused by the defendant's negligence.

(Continued)

Collateral source rule—a common-law rule that allows an injured party to recover damages from the defendant even if he or she is also entitled to receive them from a third party.[45] Common third parties, that is, collateral sources, include a health insurance company, an employer, the government, and a wage continuation plan or pension benefits. For example, an injured party could recover from both a health insurer and the defendant without having the award for damages from the tort suit offset or reduced by the amount collected from the health insurer. Abolishing the collateral source rule would allow (or require) courts to reduce damages by the amounts a plaintiff receives or is entitled to receive from collateral sources.

Subrogation—is "[t]he principle under which an insurer that has paid a loss under an insurance policy is entitled to all the rights and remedies belonging to the insured against a third party with respect to any loss covered by the policy."[46] For example, if a Medicare beneficiary is injured by another party in a car accident, the Medicare program is entitled to recover any medical expenses it has paid on behalf of the Medicare beneficiary if the Medicare beneficiary is reimbursed for medical expenses by the other party's insurer as part of any settlement.

What Is Known about Medical Malpractice?

Because of the variety of studies and viewpoints that exist in the debate surrounding medical liability reform, this section attempts to identify what is known about medical malpractice. In particular, this covers (1) the number and frequency of suits, (2) the cost of awards, (3) the underwriting cycle, (4) the cost of malpractice insurance, (5) the costs of defensive medicine, and (6) the efficiency of the tort system. This section principally addresses physicians because most of the academic research has focused on physicians. This section concludes with a brief discussion of what is known about physicians' perceptions of malpractice risk and the randomness of being subject to a malpractice law suit.

Number and Frequency of Suits

In 2009, it is estimated that there were 10,739 paid medical malpractice claims in the United States—29.5% fewer than in 2003.[47] Some of these claims were settled and paid without a trial. Paid claims represented only a part of total claims; in fact, most claims were either dropped or resolved through litigation in which the defendant provider was not found liable. At least one study found that in roughly 80% of the cases that went to trial, the alleged wrongdoer in a medical malpractice case was exonerated.[48] Table 1 shows the percentage change in the number of paid medical malpractice claims between 2003 and 2009 by state. Only two states, Massachusetts and New Mexico, experienced an increase in the number of paid claims. Six states—Connecticut, Delaware, Indiana, Kentucky, Ohio, and Texas—and the District of Columbia experienced a 50% or greater percentage decline in paid claims.

There is also considerable variation across states in the number of paid claims per 100,000 population (Table 1). In 2009, there was less than one case per 100,000 population in Alabama. This is contrasted to states like New Jersey, Pennsylvania, and New York, with rates of six cases or more per 100,000 population.[49]

The Department of Justice, Bureau of Justice Statistics, reported that in "2005 an estimated 2,449 medical malpractice cases were disposed of by trial in state courts of general jurisdiction throughout the country with plaintiffs prevailing in less than a quarter of trials."[50] In federal court, there were about 2,728 cases filed in 2009.[51] Therefore, it appears that a minority of all cases involving a paid claim result from a judge or jury trial determination for the plaintiff—slightly more than half of the claims paid appear to have been settled out of court or pretrial.

Table 1. Percentage Change in the Number of Paid Medical Malpractice Claims (2003-2009) and Claims Per 100,000 Population (2009)

State	% Change in Number of Claims (2003-2009)[a]	Claims Per 100,000 (2009)	State	% Change in Number of Claims (2003-2009)	Claims Per 100,000 (2009)	State	% Change in Number of Claims (2003-2009)	Claims Per 100,000 (2009)
AL	-37.5	0.650	KY	-53.2	2.414	ND	-45.5	2.857
AK	-36.8	1.770	LA	-02.9	6.080	OH	-65.4	1.744
AZ	-43.6	2.630	ME	-16.7	2.306	OK	0.00	3.677
AR	-29.4	1.694	MD	-36.0	3.184	OR	-34.2	1.931
CA	-30.7	2.499	MA	23.7	4.741	PA	-38.3	6.203
CO	-23.0	2.515	MI	-40.2	3.477	RI	-40.8	4.057
CT	-51.9	2.980	MN	-40.4	1.078	SC	-28.3	2.559
DE	-71.9	2.070	MS	-34.0	2.361	SD	-35.1	3.027
DC	-52.4	3.393	MO	-26.9	2.776	TN	-12.3	2.182
FL	-38.7	4.232	MT	-37.9	3.759	TX	-56.5	1.910
GA	-35.6	2.116	NE	-41.5	2.723	UT	-08.8	3.012
H1	-35.4	2.517	NV	-35.0	2.490	VT	-34.6	2.763
ID	-28.1	1.513	NH	0.00	3.591	VA	-35.5	1.544
IL	-42.4	2.225	NJ	-19.9	5.441	WA	-37.3	1.848
IN	-56.4	2.913	NM	13.7	4.201	WV	-23.8	4.462
IA	-39.7	2.367	NY	-26.5	6.712	WI	-42.0	1.168
KS	-29.4	2.612	NC	-47.8	1.191	WY	-45.8	2.436

Source: CRS analysis of Kaiser Family Foundation data, http://www.statehealthfacts.org/compare-maptable.jsp? ind=436&cat=8.

a. Number of malpractice cases in 2003 minus the number of malpractice cases in 2009, divided by the number of malpractice cases in 2003.

Though physicians surveyed express high levels of concern about the risk of malpractice litigation, statistics indicate that physicians may be inaccurately assessing the likelihood of being sued. Noted above, the Kaiser Family Foundation estimated that in 2009, there were 10,739 paid medical malpractice claims in the United States, including the Armed Forces and Samoa.[52] The Kaiser Family Foundation also reported that there are more than 1 million non-federal physicians, so there was about a half of one percent probability of participating in a malpractice trial in a given year. Assuming a 4:1 ratio of defendant to plaintiff judgments in favor of defendants,[53] physicians faced an even smaller likelihood of an adverse judgment.

Though the probabilities of participating in a trial appear relatively low generally, the probability of being threatened with a suit is larger. Moreover, we do not want to minimize the economic impacts or stress that a physician may experience being sued or being threatened with a suit.

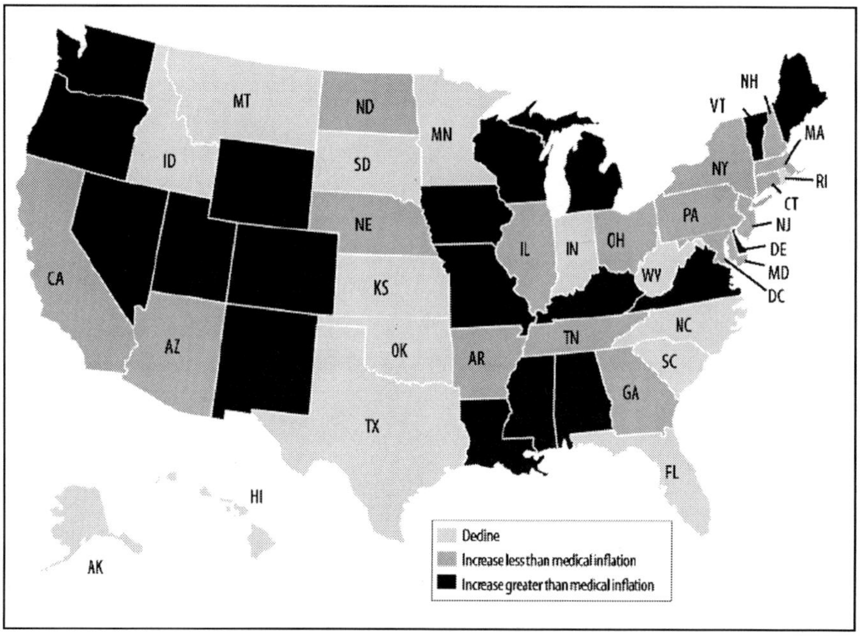

Source: http://www.statehealthfacts.org.

Notes: *Decline* indicates state experienced actual decline in the average total dollars in medical malpractice claims paid. *Increase less than medical inflation* indicates state experienced an increase in the average total dollars in medical malpractice claims paid but the increase was less than the rate of medical inflation during the 2003-2009 period. *Increase greater than medical inflation* indicates state experienced an increase in the average total dollars in medical malpractice claims paid and the increase exceeded the rate of medical inflation during the 2003-2009 period.

Figure 1. Change in the Average Paid Medical Malpractice Claim 2003-2009.

Cost of Awards

The average claim paid in the United States in 2009 was $323,273. While the 2009 figure is up from $289,891 in 2003, the rate of increase over this time period mirrors medical inflation generally.[54] These averages, however, mask the considerable variation across states. For instance, in Kansas the average claim paid in 2009 was roughly $155,622 (72 cases), while in Wisconsin it was almost $761,000 (65 cases).[55] Figure 1 shows the general change in individual states in the average medical malpractice claim paid from 2003 through 2009.[56] Sixteen states saw a decline in their average medical malpractice claim paid, ranging from roughly 5% to 50%. Seventeen states saw their average medical malpractice claim paid from 2003 through 2009 rise slower than medical inflation. Eighteen states saw their average medical malpractice claim paid from 2003 through 2009 rise faster than medical inflation.

Underwriting Cycles

Empirical studies of property and liability insurance markets have revealed underwriting cycles resulting in a sequence of rising and then falling profits for insurers.

> In the rising phase of the underwriting cycle, when ... profits are increasing, underwriters ... realize that they have more financial capacity than before. Competition for business ... encourage[s] underwriters to ease up on underwriting standards ...[which] tends to produce adverse loss experience and the cycle ultimately turns down.... Insurers [then] tighten underwriting standards, reject marginal risks and attempt to lessen underwriting losses ... but these loss data generally take two to three years to develop. In the intervening time underwriting losses mount. The decline in underwriting profits is stopped by a combination of tightened underwriting standards and rate increases which ultimately occur. Then the cycle begins its upward movement once again.[57]

The same underwriting cycles can be found in the professional liability and malpractice insurance market, and these cycles, like those elsewhere, can also be exacerbated or mitigated by investment returns with "hard" markets made worse by relatively low returns on insurer investments and "soft" markets typically marked by higher returns.[58]

While there are likely to be future hard markets, with rising premiums, the 2009 market for medical malpractice liability insurance appears soft and has been so since the mid-2000s. Table 2 shows for the period 1995-2009 premiums earned (column A); direct losses incurred (column C); direct defense and cost containment expenses incurred (column D); and the ratio of direct losses plus defense and cost containment incurred to premiums [(Columns C plus D)/Column A].[59] First, one can see the transition from a soft market in the mid-1990s to a harder market with a rising losses and rising premiums. Costs peaked in 2003 (column B), but total direct premiums earned continued to rise, peaking in 2006. Between 2006 and 2009, total direct premiums earned declined 11%. At the same time, total costs over the 2003 through 2009 period declined 47%, with a disproportionate share of the decline from a 53% decline in direct losses incurred, meaning that fewer awards or lower awards were being paid out in relation to the premiums earned. Defense costs did not decline as rapidly.[60] While there may be specific states or specialties experiencing either premium increases or difficulties purchasing insurance, Table 2 suggests, based on these national aggregated data, that the country was *not* experiencing a widespread crisis similar to previous crises in this time period.

Costs of Medical Malpractice Insurance

As shown in Table 2, the National Association of Insurance Commissioners (NAIC) reported that direct earned premiums for medical malpractice insurance totaled $10.6 billion in 2010, or an average national increase of 5.5% per year over the 2000-2009 time period.[61] Like the average awards paid out in medical malpractice, these aggregate figures of direct premiums earned mask somewhat different experiences across specialties with states or across states. For example, an internist in Los Angeles, insured by The Doctors Company, who paid $10,097 in malpractice premiums in 2000 for a $1 million/$3 million claims made policy paid $10,343 in 2009—an annual increase of less than a one-quarter of one percent.[62]

During the 2000-2009 time period, an OB/GYN in San Diego, insured by Medical Insurance Exchange of California would have experienced a 6.4% average annual increase in premiums and paid $76,188 in 2009 for malpractice insurance.

In Minnesota, over the same 2000-2009 time period, internists and OB/GYN insured by the Midwest Medical Insurance Company experienced an average annual increase of 2.5% in premiums, while general surgeons experienced a 3.7% average annual increase in premiums (see Figure 2). These figures compare favorably to the average annual increase in medical inflation of 3.7% over the same time period. However, as Figure 2 shows, while over the long-run (comparing 2000 to 2009) malpractice premiums in Minnesota have risen at or below, the rate of medical inflation (Med Index), for most of the past decade, OB/GYNs (OB Index) and general surgeons (GS Index) paid annual premiums that grew faster than the rate of inflation (Med Index) (most years their curves are above medical inflation). It is only because of a drop in premiums beginning in 2007 that the change in premiums at the end of the 10-year period appear moderate relative to inflation. Appendix B contains several additional figures depicting the experiences of California, Alabama, and Wisconsin over the same time period.

The Pennsylvania malpractice insurance market, like the California market and other markets in some other states, distinguishes premiums based on the location of the physician. Different locations can have different experiences. For instance, physicians (internists, general surgeons, and obstetrician/ gynecologists) insured by the Pennsylvania Medical Society Liability Insurance Company, over the 2000 to 2009 time period, experienced average increases of 7.6% per year in Philadelphia and 8.5% in Pittsburgh.[63] While the California, Minnesota, and Pennsylvania experiences are indicative of the variations across localities and specialties, it is difficult to generalize across states, given each state's unique experiences.

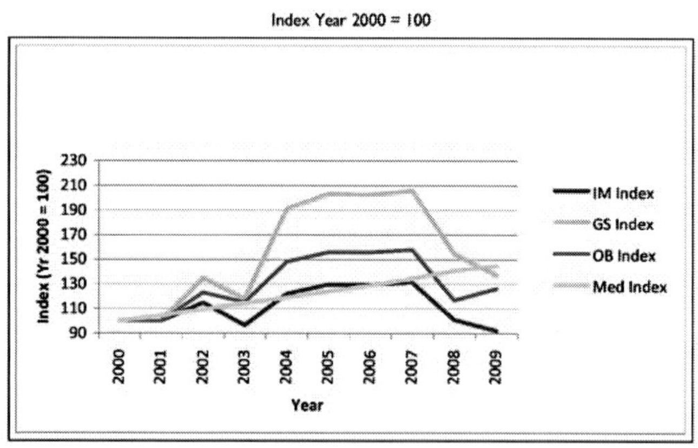

Source: http://mymedicalmalpracticeinsurance.com/medical-malpractice-insurance-rates.php.

Notes: The values on the vertical axis are index numbers that measure the magnitude of change from 2000—the base year. Index numbers are similar to percentages, and an index number of 130 would indicate, in this context, that the premium was 30% higher than the base year. IM refers to premiums for internal medicine; GS refers to premiums for general surgery; OB refers to premiums for OB/Gyn. Med Index refers to medical inflation as calculated by the Bureau of Labor Statistics.

Figure 2. Change in Malpractice Premiums, by Specialty—Minnesota.

While Medicare providers do not receive a separate payment from Medicare for their malpractice insurance costs, Medicare pays its proportionate share of each Medicare provider's malpractice insurance premium as a part of each Medicare payment for services rendered. While the exact amount paid to physicians for each service varies by geographic location and the risk associated with the service being provided, on average 3.9% of the physician fee is designated to reimburse physicians for the cost of their medical malpractice insurance.[64] MedPAC (the Medicare Payment Advisory Commission) reported that Medicare payments to physicians under the Part B fee schedule totaled $64 billion in 2009, of which roughly $2.5 billion was for malpractice coverage.[65]

Table 2. Countrywide Summary of Medical Professional Liability Insurance 1995-2009

Year	Direct Premiums Earned(A)	Cost B=(C + D)	Direct Losses Incurred (C)	Direct Defense and Cost Containment Expense Incurred(D)	Loss Ratio[a] (C+D)/A
1995	$6,137,209,298	$4,884,856,517	$3,330,613,605	$1,554,242,912	79.59
1996	$6,027,958,481	$5,039,167,602	$3,632,388,312	$1,406,779,290	83.60
1997	$5,949,688,215	$4,664,896,733	$3,222,735,496	$1,442,161,237	78.41
1998	$6,218,164,376	$6,042,303,067	$4,457,099,226	$1,585,203,841	97.17
1999	$6,167,948,760	$6,386,694,614	$4,659896,010	$1,726,798,604	103.55
2000	$6,373,039,337	$6,756,125,110	$5,098,753,650	$1,657,371,460	106.01
2001	$7,054,509,032	$8,947,198,106	$6,972,294,879	$1,974,903,227	126.83
2002	$9,631,548,967	$10,613,157,176	$8,200,307,513	$2,412,849,663	110.19
2003	$11,277,448,229	$11,307,238,584	$8,459,389,539	$2,847,849,045	100.26
2004	$11,538,819,200	$9,738,960,478	$7,224,164,963	$2,514,795,515	84.40
2005	$11,874,907,423	$8,865,683,185	$6,151,942,930	$2,713,740,255	74.66
2006	$12,167,900,762	$7,937,049,898	$5,285,472,723	$2,651,577,175	65.23
2007	$11,744,160,781	$7,089,411,154	$4,787,669,711	$2,301,741,443	60.37
2008	$11,353,905,915	$6,201,294,693	$4,092,787,274	$2,108,507,419	54.62
2009	$10,835,284,565	$6,030,844,814	$4,012,060,052	$2,018,784,762	55.66
2010	$10,600,322059	$5,393,203,822	$3,530,690,513	$1,862,513,309	51.13

Source: National Association of Insurance Commissioners, 2011.

a. Loss Ratio = (Direct Losses + Direct Defense and Cost Containment Expenses Incurred)/Direct Premiums Earned.

Cost of Defensive Medicine

There are various definitions of defensive medicine and a wide range of dollar estimates of the cost of defensive medicine. The Congressional Budget Office (CBO) reported that "recent literature generally uses defensive medicine only to refer to those extra tests and procedures undertaken out of fear of liability."[66] Physician surveys of defensive medicine, some of which use broader definitions of defensive medicine, often generate different results. For instance, a recent survey of orthopedic surgeons in Pennsylvania found that one in five tests were conducted for defensive reasons and that surgeons who had been sued in the past were more likely to order such tests.[67] Another survey conducted by Gallup and commissioned by Jackson Health care concluded that the costs of defensive medicine could be as high as $650 billion to $850 billion per year.[68]

The most recent academic studies suggest a lower dollar estimate for the cost of defensive medicine. One recent study in *Health Affairs* addressed the cost of defensive medicine, and another study addressed whether tort reform would lower health care costs by reducing defensive medicine. In the first study, the authors estimated that the total costs of defensive medicine in 2008 were $45.6 billion—a figure not widely different from the less than the 2% of health care spending number used by the CBO.[69] Moreover, as the article notes, some of these medical services, while motivated by a desire to avoid liability, may actually be beneficial. These benefits, along with any benefit associated with deterrence generally from the tort system, are not included to produce a net cost.

In a second study in *Health Affairs*, the authors used claims from more than 35 million episodes across 30 states to examine the tests and procedures ordered in 35 clinical specialties to see if malpractice reforms would reduce health care costs.[70] This study concluded that while "defensive medicine practices exist and are widespread ... their impact on medical care costs is small and that a 30% reduction in malpractice premiums would reduce medical costs by only 0.4 percent." This study noted that their results were similar to other studies and the CBO. Other studies also suggest that malpractice suits have a relatively short-term effect on physician practice patterns.[71]

From these studies, it can be generally concluded that while the dollars spent on defensive medicine do not appear to be insignificant and the health care system would benefit from saving some of these costs, the total impact of reducing defensive medicine on total health care expenditures may be relatively small.

Efficiency

Although one goal of the tort system is to promote efficiency by properly allocating the costs of injuries (so responsible parties face the proper set of economic incentives), there are several dimensions of efficiency on which tort system can be assessed: (1) time to resolve cases, (2) the costs of lawsuits, and (3) whether the system correctly identifies meritorious from non-meritorious suits. Faster resolution of cases means that injured parties are more promptly made whole by the legal system; reduced costs means that injured parties receive more of the compensation paid; and correctly identifying injured parties and properly compensating them reduces the administrative overhead of using the tort system to make these determinations.

The first dimension to consider is the time taken to resolve cases. Ideally, resolutions that occurred more quickly would be more efficient. In the state of Washington, where good statistics are available, one-third of medical malpractice claims are settled within a year, but some 8.2% of cases extended for more than seven years.[72] Others report that the average time between injury and resolution was five years and that one-third of claims took six or more years to resolve.[73] Although shorter times to resolution would be desirable to achieve efficiency, evidence suggests that some reforms, such as caps, may actually create incentives for insurers to delay settlement because their expected loss is capped.[74]

A second dimension for assessing efficiency is the costs associated with resolving a claim. It is often assumed that the medical malpractice system is inefficient since attorneys, experts, and insurance companies each have their hand in the process and each taking a share of any compensation. One 2006 study estimated that costs (both contingent fees and defense—a measure of systemic overhead) consumed 54% of the compensation paid to plaintiffs in a sample of resolved claims.[75] The CBO concluded that caps on contingent attorneys' fees would reduce nuisance suits (see below) but make it harder for poor plaintiffs to find legal representation to advance legitimate claims.[76] Moreover, these calculations of cost do not take into account how the tort system may potentially deter risky behavior.

Another indicator of efficiency is whether the tort system and health care system are equipped to deal with individuals who frivolously bring suits without merit.[77] The argument often advanced by the legal community is that because attorneys in these cases are most often retained on a contingency fee, they have a strong incentive to screen cases and pursue only those that are most likely to be meritorious. One review of the literature found that attorneys tend to reject 70% to 97% of all individuals who present with a medical malpractice claim.[78]

The same study also reviewed the literature analyzing whether the "right people received the right award"(i.e., were those who were truly injured more likely to be properly compensated and were those whose injuries were questionable less likely to be compensated). Here, the academic literature is in near universal agreement: "the merits of a claim are the best predictor of the likelihood of payment and the amount received," even though there may be both legal and medical errors in paying undeserving individuals.[79] For instance, one major study of closed insurance claims found that injured and non-injured individuals were properly compensated in a collective total of 73% of the cases. When an error was made, it was 1.6 times more likely that an injured individual would not receive compensation than it was that a non-injured individual would receive compensation. However, the amount a non-injured individual received when compensated in error was almost half that received by those truly injured.[80]

Physicians' Perspectives on Malpractice and the Randomness of Suits

Physicians and their insurance companies typically are the key groups that advocate for malpractice reforms. A recent national survey of physicians found "high levels of concern about the risk of malpractice litigation among physicians across a range of specialties, practice settings, and geographic areas and even among physicians practicing in relatively low risk environments."[81] Moreover, the study found that "physicians' assessment of their risk is driven less by the true risk of malpractice claims or the cost of malpractice insurance, and more by the perceived arbitrary, unfair, and adversarial aspects of the tort process—which most traditional state reform efforts do not address."[82] The study concluded that "[p]hysicians tend to view lawsuits as random events, unpredictable and uncontrollable, because they are not viewed as related to the quality of care provided."[83]

With respect to randomness, given that most individuals injured do not sue, some providers may perceive that being sued is part of a random process drawing from the pool of injured individuals. Second, because defendants appear to win most cases, it is often perceived that being sued is independent of any actual negligence. In support of the non-randomness of suits, there is evidence that there are certain "claims-prone" physicians.[84] Moreover, if medical malpractice suits were truly random, they would have been independent of preventable injuries. However, a 2010 Rand Corporation study of malpractice in California found that a reduction of in-hospital events associated with the occurrence of preventable injuries during care (patient safety indicator, or PSI, events) was strongly associated with a reduction in the number of medical malpractice suits; fluctuations in such events over time are associated with fluctuations in malpractice claims.[85] In fact, three-fourths of the variation in annual malpractice claims is explained by changes in PSI events. These findings held even when researchers looked at subgroups of physicians such as specialists, surgeons, and OB-GYNs. The Rand study concluded that "to the extent that improved safety performance can be shown to have a demonstrable impact on malpractice claims, [this] offers another focal point for policymakers in seeking to address the malpractice crisis."[86]

REFORM EFFORTS

While there are numerous legislative proposals for reforming medical liability, most of the state efforts and most current proposed federal legislation involve, either singularly or in combination, caps on noneconomic damages, caps on punitive damages, shorter statute of limitations, changes to joint and several liability, changes to the collateral source rule, enterprise liability, and safe harbors. Each of these are discussed below.

Caps on Noneconomic Damages

As described in Text Box 2 Text Box 2 Text Box 2 Text Box 2, noneconomic damages are typically awarded to make an individual whole. Noneconomic damages seek to compensate the injured party for the non-monetary losses, but losses nonetheless, such as pain and suffering; loss of a spouse, child, or partner; or disfigurement.

The Physician Insurers Association of America (PIAA) identified 23 states as having a cap on noneconomic damages and an additional 5 states as having a cap on total damages in medical malpractice lawsuits as of November 2010.[87] State caps on noneconomic damages range from $250,000 to a maximum of $1.5 million. Some states, but not all, index the capped amount for inflation.

The foremost practical argument in favor of caps on noneconomic damages is that they lower the total value of any particular award, lower insurers' costs, and ultimately malpractice premiums.[88] In addition, there are several theoretical reasons to either cap or otherwise limit noneconomic damages.[89] First, noneconomic damages are difficult to estimate either because the loss cannot easily be monetarized (e.g., value of scaring or loss of consortium [a loss of the benefits of family relationships due to an injury by a tortfeasor]), or they are speculative (mental anguish). Second, individuals generally do not insure themselves against noneconomic losses, and therefore it may not be reasonable for tortfeasors to be liable for these losses. For instance, many parents do not buy life insurance on their children's lives to insure the parents for the non-monetary damages associated with the loss of a child. Rather, when parents do buy insurance, the amount is generally small and often reflects the economic costs associated with a funeral.

Conversely, there are several arguments that are made against caps on noneconomic damages in medical malpractice lawsuits. First, it is asserted that caps on noneconomic damages in medical malpractice lawsuits may violate state and federal constitutional rights to equal protection by treating different litigants differently.[90] For instance, if two litigants have identical injuries and one set of injuries is caused by professional negligence of a medical provider and the second is caused by the negligence of someone other than a medical provider, the cap on noneconomic damages in a medical malpractice suit would result in a lower award for the litigant injured by the medical provider. A second argument is that caps on noneconomic damages unfairly burden women, children, and the poor who receive lower awards because their economic losses are generally less due to their limited incomes and earnings potential.[91] A third argument made against caps on noneconomic damages is that they create the wrong sets of incentives by encouraging an underinvestment in safe practices.

Research studies of the actual impact of caps on noneconomic damages suggest a mixed result. Some studies show caps on noneconomic damages reduce total awards, while other studies show that caps actually increase total awards because juries tend to find greater economic damages when faced with caps on noneconomic damages.[92]

There is similarly a varied literature with respect to the effect of noneconomic damage caps on health care expenditures, premiums, access to physicians, and physician supply. With respect to expenditures, the CBO has concluded that the "weight of empirical evidence now demonstrates a link between tort reform and the use of health care services—reducing national health care spending in response to a package of proposals, including caps on noneconomic damages, punitive damages and other reforms, by roughly 0.5 percent."[93] However, as the CBO noted, these savings are not without consequences, as some studies have found that overall national mortality would increase by 0.2%.

While caps on noneconomic damages reduce malpractice premiums, the impact varies, with studies showing reductions of between 6% and 25%.[94] However, the CBO concluded that the reduction in total national premiums would be approximately 10% if caps and other reforms were implemented.[95]

With respect to access to care, several studies of caps on noneconomic damages found that caps on liability improved access to physicians and that unlimited liability reduced access. For instance, one study found that caps encouraged physicians to work more hours, which has the impact of improving access to care;[96] another study found that increased driving distances and waiting times were associated with professional liability costs generally. For example, in high-risk counties surrounding Philadelphia, as malpractice premiums increased, physicians sought to manage their exposure by avoiding higher-risk patients. As a result, more patients switched physicians and consolidation of some high-risk specialty practices increased, leading to longer driving times for patients.[97] As noted below, caps on damages is also expected to improve access to care in rural areas by increasing the supply of physicians in those areas.

With respect to physician supply, again studies find mixed results. One study, examining the impact of all caps, found that caps had no significant effect on physician supply for most Americans but did increase the supply of physicians in rural areas.[98] Another study, examining the medical malpractice crisis in Pennsylvania found that while "claims of a physician exodus from Pennsylvania due to rising liability costs are overstated ... physicians are adjusting to liability by consolidating, adjusting patient mix, among other things, and that the impacts are greatest among specialist providers."[99] Interestingly, a recent Rand Corporation working paper found that "a favorable malpractice reform environment in a given state appears to attract riskier physicians to practice medicine there and that while local reform could lower malpractice costs they could also increase the exposure of patients in the area to risk. A logical consequence of this research is that national reform would lower costs in all areas but have no negative effect on the total risk that patients faced."[100]

The 2010 MedPAC study, which studied a variety of proposed medical malpractice reforms, concluded that the states have the most experience with caps on damages. Thus far, the evidence and literature strongly suggest that the impact of caps can best be characterized as mixed, with the overall impact modest in constraining malpractice premiums generally.[101]

Cap on Punitive Damages

As noted in Text Box 2, "[p]unitive damages are damages, other than compensatory or nominal damages, awarded against a defendant to punish him or her for outrageous conduct and to deter the defendant and others similarly situated from engaging in such conduct in the future."[102] A recent 50-state survey revealed that 10 states prohibit punitive damages either under state constitutions or state common law, 24 states enacted limits on punitive damages since 1985, and 2 states—Alabama and Ohio—overturned caps as unconstitutional.[103] Second, punitive damage awards in medical malpractice cases are rare—with one study finding punitive damage awards in just 2.52% of cases that ended with judicial determinations.[104] Even though an award of punitive damage is rare, claims for punitive damages are likely to be particularly disturbing to a defendant-physician because they allege outrageous behavior and in some states professional liability insurance does not cover punitive damages.

There are mixed empirical findings regarding the impact of caps on punitive damages. One study found that states that prohibited punitive damages had 8% lower premiums as compared to other states. While this study found that caps generally lowered premiums (by 11% to 17%), there was no significant relationship between caps or prohibitions on punitive damages and losses or earned premiums.[105] Thus, it seems that any impact that a cap on punitive damages would have on premiums may be minimal, given the infrequency of such awards.

Shorter Statute of Limitations

All states have statute of limitation rules, many of which were amended, and shortened, since the early 1970s in response to medical malpractice concerns. Some states, such as Idaho, adopt a general two-year statute of limitations for medical malpractice but toll, or extend the time limitation, if the claim is based on a foreign object left in the body, in which case a suit must be brought either within two-years or one-year following discovery, whichever is later.[106] Mississippi, for example, has a relatively long statute of limitations that requires a suit be brought within seven years of occurrence or two years from discovery.[107]

The length of the statute of limitations is important because most medical malpractice insurance that is written is *claims-made* insurance, whereby the insured is covered by his or her insurer, who provides coverage on the date the insured becomes aware of the claim against them during the policy period.[108] A physician who is insured by the same insurance carrier is generally protected against claims going back to the date the policy first became effective. If a policy is not renewed, the physician is covered up to the date the policy terminates. In addition, insurers generally offer what is called *tail insurance* to physicians to cover any claims that arise after they retire. A shorter statute of limitations should allow insurers to limit their potential losses due to claims and "more accurately account and reserve for any potential claims." A longer statute of limitation would generally favor claimants.

The MedPAC evaluation of malpractice reform options reviewed the literature on shortening the statute of limitations and concluded that

> [t]he weight of the evidence suggests that this reform does not significantly affect claims payouts, defensive medicine, or physician supply. A limited amount of evidence suggests a beneficial effect on liability premiums. The evidence on claim frequency is equivocal. The evidence concerning overhead costs and quality of care is too limited to ground firm conclusions.[109]

Theoretically, one would expect that shorter statute of limitation periods would reduce the number of claims and the reduction in the number of claims should reduce premiums. Given that many states have already enacted or reformed their statutes of limitations for medical malpractice cases, it is unknown what additional effect, if any, a national standard might have going forward.

Changes to Joint and Several Liability

As noted in Text Box 2, the principle of joint and several liability allows a claimant to recover the entire amount of a damage award from any of the parties found to be responsible for an injury, regardless of each party's degree of responsibility for that injury. The CBO reports that as of 2003, 35 states had either modified or eliminated the doctrine of joint and several liability.[110]

The MedPAC study concluded that

> [t]here is a good evidence base regarding the effects of joint and several liability reform. Although research findings are somewhat mixed, on balance, the evidence suggests that it has no significant effect on claims payouts, defense costs, liability insurance premiums, physician supply, or quality of care. It may be associated with lower health insurance premiums. The evidence concerning the effect on claim frequency and defensive medicine is equivocal.[111]

In some states, the doctrine of joint and several liability has been modified in some manner, so that defendants are responsible for only their share of the injury.[112]

Changes to the Collateral Source Rule

As noted earlier, the collateral source rule is the common-law rule that allows an injured party to recover damages from the defendant even if he or she is also entitled to receive them from a third party. Over the past 35 years, states have been particularly active in modifying the collateral source rule. As of the end of 2010, 19 states have altered the rule to require mandatory setoffs,[113] while other states have varying rules governing the admissibility of evidence regarding collateral sources and subrogation of claims.[114] Medicare and Medicaid maintain a right to subrogate payments that the federal government has made on behalf of individuals covered by these programs and injured by someone else. At least five states (Georgia, Kansas, Kentucky, New Hampshire, and Wisconsin) have had their collateral source rule changes declared unconstitutional or nullified by their states' supreme courts.[115]

The 2010 MedPAC study concluded that reforms of the collateral source rule "[do] not significantly affect claim frequency, claims payouts, overhead costs, liability insurance premiums, defensive medicine, physician supply, or patient outcomes. It may reduce health insurance premiums."[116]

Enterprise Insurance or Enterprise Liability

A newer proposal to address medical liability is enterprise liability, which would make the enterprise rather than providers liable for any negligence, because "[e]nterprise insurance would obligate hospitals and similar organizations to provide insurance covering all liabilities arising out of services performed, or to be performed, in their facilities."[117] The presumption is that the incentives on the part of the enterprise are stronger.

This concept may be increasingly attractive, given that more and more physicians are employed by hospitals, a trend that may accelerate with any widespread rollout of accountable care organizations.[118] The American Hospital Association reports that hospitals currently employ some 200,000 physicians and that many more are employed in group practices.[119] Moreover, it is estimated that 80% of medical treatment of injuries take place in hospitals.[120]

An enterprise insurance system would continue the current medical malpractice insurance system but shift financial responsibility to the employing enterprise. Such a system would create a greater incentive for the enterprise to police providers because its insurance costs (either in premiums or through self-insurance) are directly a function of actual claims, as hospitals are more likely to be experience rated than physicians. Hospitals and larger entities such as health plans and group practices also are perhaps better positioned to deal with premium cycles and to self-insure because they have a larger risk pool to draw from and greater access to capital. Furthermore, it is thought that enterprise insurance may be a better tool to encourage quality improvements that require coordination across the care delivery system and reduce the tendency of providers to engage in defensive medicine. Moreover, physicians may welcome an intermediary between themselves and potential personal liability.

Safe Harbors

While physicians may practice medicine in the belief that they are complying with current standards of care, the actual requirements can be uncertain, changing, vague, or even disputed and are only established under the tort system after the fact with a judicial determination.[121] Clinical practice guidelines could specify the appropriate treatment for specific conditions, sets of symptoms, or preventive care goals and could be evidence of the legal standard of care in medical malpractice suits. Although not yet realized on a permanent basis, the idea of safe harbors has long been in existence. Twenty years ago it was written that

> [p]ractice guidelines—systematic, scientifically derived statement of appropriate measures to be taken by physicians in the diagnosis and treatment of disease—are widely viewed as a potential panacea for many of the health care industry's most pressing problems. In addition to helping physicians obtain better medical results for their patients, practice guidelines are expected to give public and private financers of health services better tools with which to resist paying for, and thus discourage, inappropriate care. They are also being viewed hopefully as a way to ameliorate the problems associated with the law governing medical malpractice.[122]

Developing safe harbors, or clinical guidelines, has been controversial because numerous design features need to be considered including, among other things:

- Who is to develop the guidelines and how are they to be paid for?
- How is a court to reconcile potentially competing sets of guidelines?
- Should guidelines incorporate cost considerations?
- How specific should guidelines be?
- Should guidelines be national or should they reflect local practice?
- Who is to decide whether a particular guideline is applicable to a particular case?
- Must physicians participate in any safe harbor scheme?
- Is adherence to the guideline an absolute defense?
- Is failure to adhere to a guideline negligence or just evidence of potential negligence?
- How will guidelines be updated to reflect new technology and best practice?

Thus, with these questions, both lawyers and doctors share concerns with a safe harbors approach. For instance, a prominent attorney-scholar on medical malpractice wrote:

> ... there exists such heterogeneity of opinion among physicians as to proper care that it cannot be said that a single custom truly exists. The highly differentiated nature of medical problems and the differing rates at which physicians are willing to accept new technologies and treatment modalities into their practices are cited as sources of this heterogeneity.[123]

Similarly, a physician-scholar of the Harvard Medical School wrote:

> ... most guidelines, regardless of their source, are little more than general advice, applicable only under certain clinical circumstances and subject to modification by many possible medical complications, both of which the physician must determine for each patient. Guidelines are also constantly subject to revision as new evidence and new therapies emerge. So the application of even the best and most authoritative guidelines is far from straightforward. Medical judgment is always needed.[124]

If these experts are correct, even with a guidelines regime, there may still remain a significant number of malpractice cases brought where there are questions about either the applicability of particular guidelines or the physician's exercise of his or her judgment.

State vs. Federal Standards

There is a debate as to whether states should pursue reform efforts as they see fit or whether it would be better to have uniform standard to address what some argue is a national problem. Similar to other federal standards, (such as HIPAA—Health Insurance Portability and Accountability Act of 1996, P.L. 104-191), states would still have some flexibility. The division of opinion touches both on issues of states' rights and the appropriate reach of federal power, among other things.

Arguments in Favor of State-Led Standards

Arguments in favor of state-led standards include (1) tort law is a traditional area of state law, (2) medical malpractice reform is outside of the scope of the Commerce Clause of the Constitution, and (3) states are the more natural and appropriate laboratory for testing the implications of alternative reform efforts.

Traditional Area of State Law

Tort law is historically based on state common and state statutory law. In *Erie Railroad v. Tompkins*,[125] the Supreme Court held that "there is no federal general common law." Moreover, the Court held that

> [e]xcept in matters governed by the Federal Constitution or by Acts of Congress, the law to be applied in any case is the law of the State.... There is no federal general common law. Congress has no power to declare substantive rules of common law applicable in a State whether they be local in their nature or "general," be they commercial law or a part of the law of torts.... [126]

As the Cato Institute has written with respect to tort law reform, "[o]ur federal government is one of limited and enumerated powers. The making of tort law is not one of those powers. Thus, Congress must defer to state and local government."[127]

Constitutional Issues

For some, there may be a constitutional concern whether Congress has the authority to make tort law under the Commerce Clause of the Constitution.[128] With respect to federalizing tort law, "the specific issue is whether the developments in the common law and state statutory law are a barrier to interstate commerce or are merely a burden on all commerce."[129] William Niskanen, now chairman emeritus of the Cato Institute, concluded:[130]

> The cost of tort law is a burden on all commerce in a state, but it is not a specific burden to commerce among the states. The effects are more like those of a retail sales tax on all products sold in a state than of a differential tariff on products imported from another state. The average effective liability tax rate is probably around 2.5 percent, but the effective rates differ substantially by product and by state. There is ample evidence that courts favor in-state plaintiffs over out-of-state defendants, but there is no evidence (to my knowledge) that the courts favor in-state defendants over out-of-state defendants. In the absence of evidence of relative discrimination against out-of-state defendants, there

> is no basis for considering the cost of tort law to be a litigation tariff. The tort law or sales tax in a state may be unduly burdensome on commerce in that state, but that should not be sufficient basis for federal measures to harmonize either tort law or sales taxes.

It is likely that the scope of the Commerce Clause will be further clarified when and if one of the several challenges to the Patient Protection and Affordable Care Act, P.L. 111-148 as amended, reaches the Supreme Court.[131]

States as Laboratories

In *New State Ice Co. v. Liebmann,*[132] Justice Brandeis described the U.S. federal system as one in which the states "serve as a laboratory; and try novel social and economic experiments without risk to the rest of the country." As seen above, the states have been very active over the past 30 years testing numerous novel proposals. For instance, many states have capped noneconomic damages, changed their statute of limitations, limited attorneys fees, or modified the collateral source rule.[133] In addition to these more broadly debated ideas, some states have tried new ideas that are beyond those traditionally proposed. For instance, four states—Minnesota, Maine, Florida, and Vermont—conducted experiments with guidelines and safe harbors in the 1990s. No state adopted these short-term experiments permanently. "About 20 states currently have prescreening panels, which review potential cases at an early stage, for medical malpractice claims while 7 others experimented with prescreening panels and either repealed them or had them overturned by their courts."[134]

One argument in favor of leaving states in charge is that the practice of medicine generally does not cross state lines and that states have traditionally regulated health care providers, physicians, dentists, nurses and allied health professionals, hospitals, and insurers.[135] Therefore, neither providers nor insurers have to conform to multiple state liability rules, and the rules that they are subject to are generally the product of established law.[136]

Judge Posner, of the U.S. Court of Appeals for the Seventh Circuit, has noted that "states have adopted or are seriously considering adopting the kind of caps being advocated in Congress" and that "federal legislation would simply stifle state experimentation with different methods for regulating physicians and prevent us from learning which is best."[137]

Arguments in Favor of Federal-Led Standards

There are several arguments in support of federal-led standards efforts, including (1) the federal government pays for a significant amount of the health care delivered in the country, including a portion of the malpractice premiums paid by Medicare providers (discussed above), and (2) medical malpractice litigation sufficiently touches interstate commerce that Congress can regulate.

The Federal Government Is Disproportionately Affected

One argument is that state policies create externalities that are principally borne by the federal government.

> As ... the federal government was directly responsible, through Medicare, Medicaid, and a handful of other programs, for about 30 percent of nationwide health care spending (in 2006) ... the federal government thus pays directly for one-third of a state's health care consumption, including one-third of malpractice induced inefficient utilization (both "defensive medicine" and follow-up care after injury. Additionally, because the federal tax code subsidizes private health care spending, most significantly through the targeted tax exemption for employer-sponsored insurance, a portion of even state-created private costs become federal public costs in the form of lost tax revenue ... The federal government, thus, should intervene in malpractice reform because the federal government is the only institution that fully internalizes the cost-benefit tradeoffs of malpractice policy. [138]

While the federal government is responsible for a substantial share of health care expenditures in the United States,[139] the licensing and regulation of health care providers, physicians, dentists, nurses and allied health professionals, hospitals, and insurers has generally been a state function.[140]

Constitutional Issues

A second argument is that Congress, under the Commerce Clause, has the power to regulate medical malpractice because it touches interstate commerce since "physicians are forced to move from one state to another, or retire from practice altogether (thus removing their services from the stream of interstate commerce)."[141] An additional rationale for federal intervention, perhaps on weaker constitutional grounds, is simply that medical malpractice is a national problem and requires a national solution.[142]

The Connection between Quality and Malpractice: The Experience of Anesthesiologists and Others

The American Society of Anesthesiologists (ASA) reports that real malpractice premiums for anesthesiologists declined from $36,224 in 1985 (in 2008 dollars) to $21,480 in 2009 (in 2008 dollars), or slightly more than 40% in real terms in 25 years.[143] As discussed below, this decline in malpractice premiums on the part of anesthesiologists provides some evidence of the connection between patterns of care, quality improvement, and malpractice premiums.

Beginning in 1985, the ASA started the Closed Claims Project in response to rising medical malpractice premiums, too many claims, and difficulties procuring insurance.[144] Even in the 1980s, patient deaths were 1 in 5,000 cases and the profession recognized that to permanently address the problem, it needed to identify causes of loss and improve patient safety. The project involved in part looking at closed claims to see what practices where causing liability and then developing new methods to improve the safety of anesthesiology. By 2005, the death rate from anesthesiology had declined to less than 1 in 200,000 cases.

As the *Wall Street Journal* reported:[145]

> According to recent study conducted by Public Citizen, anesthesiologists in 1972 accounted for 7.9% of total malpractice lawsuits, compared with 3.8% between 1985 and 2001. In addition, the amount of payments from malpractice lawsuits against anesthesiologists also has decreased. According to ASA, the median payment from

malpractice lawsuits against anesthesiologists in the 1990s was $179,010, a 46% decrease from the 1970s after adjustment for inflation.

In addition, the experience of anesthesiologists has continued through 2009, with real premiums for anesthesiologists declining 6% between 2005 and 2009.[146] Despite the downward trend, the ASA warned that premiums were likely to rise in 2010, attributing the increase to the current economic crisis and the decline in investment income earned by the insurance companies.

The experience of anesthesiologists is not unique. A recent RAND Corporation study found that "improvements in patient safety reduce malpractice claims." Specifically the study, conducted at the county level in California, found that a county, which "saw a decrease of 10 adverse events (achieved through improvements in the quality of care provided) in a given year also saw a decrease of 3.7 malpractice claims."[147] Furthermore, in 2010, the Virginia Mason Medical Center in Seattle, WA, was named Hospital of the Decade by the Leapfrog Group, along with the University of Maryland Medical Center, for "major achievements in reducing medical errors and other innovations in patient safety and quality."[148] The Virginia Mason Medical Center reported that

> with improving quality of care and preventing errors, we have seen a decline in our medical malpractice premiums. We have seen decreases in medical malpractice premiums every year since 2005. As of 2011, our premiums have dropped by 52% since 2005, saving us literally millions of dollars.[149]

While other medical systems have also achieved similar improvements by linking quality and preventing medical errors,[150] there is evidence that more might be done to ensure that hospitals fully internalize the costs of their errors, such that they have a solid business case to continue improving quality and reducing errors.[151]

CONCLUSION

The United States has experienced three national modern medical malpractice crises in the past 40 years, with the latest ending just a few years ago. While advocates of reform have proposed numerous changes to the tort system, including the joint and several liability doctrine; changes to statutes of limitations; caps on noneconomic damages; caps on punitive damages; enterprise liability or enterprise insurance; and others, with the exception of caps on noneconomic damages, the evidence in support of one or more of these reform proposals is generally mixed at best or non-existent at worst.

Research on the effects of reform, and general studies on the impact of medical malpractice on the cost and provision of health care, suggest that even if some of the above reforms are found to be promising, in aggregate, the impact of any reform effort is not likely to be that significant—either at reducing premiums for providers or reducing health care costs to payers.[152]

Evidence also suggests that quality improvement initiatives that reduce medical errors reduce claims and that such efforts are increasingly being rewarded in the liability insurance market place with lower malpractice premiums. This trend is particularly evident among entities that are subject to experience ratings, such as hospitals and large provider groups, and among particular specialties.

Finally, while surveys reveal that physicians' perception of the risk of malpractice litigation is high, changing the perceptions of health care providers is key to any reform efforts. However, this may prove difficult, given that studies show that physicians tend to over estimate their likelihood of being sued. Moreover, physician malpractice concerns appear to be relatively insensitive to their states' malpractice reforms, including caps on noneconomic and punitive damages. Thus, even following reform, there may be few changes in practice patterns or savings from reduced defensive medicine.

APPENDIX A. THE ROLE OF TORT LAW IN A MARKET ECONOMY

Introduction

Economists began integrating law and economics as early as the late 1950s,[153] and applying their analysis to accidents and tort liability soon afterwards.[154] Learned Hand's formulation of negligence has intuitive appeal to economists because Hand's appropriate standard of care, adopted in the Second Restatement of Torts,[155] can be restated by employing economists' familiar marginal cost-benefit analysis. Under this analysis, an "injurer is liable if the marginal cost of his or her precaution is less than the resulting marginal benefit."[156]

While obtaining compensation for a plaintiff's injury may be the principle focus of lawyers under the tort system, economists and others also tend to analyze the tort system and its impact on behavior in the broader market. From an economist's perspective, liability rules create incentives for all individuals engaged in potentially harmful activities to alter their behavior. The tort system can aid the proper functioning of a market by

- forcing sellers to incorporate the costs of any negative externalities into their prices;
- improving consumer decisions through better pricing; and
- deterring poor performance on the part of providers who would face additional costs associated with higher premiums.

In addition, some economists may perceive the tort system as functioning as a private regulatory system to protect individuals. Scholars have observed that "[a]s opposed to governmental bureaucracies in Europe and Japan, which are typically responsible for extensive regulation of the private sector ... American tort law acts as a primary—if not *the* primary—means by which private parties monitor and limit the behavior of other private parties."[157]

Compensation

While a primary function of the tort system is to compensate plaintiffs where the provider is found legally liable, it has been argued that the tort system does not adequately compensate those injured by the professional negligence of health care providers. There are several reasons for this. First, despite public perceptions to the contrary, most injured parties do not sue.[158] A 2002 Harvard Medical Practice study found that "[a]pproximately 2% of those who were negligently injured filed a claim, although a substantially greater percentage of claims were filed in cases where the injury was more severe."[159] Due to the low number of claims filed, it can be concluded that a majority of individuals are not being compensated via the tort system, giving rise to the observation that it may not be an effective mechanism for compensation. Moreover, as discussed below, if too few bring suit, this, too, has an impact on the system's deterrent effects.

A second critique of the tort system is that it compensates some plaintiffs who were either not injured, or if injured, their injuries were not caused by negligence. In one study of 1,452 closed malpractice claims researchers found that "3% of the claims had no verifiable medical injuries and 37% did not involve errors."[160] However, 16% of those claims not associated with an injury (6 out of 1,452) and 28% of those not associated with an error (145 out of 1,452) were compensated.[161] These payments, associated with no error, were estimated to account for 13 to 16% of the system's total monetary cost.

A third situation that questions the effectiveness of the tort system for obtaining compensation is the perception that injured parties do not receive appropriate compensation, with some plaintiffs potentially being overcompensated and others being undercompensated. Thus, when considering tort reform, one question may be how to reduce or lower the costs related to these types of payments. While overcompensation is difficult to cull from any data, undercompensation is perhaps more identifiable because every claimant, who is victorious and properly compensated, must bear any costs of their own representation even if on a contingent basis, thus leaving them undercompensated. For instance, a successful litigant with a meritorious $100,000 judgment, that accurately represents his compensable economic loss, may share more than $30,000 of the judgment with their attorney leaving the litigant undercompensated in the end.[162] The system of compensation also creates an incentive for "claimants try to make up for these fees, in part, by inflating medical damages and seeking pain and suffering damages."[163] Again, while the incentive exists, it is difficult to estimate the extent of this potential problem.

Deterrence

As noted, for economists, "[d]eterrence is the primary theoretical rationale for the tort liability system—the threatened costs of litigation, both economic and psychological, [are assumed to] create an incentive to take safety precautions," and under a negligence rule additional precautions should be taken until the marginal value of the additional precautions equals their marginal cost.[164]

There is mixed evidence about the effectiveness of the tort system in deterring behavior. To be an effective deterrent, that is to alter behavior and encourage an appropriate investment in quality and improvement in safety, the economic model assumes that individuals actually sue, which as noted above happens rarely.[165] A second argument that the tort system's impact on deterrence is imperfect is that almost all providers are insured and most medical malpractice insurers tend to not to use the number of malpractice claims as a factor when rating providers, known as experience rating.[166] Therefore, physicians, who have had a higher number of malpractice claims against them, may not be affected by either changes in premiums and actual payments made on their behalf by their insurer.

While physicians may not face higher premiums or actual losses, the tort system may be an effective deterrent in other ways. First, the fear of litigation and the associated stress of being sued, or seeing others being sued, can serve as an incentive.[167] Second, physicians may face non-monetary costs such as a decline in professional reputation when sued. One study found that obstetricians who are sued lose patients and subsequently tend to accept more lower-paid Medicaid and HMO patients. The combination of these effects can reduce a physician's income by roughly $10,000 to $20,000 per year for about five years.[168]

Generate Information

The field of *information economics* has focused attention on the importance of information because a market economy requires information both about the prices and the quality of good and services in the market. For example, a former Federal Trade Commissioner stated:

> One of the fundamentals of a market economy is the free flow of information about goods and services offered for sale. The underlying theory is that the more fully consumers are informed, the better equipped they will be to make purchase decisions. Unwanted goods and services eventually will disappear from the market, and prices that are too high to induce purchase ultimately will be lowered as firms seek to attract buyers. Most of the time, advertising enhances market performance by transferring useful information to consumers and by enabling firms to promote the attributes of their products and services and, thereby, to compete better with each other. On the other hand, advertising may adversely affect market performance when firms use it to transmit deceptive or fraudulent messages on which reasonable consumers are induced to rely to their detriment. When this happens, we tend to refer to the result as "market failure."[169]

The health care market suffers from many well-studied potential "market failures."[170] One informational problem identified "is the problem that doctors' actions are often hidden and the patient is unable to tell, even after the fact, whether the doctor has acted optimally or provided substandard care. Another problem is that patients are often unable to assess the practitioner's level of professional skills and thus cannot effectively choose among doctors."[171]

The tort system, via cases, has the potential to provide information to the market about the safety of services and products. First, the open nature of court filings, at least initial court filings, allows for some degree of public scrutiny of the alleged claims. Court filings can be viewed as encouraging some injured parties to bring suit when they ascertain that others have been similarly injured, and deterring others from bringing suit when similar suits are either not found in the public record or have not been successful in the past. As evidence of this effect, in the Firestone Tire litigation, "[o]fficials at the [U.S.] Department of Transportation [said] the sealing of documents in settled lawsuits is one reason they did not spot the pattern of scores of rollover deaths in Ford Explorers equipped with Firestone tires that failed."[172] Had the records been unsealed, better information would have been available to consumers about the relative safety of their purchases.

Appendix B. Change in Malpractice Premiums, by Specialty in Selected States

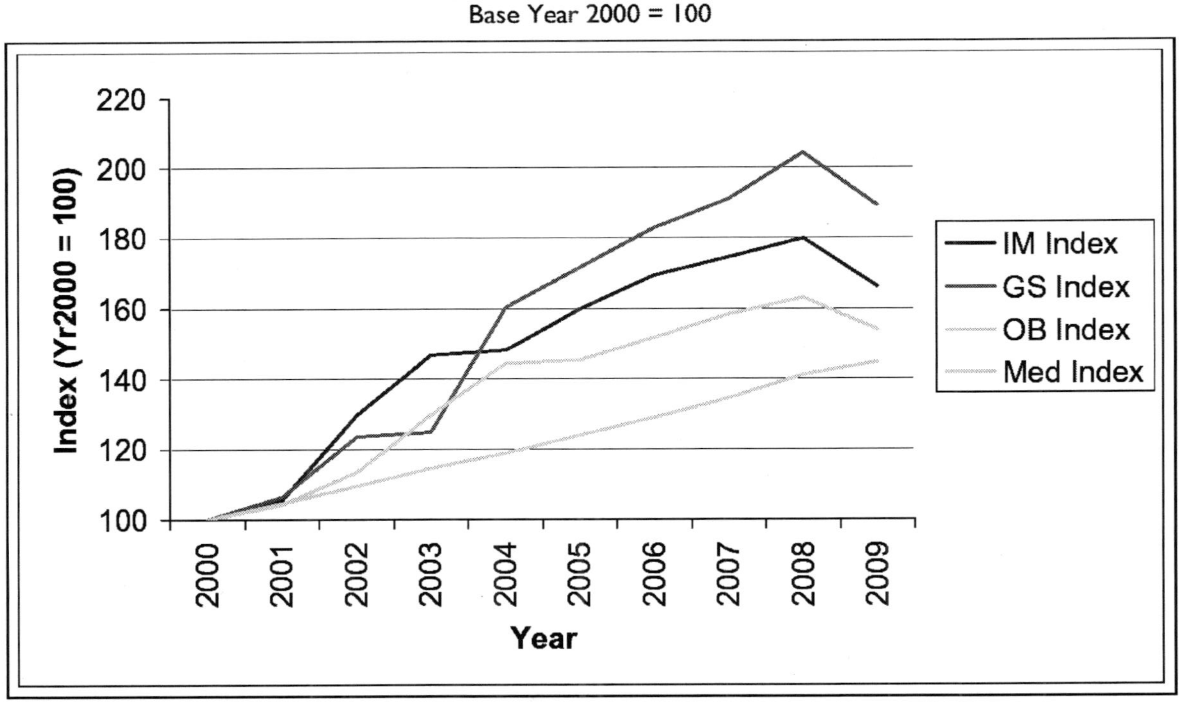

Source: CRS analysis of http://mymedicalmalpracticeinsurance.com/medical-malpractice-insurance-rates.php.

Notes: The values on the vertical axis are index numbers which measure the magnitude of change from 2000—the base year. Index numbers are similar to percentages and an index number of 130 would indicate, in this context, that the premium was 30% higher than the base year. IM refers to premiums for internal medicine; GS refers to premiums for general surgery; OB refers to premiums for OB/Gyn. Med Index refers to medical inflation as calculated by the Bureau of Labor Statistics.

Figure B-1. Change in Malpractice Premiums, by Specialty—California.

Base Year 2000 = 100

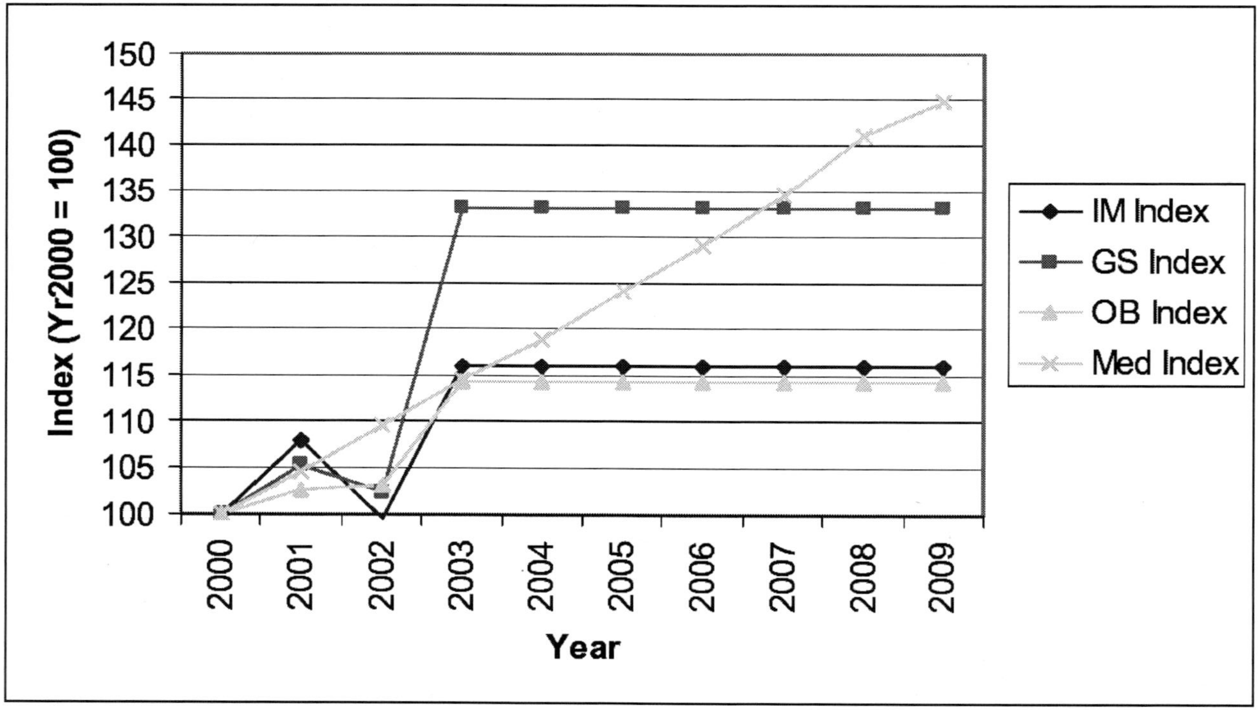

Source: CRS analysis of http://mymedicalmalpracticeinsurance.com/medical-malpractice-insurance-rates.php.

Notes: The values on the vertical axis are index numbers which measure the magnitude of change from 2000—the base year. Index numbers are similar to percentages and an index number of 130 would indicate, in this context, that the premium was 30% higher than the base year. IM refers to premiums for internal medicine; GS refers to premiums for general surgery; OB refers to premiums for OB/Gyn. Med Index refers to medical inflation as calculated by the Bureau of Labor Statistics.

Figure B-2. Change in Malpractice Premiums, by Specialty—Alabama.

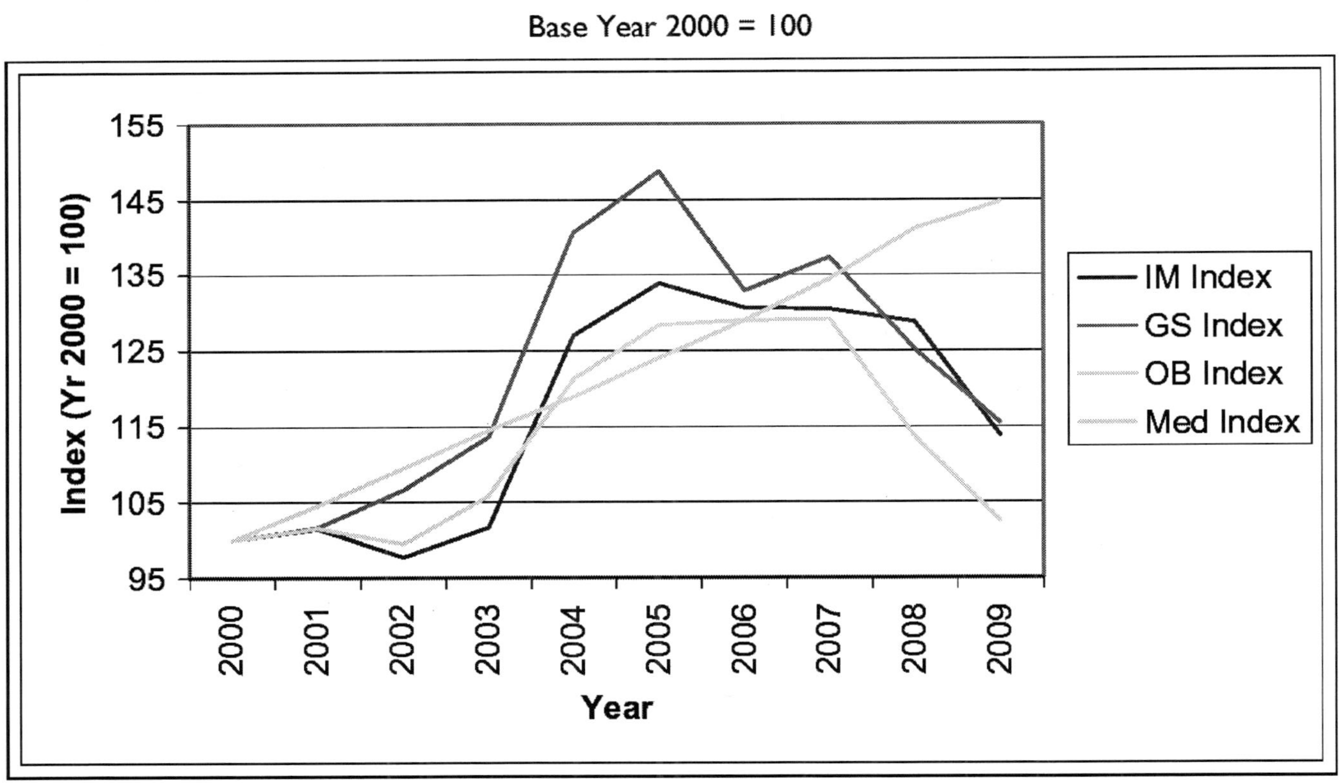

Source: CRS analysis of http://mymedicalmalpracticeinsurance.com/medical-malpractice-insurance-rates.php.

Notes: The values on the vertical axis are index numbers which measure the magnitude of change from 2000—the base year. Index numbers are similar to percentages and an index number of 130 would indicate, in this context, that the premium was 30% higher than the base year. IM refers to premiums for internal medicine; GS refers to premiums for general surgery; OB refers to premiums for OB/Gyn. Med Index refers to medical inflation as calculated by the Bureau of Labor Statistics.

Figure B-3. Change in Malpractice Premiums, by Specialty—Wisconsin.

Second, in a market economy both pre-trial settlements and post-trial judgments are assumed to drive up a firm's costs, making its products more expensive, and signaling to consumers, through the price mechanism to shift to alternative producers. Similarly, even if the firm is fully insured, so long as firms in the industry are experience rated for their liability insurance, as opposed to community rated,[173] the price mechanism is assumed to work since firms will face higher insurance costs equal to their expected claims and the administrative costs associated with the insurance.

Finally, and perhaps most importantly, the systematic analysis of "closed claims" can provide valuable information to providers and consumers about the relative performance of different organizations or providers, or the safety of different procedures.[174] For instance, anesthesiologists used closed claim files to identify a "disproportionate number of respiratory system-related claims, many based on inadequate or problematic ventilation, esophageal intubation, or tracheal intubation."[175]

End Notes

[1] While several legislative proposals, including H.R. 5, the Help Efficient, Accessible, Low-cost, Timely Healthcare (HEALTH) Act of 2011, address both medical malpractice and product liability, this report is limited to provider medical malpractice.

[2] The tort system is held out by some economists and legal scholars to play a broader role than simply compensating for wrongs. See Appendix A for a discussion of the role of the tort system in a market economy.

[3] The cost of capital is an accounting concept which is "a weighted average of the opportunity cost of the debt and equity components of a firm's capital structure." See J. J. Launie, "The Cost of Capital of Insurance Companies," *The Journal of Risk and Insurance*, vol. 38, no. 2 (June 1971), pp. 263-268.

[4] See CRS Report R41693, *Medical Malpractice: Background and Legislation in the 112th Congress*, by Baird Webel, Vivian S. Chu, and David Newman, pp. 6-8.

[5] A medical malpractice crisis can be narrowly defined, focusing on insurance, as an environment of rapidly rising premiums or a reduction in the number of firms offering professional liability insurance to medical providers or more broadly defined to include the number of malpractice suits, the dollar amounts of awards, and the impact of the availability and cost of insurance and frequency of law suits on access to care and the practice of medicine, among other things. See Kenneth E. Thorpe, "The Medical Malpractice 'Crisis': Recent Trends And The Impact Of State Tort Reforms," *Health Affairs*, January 21, 2004, pp. W4-W20.

[6] Allen D. Spiegel and Florence Kavaler, "America's First Medical Malpractice Crisis, 1835-1865," *Journal of Community Health*, vol. 22, no. 4 (August 1997), pp. 283-303.

[7] William M. Sage, "The Forgotten Third: Liability Insurance And The Medical Malpractice Crisis," *Health Affairs*, vol. 23, no. 4 (2004), pp. 10-21.

[8] Mutual legal defense societies emerged and private medical malpractice insurance first became available around 1900. See Kenneth A. DeVille, *Medical Malpractice in Nineteenth-Century America: Origins and Legacy* (New York: New York University Press, 1990), p. 205.

[9] David A. Hyman, "What Lessons Should We Learn from the First Malpractice Crisis of the Twenty-First Century," *Drexel Law Review*, vol. 1 (2009), p. 262.

[10] Daniel R. Levinson, Inspector General, *Adverse Events in Hospitals: National Incidence Among Medicare Beneficiaries*, Department of Health and Human Services, Office of Inspector General, OEI-06-09-00090, Washington, DC, November 2010, http://oig.hhs.gov/oei/reports/oei-06-09-00090.pdf.

[11] Ibid.

[12] http://www8.nationalacademies.org/onpinews/newsitem.aspx?recordid=11623.

[13] Institute of Medicine, *To Err is Human: Building a Safer Health Care System* (Washington, DC: National Academies Press, 2000).

[14] Some *wrongs* can give rise to both potential criminal and civil liability such as an accident involving injuries caused by a drunk driver. Generally, civil actions are brought by the injured party and criminal actions are brought by the State. Absent victim compensation schemes, fines and penalties imposed through the criminal actions inure to the benefit of the state and not the injured party.

[15] "New ... torts are being recognized constantly, and the progress of the common law is marked by many cases of first impression, in which the court has struck out boldly to create a new cause of action, where none had been recognized before. ... When it becomes clear that the plaintiff's interests are entitled to legal protection against

the conduct of the defendant, the mere fact that the claim is novel will not itself operate as a bar to the remedy." W. Page Keeton, Prosser & Keeton on the Law of Torts, § 1 (5th ed. 1984) [hereinafter Prosser & Keeton, Torts].

16 George C. Christie and James E. Meeks, Cases and Materials on the Law of Torts, at 5 (2d ed. 1990).

17 Michael Shapo, Principles of Tort Law, § 1.03(A) (2d ed. 2003).

18 Restatement (Second) of Torts § 282 (1965).

19 Black's Law Dictionary 716 (6th ed. 1991). In a landmark decision from 1850 where the court considered an action for trespass for assault and battery, the court held that *ordinary care* would "vary with the circumstances of the case and it means that kind of degree of care, which prudent and cautious men would use, such as is required by the exigency of the case, and such as is necessary to guard against probable danger." Thus, to avoid liability, a tortfeasor must have "used the kind and degree of care necessary to the exigency, and in the circumstances in which he was placed" Brown v. Kendall, 60 Mass. (1 Cush) 292 (Mass. 1850).

20 Black's Law Dictionary 717 (6th ed. 1991).

21 Black's Law Dictionary 717-718 (6th ed. 1991).

22 Black's Law Dictionary 717 (6th ed. 1991).

23 H.R. 5, the Help Efficient, Accessible, Low-cost, Timely Healthcare (HEALTH) Act of 2011 would not alter any existing standards of negligence or defenses to claims of negligence. H.R. 5, § 11(b)(1) provides "Any issue that is not governed by any provision of law established by or under this Act (including State standards of negligence) shall be governed by otherwise applicable State or Federal law."

24 159 F.2d 169 (2d. Cir. 1947).

25 Shapo, *supra* note 17, at § 19.02.

26 Another balancing test to determine the standard of care is the risk-utility analysis as set forth in the Restatement (Second) of Torts. Section 291 states that "risk is unreasonable and the act is negligent if the risk is of such magnitude as to outweigh what the law regards as the utility of the act or of the particular manner in which it is done." Section 292 further lists several factors important in determining "the utility of the actor's conduct," and the "magnitude of the risk," one of which is "the social value which the law attaches to the interest" that is to be protected or imperiled, respectively. Where this type of balancing test differs from the *Learned Hand test* is that "the *Hand* test is essentially a cost/cost test rather than one weighing costs or risks against utility or benefits." Shapo, *supra* note 17, at § 19.02(D).

27 Richard A. Posner, *Economic Analysis of Law*, 6th ed. (New York: Aspen Publishers, 2003), p. 169.

28 Grimshaw v. Ford Motor Co., 174 Cal. Rptr. 348 (Cal. Ct. App. 1981).

29 This description of the Ford Pinto case is taken from Gary T. Schwartz, "The Myth of the Ford Pinto Case," *Rutgers Law Review*, vol. 43 (1991), pp. 1013-1068.

30 See also Douglas Birsch and John H. Fielder, The Ford Pinto Case: A Study in Applied Ethics, Business, and Technology (1994).

31 Shapo, *supra* note 17, § 23.01.

32 http://www.randcompare.org/glossary/16/letterm.

33 The term "express or implied" means that the contract or agreement between a physician and a patient does not need to be formal or written. Rather, it can be implied by the actions of the parties. For instance, see http://www.texmed.org/ Template.aspx?id=16146#_ftn2.

34 65 Corpus Juris Secundum § 162 (2010).

35 To account for the difference between urban and rural medical treatment and facilities, courts acknowledged different standards of care for physicians in different locations. The "strict locality rule" required the physician to use "such skill as doctors in the same general neighborhood, in the same general lines of practice, ordinarily have and exercise in like cases." Tefft v. Wilcox, 6 Kan. 46 (1870). A more modified locality rule required one's practice to align with "similar localities." Small v. Howard, 128 Mass. 131 (Mass.1880), *overruled by* Brune v. Belinkoff, 235 N.E.2d 793 (Mass. 1968). An example of a "national" standard of care is "whether the physician, if a general practitioner, has exercised the degree of care and skill of the average qualified practitioner, taking into account the advances in the profession. ... Under this standard some allowance is thus made for the type of community in which the physician carries on his practice." See Prosser, Torts § 32 (3d ed.).

36 Michael Shapo, Principles of Tort Law, § 23.04. Some states will require the expert witness to be licensed to practice in the jurisdiction, with exceptions that allow the trial court to admit an out-of-state witness "when it determines that the appropriate witnesses would otherwise not be available." See, e.g., Tenn. Code Ann. § 29-26-115(b).

37 Shilkret v. Annapolis Emergency Hospital Ass'n, 349 A.2d 245 (Md. 1975).

38 This conclusion is clearer if we consider the following terms:

(1) Adverse event: an injury caused by medical management rather than the underlying condition of the patient,

(2) Error: the failure, for reasons which are preventable, of a planned action to be completed as intended (i.e. error of execution), or the use of a wrong plan to achieve an aim (i.e. error of planning),

(3) Preventable adverse event: an adverse event attributable to error, and

(4) Negligence: negligent adverse events represent a subset of preventable adverse events that satisfy legal criteria used in determining negligence.

With respect to medical malpractice, in a well-functioning system, non-preventable adverse events should not give rise to negligence nor should an outcome fully depend on the patient's condition. See Aziz Sheihk and Brian Hurwitz, "Setting up a database of medical error in general practice: conceptual and methodological considerations," *British Journal of General Practice*, vol. 51 (2001), pp. 57-60.

[39] 471 A.2d 758 (Md. Ct. Spec. App. 1984)

[40] 54 Corpus Juris Secundum, § 1.

[41] Ibid. at § 3.

[42] 25 Corpus Juris Secundum, § 1.

[43] Jerome H. Notes, Clark D. Kimball, and Diana T. Axelrod, et al., *Damages in Tort Actions* (New York: LexisNexis, 2010), § 3.05(2) .

[44] James Granelli, "The Attack on Joint and Several Liability," *ABA Journal, The Lawyer's Magazine*, vol. 71 (July 1985), pp. 61-63.

[45] Charles W. Peckinpaugh, Jr., "An Analysis of the Collateral Source Rule," *Insurance Law Journal*, 1966, pp. 545-555. (The collateral source rule declares that "benefits received by an injured party from a collateral source wholly independent of the wrongdoer will not operate to lessen the damages recoverable from the party causing the injury, and evidence of the receipt of such benefits is inadmissible for mitigation purposes.")

[46] Black's Law Dictionary (8th ed. 2004).

[47] These figures are from the Kaiser Family Foundation analysis of data from the National Practitioner Data Bank (NPDB). See http://statehealthfacts.kff.org/comparemaptable.jsp?ind=436&cat=8.

[48] David A. Hyman and Charles Silver, "Medical Malpractice Litigation and Tort Reform: It's the Incentives, Stupid," *Vanderbilt Law Review*, vol. 59, no. 4 (2006), p. 1107.

[49] CRS analysis of Kaiser Family Foundation data, *available at*, http://statehealthfacts.kff.org/.

[50] See http://bjs.ojp.usdoj.gov/index.cfm?ty=tp&tid=2234.

[51] Federal court statistics are not very detailed and report only the broad category of torts. An analysis of a sample of 7,688 federal court cases filed between October 1, 2005 and September 30, 2006 revealed only 58 malpractice cases or 0.75 percent of all cases. In 2009, there were 363,774 cases filed in federal district courts so one might estimate that about 2,728 medical malpractice cases were filed in federal court. See Jordan M. Singer, *Civil Case Processing in the Federal District Courts: A Twenty-First Century Analysis,* The Institute for the Advancement of the American Legal System, Denver, CO, January 21, 2009, pp. 1-108, http://papers.ssrn.com/sol3/papers.cfm?abstract_id=1331024& download=yes.

[52] http://www.statehealthfacts.org/comparemaptable.jsp?ind=436&cat=8#notes-1.

[53] A ratio generally acknowledged in the industry. See Medical Protective Company Website, http://www.medpro.com/ about-medical-protective, where the company claims that 79% of all claims between 2000 and 2009 were closed without payment and 90% of all cases that went to trial were won by the defense.

[54] The Bureau of Labor Statistics estimates inflation for medical care services and includes changes in prices for professional services, hospital and related services, and health insurance. The measure is described at http://www.bls.gov/cpi/cpifact4.htm.

[55] http://www.statehealthfacts.org.

[56] These figures are in nominal dollars and are not adjusted for inflation. The actual number of cases in some states, particularly those with a small number of cases each year on average can vary considerably from year to year just as the average dollar amount of claims paid in Figure 1 can be dependant on the nature of the claims settled in any one year.

[57] LeRoy F. Simmons and Mark L. Cross, "The Underwriting Cycle and the Risk Manager," *The Journal of Risk and Insurance*, vol. 53, no. 1 (March 1986), pp. 155-163.

[58] See CRS Report RL31886, *Medical Malpractice Insurance: An Economic Introduction and Review of Historical Experience*, by Baird Webel. Also see Tom Baker, "Medical Malpractice Insurance Reform," in *Medical Malpractice and the U.S. Health Care System*, ed. William M. Sage and Roger Kersh (New York: Cambridge University Press, 2006), pp. 267-290.

[59] One shortcoming of the National Association of Insurance Commissioners data is that it does not capture the impact of changes in the market such as the potentiality that more physicians are now employed by organizations that self insure for all or part of the risk.

[60] There is some evidence to suggest "that tort and government reforms in the medical malpractice market have a significant, and counter-intuitive, impact on the resources that insurers devote to defending malpractice claims with damage limits and attorney fee limits being associated with greater levels of spending on claims defense expenses" since the downside of an adverse jury decision is capped at the statutory limit. See Jan M. Ambrose and Anne Carrol, "Medical Malpractice Reform and Insurer Claim Defense: Unintended Effects?," *Journal of Health Politics, Policy and Law*, vol. 32, no. 5 (October 2007), pp. 843-865.

[61] Statistics provided to CRS by the National Association of Insurance Commissioners. Direct earned premiums are the proportion of premiums paid that, for accounting purposes, are recognized as income during a period.

62 All premium data are from http://mymedicalmalpracticeinsurance.com/medical-malpractice-insurance-rates.php. A $1 million/$3 million policy is a typical medical malpractice policy and "pays up to $1 million for each individual claim and up to $3 million in any given insurance year for multiple claims against the insured."

63 Some states have statewide premiums, whereas insurers in other states set premiums geographically and often by county. In Pennsylvania, these percentage increases do not include physician funding of the MCARE program enacted in 2002 to compensate individuals injured by medical malpractice.

64 For a discussion of how the Centers for Medicare & Medicaid Services calculates the malpractice RVU (relative value units) attached to services, see https://www.cms.gov/PhysicianFeeSched/Downloads/MP-RVU-Report_v11_508v5.pdf/. The 2011 Medicare Physician Fee Schedule provides for the 3.9% figure. See Department of Health and Human Services, "42 CFR Parts 405, 409, 410 et al. Medicare Program; Payment Policies Under the Physician Fee Schedule and Other Revisions to Part B for CY 2011; Final Rule," 75 *Federal Register* 73260, November 29, 2010.

65 http://www.medpac.gov/documents/MedPAC_Payment_Basics_10_Physician.pdf. CMS periodically surveys medical malpractice carriers and updates the payments to reflect the then current premiums and mix of providers performing particular services (https://www.cms.gov/PhysicianFeeSched/Downloads/MP-RVU-Report_v11_508v5.pdf.). The latest update was implemented in 2010. Similarly, the Medicare Inpatient Prospective Payment System (IPPS) payment rates to hospitals are adjusted annually to reflect changes in the goods and services hospitals purchase to provide patient care, including medical malpractice insurance, as estimated by changes in the CMS professional liability insurance premium index.

66 Congressional Budget Office, *Medical Malpractice Tort Limits and Health Care Spending*, Background Paper, Washington, DC, April 2006, http://www.cbo.gov/ftpdocs/71xx/doc7174/04-28-MedicalMalpractice.pdf.

67 Marilynn Marchione, "Study: Doctors order tests out of fear of lawsuits," *The Washington Post*, February 16, 2010, http://www.washingtonpost.com/wp-dyn/content/article/2011/02/16/AR2011021604384_pf.html.

68 http://www.jacksonhealthcare.com/healthcare-research/healthcare-costs-defensive-medicine-study.aspx. Also see Statement of Stuart L. Weinstein, M.D., U.S. Congress, House Committee on the Judiciary, hearing on the Subject of Medical Malpractice Reform: Cutting Costs, Spurring Investment, Creating Jobs, 112th Cong., 1st sess., January 20, 2011, p. http://judiciary.house.gov/hearings/pdf/Weinstein01202011.PDF.

69 Michelle M. Mello, Amitabh Chandra, and Atul A. Gawande, et al., "National Costs Of The Medical Liability System," *Health Affairs*, vol. 29, no. 9 (September 2010), pp. 1569-1577.

70 J. William Thomas, Erika C. Ziller, and Deborah A. Thayer, "Low Costs Of Defensive Medicine, Small Savings From Tort Reform," *Health Affairs*, vol. 29, no. 9 (September 2010), pp. 1578-1584.

71 David Dranove and Yasutora Watanabe, "Influence and Deterrence: How Obstetricians Respond to Litigation Against Themselves and their Colleagues," *American Law and Economics Review*, vol. 12, no. 1 (2010), pp. 69-94.

72 http://www.insurance.wa.gov/legislative/reports/medmal2010.pdf.

73 David M. Studdert, Michelle M. Mello, and Atul A. Gawande, et al., "Claims, Errors, and Compensation Payments in Medical Malpractice Litigation," *The New England Journal of Medicine*, vol. 354, no. 19 (May 11, 2006).

74 Jan M. Ambrose and Anne Carrol, "Medical Malpractice Reform and Insurer Claim Defense: Unintended Effects?," *Journal of Health Politics, Policy and Law*, vol. 32, no. 5 (October 2007), pp. 843-865.

75 David M. Studdert, Michelle M. Mello, and Atul A. Gawande, et al., "Claims, Errors, and Compensation Payments in Medical Malpractice Litigation," *The New England Journal of Medicine*, vol. 354, no. 19 (May 11, 2006).

76 Congressional Budget Office, *The Economics of U.S. Tort Liability: A Primer*, October 2003, p. 28, *available at*, http://www.cbo.gov/ftpdocs/46xx/doc4641/10-22-TortReform-Study.pdf.

77 Another aspect of efficiency, which we do not deal with here, is the degree to which those with actual injury experience difficulties retaining counsel and being adequately compensated.

78 David A. Hyman and Charles Silver, "Medical Malpractice Litigation and Tort Reform: It's the Incentives, Stupid," *Vanderbilt Law Review*, vol. 59, no. 4 (2006), pp. 1085-1135.

79 David A. Hyman and Charles Silver, "Medical Malpractice Litigation and Tort Reform: It's the Incentives, Stupid," *Vanderbilt Law Review*, vol. 59, no. 4 (2006), p. 1100.

80 Hyman and Silver, 2006, p.1100 citing David M. Studdert, Michelle M. Mello, and Atul A. Gawande, et al., "Claims, Errors, and Compensation Payments in Medical Malpractice Litigation," *The New England Journal of Medicine*, vol. 354, no. 19 (May 11, 2006). See also David M. Studdert, Michelle M. Mello, and Atul A. Gawande, et al., "Claims, Errors, and Compensation Payments in Medical Malpractice Litigation," *The New England Journal of Medicine*, vol. 354, no. 19 (May 11, 2006) at 2031 and Patricia Danzon, *Medical Malpractice: Theory, Evidence and Public Policy* (Cambridge, MA: Harvard University Press, 1985), a somewhat dated study that found that between 39% and 53% of the law suits filed but dropped lawsuits during the pendency of proceedings would have produced an award for the plaintiff.

81 Emily R. Carrier, James D. Reschovsky, and Michelle M. Mello, et al., "Physicians' Fears Of Malpractice Lawsuits Are Not Assuaged By Tort Reforms," *Health Affairs*, vol. 29, no. 9 (September 2010), pp. 1585-1592.

[82] Ibid.

[83] Ibid.

[84] See John E. Rolph, John L. Adams, and Kimberly A. McGuigan, "Identifying Malpractice Prone Physicians," *Journal of Empirical Legal Studies*, vol. 4, no. 1 (March 2007), p. 127 for citations to this literature.

[85] Michael D. Greenberg, Amelia M. Haviland, and J. Scott Ashwood, et al., *Is Better Patient Safety Associated with Less Malpractice Activity? Evidence from California*, Rand Corporation, Santa Monica, CA, 2010, http://www.rand.org/content/dam/rand/pubs/technical_reports/2010/RAND_TR824.pdf.

[86] Ibid. at 19.

[87] Physician Insurers Association of America, *State Enactments of Selected Health Care Liability Reforms*, Rockville, MD, November 1, 2010. See also the National Conference of State Legislatures' state summary of medical malpractice laws at http://www.ncsl.org/default.aspx?tabid=18516.

[88] Catherine M. Sharkley, "Caps and the Construction of Damages in Medical Malpractice Cases," in *Medical Malpractice and the U.S. Health Care System*, ed. William M. Sage and Roger Kersh (New York: Cambridge University Press, 2006), pp. 154-172.

[89] Some states, such as Texas, cap noneconomic damages at a dollar amount per claimant ($250,000);some states cap noneconomic damages at a dollar amount but also limit the total amount that can be awarded for noneconomic damages (for instance, in 2010 South Carolina capped damages per provider at $397,175 and any total to $1.191 million). Some states, such as Virginia, cap just the total.

[90] See *Carson v. Maurer*, 424 A.2d 825 (N.H. 1980) in which the New Hampshire Supreme Court struck down a $250,000 cap on noneconomic damages as violating equal protection.

[91] See Center for Justice and Democracy, *How "Caps" and Other Liability Limits Shift Costs to Taxpayers*, New York, NY, http://www.centerjd.org/archives/issues-facts/NYMedicaidCapCosts.pdf.

[92] See Catherine M. Sharkley, "Unintended Consequences of Medical Malpractice Damage Caps," *New York University Law Review*, vol. 80, no. 2 (May 2005), pp. 412-432.

[93] See Douglas W. Elmendorf, *Letter to the Honorable Orrin G. Hatch*, Congressional Budget Office, October 9, 2009, *available at*, http://www.cbo.gov/ftpdocs/106xx/doc10641/10-09-Tort_Reform.pdf and Congressional Budget Office, *Congressional Budget Office Cost Estimate: H.R. 5 Help Efficient, Accessible, Low-cost, Timely Healthcare (HEALTH) Act of 2011* , May 23, 2011, http://cbo.gov/ftpdocs/122xx/doc12209/HR5.pdf.

[94] See Michelle M. Mello and Allen Kachalia, *Evaluation of Options for Medical Malpractice System Reform*, Medicare Payments Advisory Commission, 10-2, Washington, DC, April 2010, p. 5, *available at*, http://www.medpac.gov/documents/Apr10_MedicalMalpractice_CONTRACTOR.pdf.

[95] Douglas W. Elmendorf, *Letter to the Honorable Orrin G. Hatch*, Congressional Budget Office, October 9, 2009, *available at*, http://www.cbo.gov/ftpdocs/106xx/doc10641/10-09-Tort_Reform.pdf. However, it should be noted that there may be a differential impact on some high-risk specialties. See Jonathan Klick and Thomas Stratmann, "Medical Malpractice Reform and Physicians In High-Risk Specialties," *Journal of Legal Studies*, vol. 36 (June 2007), pp. S121-S142.

[96] Eric A. Helland and Mark Showalter, "The Impact of Liability on the Physician Labor Market," *Rand Working Paper*, 2006, *available at*, http://www.rand.org/content/dam/rand/pubs/working_papers/2006/RAND_WR384.pdf.

[97] Michelle M. Mello, David M. Stoddert, and Catherine M. DesRoches, et al., "Effects of a Malpractice Crisis on Specialist Supply and Patient Access to Care," *Annals of Surgery*, vol. 242, no. 5 (November 2005), p. 621 628.

[98] For instance, see David A. Matsa, "Does Malpractice Liability Keep the Doctor Away? Evidence from Tort Reform Damage Caps," *Journal of Legal Studies*, vol. 36, no. 2 (June 2007), p. S143–S182.

[99] Michelle M. Mello, David M. Stoddert, and Catherine M. DesRoches, et al., "Effects of a Malpractice Crisis on Specialist Supply and Patient Access to Care," *Annals of Surgery*, vol. 242, no. 5 (November 2005), p. 621 628.

[100] Seth A. Seabury, *Does Malpractice Liability Reform Attract High Risk Doctors?*, Rand Institute for Civil Justice, WR-674-ICJ, Santa Monica, CA, December 2009, p. 28.

[101] See Michelle M. Mello and Allen Kachalia, *Evaluation of Options for Medical Malpractice System Reform*, Medicare Payments Advisory Commission, 10-2, Washington, DC, April 2010, p. 5, *available at*, http://www.medpac.gov/documents/Apr10_MedicalMalpractice_CONTRACTOR.pdf.

[102] Restatement (Second) of Torts § 908(1) (1979).

[103] Thomas J. Miceli and Michael P. Stone, "The Determinants of State-Level Caps on Punitive Damages: Theory and Evidence," University of Connecticut Department of Economics Working Paper Series, Storrs, CT, October 2010, *available at*, http://www.econ.uconn.edu/working/2010-25.pdf.

[104] Joni Hersch and W. Kip Viscusi, "Punitive Damages: How judges and Juries Perform," *Journal of Legal Studies*, vol. 33, no. 1 (January 2004), pp. 1-36.

[105] Kenneth E. Thorpe, "The Medical Malpractice 'Crisis': Recent Trends And The Impact Of State Tort Reforms," *Health Affairs*, January 21, 2004, pp. W4-W20.

[106] Idaho Code § 5-219.

[107] Miss. Code Ann. § 15-1-36.

[108] The alternative, and less common form of insurance, is referred to as *occurrence insurance* that relates to the date that the alleged incident occurred.

[109] Michelle M. Mello and Allen Kachalia, *Evaluation of Options for Medical Malpractice System Reform*, Medicare Payments Advisory Commission, 10-2, Washington, DC, April 2010, http://www.medpac.gov/documents/Apr10_MedicalMalpractice_CONTRACTOR.pdf.

[110] Congressional Budget Office, *Medical Malpractice Tort Limits and Health Care Spending*, Background Paper, Washington, DC, April 2006, http://www.cbo.gov/ftpdocs/71xx/doc7174/04-28-MedicalMalpractice.pdf.

[111] Michelle M. Mello and Allen Kachalia, *Evaluation of Options for Medical Malpractice System Reform*, Medicare Payments Advisory Commission, 10-2, Washington, DC, April 2010, http://www.medpac.gov/documents/Apr10_MedicalMalpractice_CONTRACTOR.pdf.

[112] See, e.g., Ariz. Rev. Stat. § 12-2506 (the liability of each defendant for damages is several only and is not otherwise joint); Fla. Stat. Ann. § 768.81 (the court shall enter judgment against each party on the basis of such party's percentage of fault and not on the basis of joint and several liability).

[113] A mandatory setoff requires "a court to subtract the amount of any collateral source benefits received, or available, to an injured plaintiff from any compensatory damage award." See Michael Flynn, "Private Medical Insurance and the Collateral Source Rule: A Good Bet?," *University of Toledo Law Review*, vol. 22 (1990), pp. 39-71.

[114] Physician Insurers Association of America, *State Enactments of Selected Health Care Liability Reforms*, Rockville, MD, November 1, 2010.

[115] Ibid.

[116] Michelle M. Mello and Allen Kachalia, *Evaluation of Options for Medical Malpractice System Reform*, Medicare Payments Advisory Commission, 10-2, Washington, DC, April 2010, http://www.medpac.gov/documents/Apr10_MedicalMalpractice_CONTRACTOR.pdf.

[117] Tom Baker, "Medical Malpractice Insurance Reform," in *Medical Malpractice and the U.S. Health Care System*, ed. William M. Sage and Roger Kersh (New York: Cambridge University Press, 2006), pp. 267-290.

[118] CRS Report R41474, *Accountable Care Organizations and the Medicare Shared Savings Program*, by David Newman.

[119] See http://www.aha.org/aha/letter/2010/101203-let-fishman-berwick.pdf and see A. Liebhaber and J.M. Grossman, *Physicians Moving to Mid-Sized, Single-Specialty Practices.* Tracking Report No. 18. Washington, D.C.: Center for Studying Health System Change, December, 2007 which reports that "physicians increasingly are practicing in mid-sized, single-specialty groups of six to 50 physicians."

[120] Robert Cooter and Thomas Ulen, *Law and Economics*, 3rd ed. (Reading, MA: Addison-Wesley, 2000), p. 371.

[121] See Havighurst, 1991, p.96 and James F. Blumstein, *Medical Malpractice Standard-Setting: Developing Malpractice "Safe Harbors"as a New Role for QIOs?*, Vanderbilt University Law School Public Law and Legal Theory Working Paper Number 06-08, Nashville, TN, April 2006, pp. 1-42, http://papers.ssrn.com/sol3/papers.cfm? abstract_id=899321.

[122] Clark C. Havighurst, "Practice Guidelines as Legal Standards Governing Physician Liability," *Law and Contemporary Problems*, vol. 54, no. 2 (Spring 1991), pp. 87-117.

[123] Michelle M. Mello, "Of Swords and Shields: The Role of Clinical Practice Guidelines in Medical Malpractice Litigation," *University of Pennsylvania Law Review*, vol. 149, no. 3 (January 2001), pp. 645-710.

[124] Arnold S. Relman, "Medical Guidelines and Malpractice," *The New York Times*, October 22, 2010 (letter by Mr. Relman in response to op-ed by Peter Orszag), *available at*, http://www.nytimes.com/2010/10/23/opinion/l23orszag.html.

[125] 304 U.S. 64 (1938).

[126] Ibid. at 78.

[127] Cato Institute, *Cato Handbook for Congress: Policy Recommendations for the 106th Congress* , Washington, DC, 1999, http://www.cato.org/pubs/handbook/hb106/hb106-29.pdf.

[128] U.S. Const., art I, § 8, cl. 3.

[129] William A. Niskanen, "Do Not Federalize Tort Law," *Regulation*, vol. 4 (1995), pp. 34-37.

[130] Ibid. at 35.

[131] CRS Report R40725, *Requiring Individuals to Obtain Health Insurance: A Constitutional Analysis*, by Jennifer Staman et al.

[132] 285 U.S. 262, 311 (1932).

[133] CRS Report R41661, *Medical Malpractice Liability Reform: Legal Issues and 50-State Surveys on Tort Reform Proposals*, by Vivian S. Chu.

[134] Michelle M. Mello and Allen Kachalia, *Evaluation of Options for Medical Malpractice System Reform*, Medicare Payments Advisory Commission, 10-2, Washington, DC, April 2010, p. 5, *available at*, http://www.medpac.gov/ documents/Apr10_MedicalMalpractice_CONTRACTOR.pdf.

[135] The federal government in many instances engages state agencies to survey nursing homes and hospitals for participation in the Medicare and Medicaid programs. Similarly, Medicare requires physicians to be state licensed.

[136] Abigail R. Moncrieff, "Federalization Snowballs: The Need for National Action in Medical Malpractice Reform," *Columbia Law Review*, vol. 109 (2009), p. 859.

[137] The Becker-Posner Blog, "Tort Reform - Posner," press release, January 16, 2005, http://www.becker-posner-blog.com/2005/01/tort-reform—posner.html.

[138] Abigail R. Moncrieff, "Federalization Snowballs: The Need for National Action in Medical Malpractice Reform," *Columbia Law Review*, vol. 109 (2009), pp. 844-892; See also Michael I. Krauss, *The Tort of Medical Malpractice: Is it Time for Law Reform in North Carolina*, John Locke Foundation, Raleigh, NC, October 2004, pp. 1-30, http://www.johnlocke.org/acrobat/policyReports/tort_of_medical.

[139] The federal government's share is actually likely to be more than the 30 percent estimated by Moncrieff once one includes federal purchases of insurance and health care for its employees through the Federal Employees Health Benefits Program, the Department of Defense, and the Department of Veterans Affairs.

[140] The federal government in some instances engages state agencies to survey nursing homes and hospitals for participation in the Medicare and Medicaid programs. Similarly, Medicare requires physicians to be state licensed.

[141] Michael I. Krauss, *The Tort of Medical Malpractice: Is it Time for Law Reform in North Carolina*, John Locke Foundation, Raleigh, NC, October 2004, pp. 1-30, http://www.johnlocke.org/acrobat/policyReports/tort_of_medical_malpractice.pdf.

[142] Krauss, citing White House, Press Release, President Proposes Major Reforms to Address Medical Liability Crisis, July 25, 2002. While federal tort reform legislation applicable to particular intrastate torts that arguably do not substantially affect interstate commerce would likely be unconstitutional, the same could not be said with respect to torts that substantially affect commerce. In *Gonzales v. Raich*, 545 U.S. 1 (2005), the Supreme Court upheld the application of a federal statute prohibiting the manufacture and possession of marijuana to the intrastate cultivation and use of marijuana for medicinal purposes, because there was a rational basis for concluding that "taken in the aggregate, [such activity] substantially affect[s] interstate commerce." Ibid at 22. This decision appears to support Congress's power to regulate medical malpractice, because it would be rational to conclude that litigation concerning this activity substantially affects interstate commerce.

[143] Karen B. Domino, *Professional Liability Insurance Premiums for Anesthesiologists: Stability Despite the Economic Crisis*, American Society of Anesthesiologists, 2010, *http://depts.washington.edu/asaccp/prof/asa73_8_44_45.pdf.*

[144] See http://depts.washington.edu/asaccp/ASA/index.shtml.

[145] Joseph T. Hallinan, "Heal Thyself," *Wall Street Journal*, June 21, 2005, p. A1, http://prdupl02.ynet.co.il/ForumFiles/12422128.pdf.

[146] Karen B. Domino, *Professional Liability Insurance Premiums for Anesthesiologists: Stability Despite the Economic Crisis*, American Society of Anesthesiologists, 2010, http://depts.washington.edu/asaccp/prof/asa73_8_44_45.pdf.

[147] Michael D. Greenberg, Amelia M. Haviland, and J. Scott Ashwood, et al., *Is Better Patient Safety Associated with Less Malpractice Activity? Evidence from California*, Rand Corporation, Santa Monica, CA, 2010, http://www.rand.org/content/dam/rand/pubs/technical_reports/2010/RAND_TR824.pdf.

[148] https://www.virginiamason.org/body.cfm?id=158&action=detail&ref=3500.

[149] E-mail from Dr. Craig Blackmore, Virginia Mason Medical Center, January 25, 2011.

[150] One major integrated health care system reported a roughly 70% decline in malpractice costs between 2005 and 2010 and attributes the decline to both the soft insurance market and its quality improvement efforts.

[151] Sheila Leatherman, Donald Berwick, and Debra Iles, et al., "The Business Case For Quality: Case Studies And An Analysis," *Health Affairs*, vol. 22, no. 2 (March/April 2003), pp. 17-30.

[152] For example, in California, as shown in Figure B-1, in the Appendix B, premiums for physicians have continued to increase at a rate far faster than medical inflation over the past decade despite California adopting malpractice reforms in 1975.

[153] See Ronald H. Coase, "The Problem of Social Cost," *Journal of Law and Economics*, vol. 3, no. 1 (1960), pp. 1-44.

[154] See Guido Calabresi, "Some Thoughts on Risk Distribution and the Law of Tort," *Yale Law Journal*, vol. 70 (1961), pp. 499-553 and Richard A. Epstein, "A Theory of Strict Liability," *Journal of Legal Studies*, vol. 2, no. 1 (1973), pp. 151-221.

[155] Restatement (Second) of Torts §§ 290-293 (1964).

[156] Robert Cooter and Thomas Ulen, *Law and Economics*, 3rd ed. (Reading, MA: Addison-Wesley, 2000), p. 314.

[157] David S. Sanson, "The Pervasive Problem of Court-Sanctioned Secrecy and the Exigency of National Reform," *Duke Law Journal*, vol. 53 (2003), pp. 807 - 832.

[158] A Kaiser Family Foundation study found that "[n]early six in ten adults (58%) said that the number of malpractice lawsuits is a "very" important factor in causing rising health care costs, and nearly two in ten (19%) said it was the most important factor when forced to choose among several." See http://www.kff.org/spotlight/malpractice/upload/ Spotlight_Dec05_malpractice-2.pdf.

[159] David A. Hyman, "Medical Malpractice and the Tort System: What Do We Know and What (If Anything) Should We Do About It?," *Texas Law Review*, vol. 80, no. 7 (June 2002), p. 1639-1656.

[160] David M. Studdert, Michelle M. Mello, and Atul A. Gawande, et al., "Claims, Errors, and Compensation Payments in Medical Malpractice Litigation," *The New England Journal of Medicine*, vol. 354, no. 19 (May 11, 2006).

[161] David M. Studdert, Michelle M. Mello, and Atul A. Gawande, et al., "Claims, Errors, and Compensation Payments in Medical Malpractice Litigation," *The New England Journal of Medicine*, vol. 354, no. 19 (May 11, 2006).

[162] A one-third attorney contingency fee has historically been the most common percentage (See http://apps.americanbar.org/tips/contingent/MedMalReport092004DCW2.pdf). While some states have imposed caps on medical malpractice contingent fees (e.g., Florida, California, Tennessee) higher figures than one-third are allowed in some states, (e.g., Oklahoma).

[163] U.S. Congress, Joint Economic Committee, *Improving the American Legal System: The Economic Benefits of Tort Reform* , 104th Cong., March 1996, p. http://www.house.gov/jec/tort/tort/tort.htm#endnot32.

[164] Michelle M. Mello and David M. Studdert, "The Medical Malpractice System," in *Medical Malpractice and the U.S. Health Care System*, ed. William M. Sage and Roger Kersh (New York: Cambridge University Press, 2006), pp. 17-21.

[165] David A. Hyman and Charles Silver, "Medical Malpractice Litigation and Tort Reform: It's the Incentives, Stupid," *Vanderbilt Law Review*, vol. 59, no. 4 (2006), pp. 1085-1135.

[166] This is not to suggest that a physician with repeated claims is never dropped by their insurer or that a physician with repeated claims may not have difficulties finding insurance. The connection is not perfect as physicians resist experience rating, and insurers have found that data other than past claims does a better job predicting future claims. See John E. Rolph, John L. Adams, and Kimberly A. McGuigan, "Identifying Malpractice Prone Physicians," *Journal of Empirical Legal Studies*, vol. 4, no. 1 (March 2007), pp. 125-153.

[167] More than 95% of physicians sued report emotional distress including anger, frustration, tension or insomnia during the pendency of a malpractice lawsuit. See Sara C. Charles, "Coping With a Medical Malpractice Suit," *Western Journal of Medicine*, vol. 174 (January 2001), pp. 55-58.

[168] David Dranove, Subramaniam Ramanarayanan, and Yasutora Watanabe, "Delivering Bad News: Market Responses to Negligence" Kellogg School of Management, Working Paper Series, 2009, http://www.kellogg.northwestern.edu/faculty/watanabe/htm/delivering.pdf

[169] Mary L. Azcuenaga, Commissioner, Federal Trade Commission, "Advertising Regulation and the Free Market," Remarks: Before the International Congress of Advertising and Free Market Freedom: *XXI Century; The Century of The Consumer*, Lima, Peru, May 11, 1995, *available at*, http://www.ftc.gov/speeches/azcuenaga/lima.shtm.

[170] The earliest seminal study is Kenneth J. Arrow, "Uncertainty and the Welfare Economics of Medical Care," *American Economic Review*, vol. 53, no. 5 (1963), pp. 941-973.

[171] Noam Sher, "New Differences Between Negligence and Strict Liability and Their Implications on Medical Malpractice Reform," *Southern California Interdisciplinary Law Journal*, vol. 16, pp. 335-377.

[172] Matthew L. Wald and Keith Bradsher, "Judge Tells Firestone to Release Technical Data on Tires," *New York Times*, September 28, 2000, p. C2.

[173] Under experience rating, an individual's premium is set in part as a function of some classification scheme and in part as a function the individual's experience within the classification scheme. Under community rating, all those in a particular *community* are charged the same premium regardless of experience.

[174] A closed malpractice claims analysis is a research methodology in which researchers systematically study the detailed record generated as part of the insurer's defense. Closed claim analysis can be used to independently assess the validity of claims and the appropriateness of damage awards, identify patterns of injury, and strategies to mitigate future losses.

[175] Wayne J. Guglielmo, "Is this the way to lower malpractice rates? Anesthesiologists have reduced their premiums by focusing on safety. But is that a realistic model for primary care and other doctors to follow?," *Modern Medicine*, December 2, 2005, *available at*, http://www.modernmedicine.com/modernmedicine/article/articleDetail.jsp?id= 253678.

In: Medical Malpractice: Considerations and Proposals
Editors: Vincent Braswell and Don Mccloud
ISBN: 978-1-61942-141-7

Chapter 2

MEDICAL MALPRACTICE: BACKGROUND AND LEGISLATION IN THE 112TH CONGRESS

Baird Webel, Vivian S. Chu and David Newman

SUMMARY

As a policy area, medical malpractice involves issues related to its prevalence in the health care system, the market for provider liability insurance, and the resolution of malpractice complaints through the tort system.

Medical malpractice has attracted congressional attention numerous times over the past decades, particularly in the midst of three "crisis" periods for the liability insurance market in the mid-1970s, the mid-1980s, and the early 2000s. These periods were marked by sharp increases in medical liability insurance premiums, difficulties in finding any insurance in some areas as insurers withdrew from providing coverage, reports of providers leaving areas or retiring following insurance difficulties, and a variety of public policy measures at both the state and federal levels to address these historic crises. Which public policy measures have been effective in addressing the difficulties in the medical malpractice liability market has been a matter of debate, in part because these difficulties have been at the intersection of the health care, tort, and insurance systems.

The overall medical liability insurance market is not currently exhibiting comparable level of disruption as in the "crisis" periods. Nonetheless, concerns persist regarding the affordability and availability of malpractice insurance in particular regions and physician specialtics (e.g., obstetricians). In addition, the fear of claims for medical malpractice may affect individual provider decisions and drive up the overall cost of health care.

In terms of *direct* costs, medical malpractice insurance adds relatively little to the overall cost of health care. According to the National Association of Insurance Commissioners (NAIC), medical malpractice premiums written in 2010 totaled approximately $10.6 billion, while overall health expenditures are estimated by the Congressional Budget Office (CBO) to total $2.6 trillion. *Indirect* costs, particularly increased use of tests and procedures by providers to protect against future lawsuits ("defensive medicine"), have been estimated to be much higher than direct premiums. CBO estimated that enacting federal tort reforms would reduce both health care spending by approximately 0.4%-0.5% (roughly $9 billion-$11 billion) and the federal budget deficit by $40 to $57 billion over a 10-year period.

The malpractice system also faces issues of equity and access. For example, some observers have criticized the current system's performance with respect to (1) compensating patients who have been harmed by malpractice, (2) deterring substandard medical care, and (3) promoting patient safety. There are differing opinions as to the extent that each of these particular areas has been affected by the current malpractice system.

The President's 2012 budget encouraged Congress to reform the medical malpractice system and requested $250 million for the Department of Justice to test a variety of reform proposals. In the 112th Congress, the specific issue of medical liability reform was addressed by the House Committee on the Judiciary and the House Committee on Energy and Commerce. Both committees have marked up and reported H.R. 5, the Help Efficient, Accessible, Low-cost, Timely Healthcare (HEALTH) Act of 2011 to the full House. A Senate companion bill, S. 218, has not been acted on to date. Among other things, the HEALTH Act would implement a cap on non-economic damages for health care lawsuits.

INTRODUCTION

Medical malpractice has attracted congressional attention numerous times over the past few decades, particularly in the midst of three "crisis" periods for medical malpractice liability insurance in the mid-1970s, the mid-1980s, and the early 2000s. These periods were marked by sharp increases in medical liability insurance premiums, difficulties in finding any liability insurance in some regions and among some specialties as insurers withdrew from providing coverage, reports of providers leaving areas or retiring following insurance difficulties, and a variety of public policy measures at both the state and federal levels to address the market disruptions. In each case, attention receded to some degree after a few years as premium increases moderated and market conditions calmed.

The overall medical liability insurance market is not currently exhibiting the same level of crisis as in previous time periods. Nonetheless, problems with the affordability and availability of malpractice insurance persist, especially in particular regions and physician specialties (e.g., obstetricians). In addition, the fear of claims for medical malpractice may affect individual provider decisions particularly through increased use of tests and procedures to protect against future lawsuits ("defensive medicine") and drive up the overall cost of health care. The malpractice system also experiences issues with equity and access. For example, some observers have criticized the current system's performance with respect to compensating patients who have been harmed by malpractice,[1] deterring substandard medical care,[2] and promoting patient safety.[3]

Which public policy measures have been effective in addressing the successive insurance market disruptions, and may be effective in the future, has been a matter of debate. Some proposals (such as the current Help Efficient, Accessible, Low-cost, Timely Healthcare (HEALTH) Act of 2011, H.R. 5/S. 218) have addressed the tort system, particularly limits on claims brought in medical liability cases; others have addressed the insurance system, particularly increased direct regulation of insurance companies, or removal of the existing partial exemption from federal antitrust laws for the "business of insurance."

RECENT ACTION AND PROPOSALS ON MEDICAL MALPRACTICE

During the 112th Congress

The 112th Congress has acted early to address health reform generally and medical malpractice issues specifically. H.R. 2, which would repeal P.L. 111-148 in its entirety, including the medical malpractice provisions discussed below (under the section "During the 111th Congress"), was introduced by Representative Eric Cantor on January 5, 2011. This bill was passed by the House on January 19, 2011. Medical liability reform was the topic of the first committee hearing in the House Committee on the Judiciary for the 112th Congress, held on January 20, 2011, and the committee has acted on H.R. 5 as discussed below.

The Help Efficient, Accessible, Low-cost, Timely Healthcare (HEALTH) Act of 2011 (H.R. 5/S. 218)

H.R. 5 was introduced by Representative Phil Gingrey on January 24, 2011.[4] The House Committee on the Judiciary marked up the bill on February 9 and February 16, 2011, and reported the bill on March 17, 2011. The bill was marked up on May 13, 2011, and reported on May 23, 2011, by the House Committee on Energy and Commerce. S. 218 was introduced by Senator John Ensign on January 27, 2011, and referred to the Senate Committee on the Judiciary, which has not acted on the bill.

H.R. 5/S. 281 as introduced would, with certain exceptions, preempt some aspects of existing state medical malpractice laws. Although the legislation seeks to address both medical malpractice and product liability, this report will discuss only provider medical malpractice. The legislation defines a "health care lawsuit" to encompass not only suits between a provider and patient, but also any claim against a health care organization, manufacturer, distributor, supplier, marketer, promoter, or seller of a medical product and any claims concerning health care goods and services or medical products affecting interstate commerce. Among other things, H.R. 5/S. 281 would mandate a uniform statute of limitations for health care lawsuits and set parameters and caps for non-economic damages,[5] punitive damages,[6] and attorneys' fees. However, the legislation would also grant states flexibility in that it would not preempt any state law that imposes greater procedural or substantive protections for health care providers and organizations from liability, loss, or damages. The legislation would also not preempt any state law that specifies a particular monetary amount of compensatory or punitive damages, regardless of whether the state's monetary amount is greater or lesser than is provided for in the act.

In the February 16, 2011, House Judiciary Committee markup of H.R. 5, an amendment to eliminate a provision in H.R. 5 that would have allowed juries to hear evidence of "collateral source benefits," such as workers' compensation payments or long-term disability insurance payments, was adopted by voice vote. The amendment also struck a provision that would have prohibited providers of collateral source benefits from recovering any amounts paid after a court award is made to a plaintiff.[7] CBO's cost estimate for this version of H.R. 5 foresees a 0.4% decrease in overall health spending and a reduction in the federal budget deficit of $40 billion over a 10-year period.[8]

In the May 11, 2011, House Energy and Commerce Committee markup of H.R. 5, the bill was amended to add a further exception to the prohibition on punitive damages for products that comply with Food and Drug Administration (FDA) standards. If enacted as reported, punitive damages would be allowed to be awarded in a health care lawsuit if the product which caused the harm was misbranded, adulterated, contaminated, mislabeled, or improperly stored. CBO's cost estimate for this version of H.R. 5 foresees a 0.5% decrease in overall health spending and a reduction in the federal budget deficit of $57 billion over a 10-year period. This increased savings is largely due to the retention of the collateral source rule that was removed in the Judiciary Committee markup. [9]

FY2012 President's Budget

The President's FY2012 budget made general reference to reforming medical malpractice:[10]

> To do more to restrain health care costs, the President is ... :
>
> Calling for a more aggressive effort to reform our medical malpractice system to reduce defensive medicine, promote patient safety, and improve patient outcomes. The President encourages Republicans to work constructively with him on medical malpractice as part of an overall effort to restrain health costs.

In addition, the President's budget "makes available $250 million in grants to states to reform the way they resolve medical malpractice disputes." These grants would be awarded in consultation with the Department of Health and Human Services.[11]

According to information from the Justice Department,[12]

> [S]tates could use the grant money to test out reforms such as:
>
> Health courts which use specially-trained judges and medical experts to review medical liability cases, rather than the traditional trial-by-jury approach.
>
> Safe harbors, which would provide physicians, hospitals, and other medical providers a legal safety net; those who adhered to best-practices standards of care would be considered non-negligent. Funding could be used toward identifying and certifying practice guidelines.
>
> Early disclosure and offer, which would require doctors and hospitals to follow a protocol after a medical error occurred that could include disclosing the error to a safety officer and the patient, apologizing to the patient, and offering fair compensation. If the patient decided to sue, the provider's disclosure and apology could not be used as evidence of liability.

States could also use the money to try out other reforms, such as a "fair share" rule that would allocate responsibility for malpractice payments that are in proportion to responsibility for the damages.

These grants are ultimately dependent on further legislative action by Congress.

During the 111th Congress

PPACA and Medical Malpractice

The Patient Protection and Affordable Care Act (PPACA; P.L. 111-148), as amended, included two provisions related to medical malpractice reform.

PPACA, § 6801, expressed the Sense of the Senate that (1) health care reform presents an opportunity to address issues related to medical malpractice and medical liability insurance; (2) states are encouraged to develop and test litigation alternatives while preserving an individual's right to seek redress in court; and (3) Congress should consider establishing a state demonstration program to evaluate alternatives to the existing civil litigation system with respect to medical malpractice claims.

PPACA, § 10607, authorized $50 million for a five-year period beginning in FY2011 for the HHS Secretary to award demonstration grants to states for the development, implementation, and evaluation of alternatives to current tort litigation for resolving disputes over injuries allegedly caused by health care providers or organizations. States that receive a grant are required to develop an alternative that (1) allows for the resolution of disputes caused by health care providers or organizations, and (2) promotes a reduction of health care errors by encouraging the collection and analysis of patient safety data related to the resolved disputes.

Prior to receiving a grant, a state will have to demonstrate that its alternative (1) increases the availability of prompt and fair resolutions of disputes, (2) encourages the efficient resolution of disputes, (3) encourages the disclosure of health care errors, (4) enhances patient safety by reducing medical errors and adverse events, (5) improves access to liability, (6) informs the patient about the differences between the alternative and tort litigation, (7) allows the patient to opt out of the alternative at any time, (8) does not conflict with state law regarding tort litigation, and (9) does not abridge a patient's ability to file a medical malpractice claim.

The demonstration grant provisions do not limit any prior, current, or future efforts of any state to establish any alternative to tort litigation. Monies for this demonstration have not been appropriated as of this time.

COSTS OF MEDICAL MALPRACTICE

In terms of direct costs, medical malpractice insurance adds relatively little to the direct cost of health care relative to total health care spending, but medical malpractice tort reform could still save, as noted below, a not insignificant amount of money over time. Medical malpractice premiums written in 2009 totaled approximately $10.8 billion,[13] while health expenditures estimated by CBO total $2.6 trillion.[14] Indirect costs, particularly increased use of tests and procedures by providers to protect against future lawsuits ("defensive medicine"), have been estimated to be much higher than direct premiums. These conclusions, however, have been controversial, in part because some synthesis studies have claimed that national estimates of defensive medicine are unreliable.[15] A recent analysis on the subject estimated that the total costs of defensive medicine in 2008 were $45.6 billion.[16]

Prior to the passage of the health care reform law, CBO conducted its own analysis, as well as synthesized and analyzed previous studies on the relationship between medical malpractice and health care costs.[17] The recent CBO analyses of H.R. 5 estimated that federal tort reforms would reduce national health care spending by 0.4%-0.5% (equivalent to approximately $9 billion to $11 billion in 2009) depending on the exact provisions included.[18] This estimate is the cumulative impact of tort reform on both lowering medical malpractice insurance premiums and reducing use of health care services, and takes into account the fact that because many states have implemented tort reforms, a significant proportion of potential cost savings already has been realized. Other earlier studies have estimated the reduction of health care spending attributable to state tort reforms. These studies compared pre- and post-reform spending within each state that implemented such reforms, and found varying impact (e.g., a set of studies found 4%-9% reduction in hospital spending for Medicare patients with heart disease; another study found that state tort reforms reduced personal health care expenditures by 3%-4%).[19]

CBO also estimated the effect of malpractice tort reform on the federal budget. In its analyses of H.R. 5, CBO estimated that such reforms would reduce spending under Medicare, Medicaid, the State Children's Health Insurance Program, and the Federal Employees Health Benefits Program by approximately $34 billion to $48 billion from 2011 to 2021. In addition, the Joint Committee on Taxation (JCT) estimated that such reforms would lead to an increase in federal revenues of $6 billion to almost $10 billion over the same 10-year period.[20] By combining the impact of tort reform on mandatory health spending and tax revenues, CBO estimated that tort reforms could reduce the federal budget deficit by approximately $40 billion to $57 billion over 10 years.[21]

Challenges in Medical Malpractice Policymaking

Addressing problems in medical malpractice can be challenging, particularly due to the interactions of three different systems, each of which is complex in its own right: health care, tort, and insurance.

Health Care System

Medical errors can lead to injury, and injury is the medical basis on which a malpractice claim is made. Reducing errors through improved medical practices and effectuating penalties against poorly performing providers may benefit the overall performance of the medical malpractice insurance system by, for example, possibly lowering premiums or improving access to insurance.

States have the primary authority to define the process for granting and renewing a medical license, and regulating the medical practice. Currently, there is a lack of uniformity across states regarding both medical licensure and the medical practice. Moreover, states face financial challenges and many are likely to lack clinical expertise to fully implement patient safety strategies. For example, current state initiatives vary regarding the existence, scope, and robustness of data-collection efforts to track and analyze medical errors and possible instances of malpractice. Federal input may be implemented through a variety of approaches, both voluntary (e.g., support for research on evidence-based medicine, and toolkits to evaluate the adoption of patient safety efforts) and mandatory (e.g., "conditions of participation" standards for institutional providers under the Medicare program).

While reducing medical errors may be a worthy goal in its own right, it is unclear to what degree medical malpractice insurance will be affected if only patient safety concerns are addressed. Multiple older studies have found that the majority of malpractice claims filed involve medical injuries not caused by negligence.[22] Moreover, only a small proportion of patients whose injuries are caused by negligent medical care actually end up filing a malpractice claim.[23] However, there is an emerging consensus in the academic literature that, while there are legal errors in paying undeserving individuals in addition to medical errors, "the merits of a claim are the best predictor of the likelihood of payment and the amount received."[24] These findings speak to the complexity of the existing medical liability system and difficulty in designing effective policies without consideration of the interrelated systems.

As noted above, some observers suggest that the current malpractice system encourages the practice of "defensive medicine," that is, the fear of liability and the potential negative outcomes associated with malpractice claims lead providers to administer additional health care treatments or avoid high-risk services primarily to reduce their liability risk. The implication is that defensive medicine results in either an increase in overall consumption of and spending on health care services that may not be medically necessary or a decrease in access to certain services or for certain patients. Multiple studies have found some evidence of defensive medicine, but even providers acknowledge that it is a difficult concept to measure.[25] Moreover, some evidence suggests that factors other than defensive medicine, such as physician payment systems (e.g., fee-for-service vs. capitation) and financial incentives, may explain the over-provision of health services.[26]

Tort System

The tort system acts as a mechanism through which a person suffering injury due to medical errors is monetarily compensated when he or she establishes that a provider provided substandard health care. Some argue that the tort system is an efficient way to both compensate those who suffer from an injury and to deter the errors that created the injury, and that the tort system is the primary way that the present system deals with such issues. However, there are those who argue that, in the case of medical malpractice, the current system does neither particularly well.[27] Some observers have suggested that the medical malpractice tort system is arbitrary in its outcome.[28] As noted above, many valid claims are never filed and many filed claims are not the result of negligence. Jury verdicts can vary significantly from case to case, with substantial variation also occurring among states and among counties within states.

Insurance System

Liability insurance insulates providers from the direct cost of medical malpractice. It acts as a buffer between the actual award for malpractice determined under the tort system and the provider who may have committed malpractice. The vast majority of providers have liability insurance, although there is anecdotal evidence about some providers practicing medicine without malpractice insurance. By its nature, insurance spreads the costs across a wide base of providers in a particular specialty or geographic area, so that the actions of a relatively small number of providers can have a wider impact.

(in billions of nominal dollars)

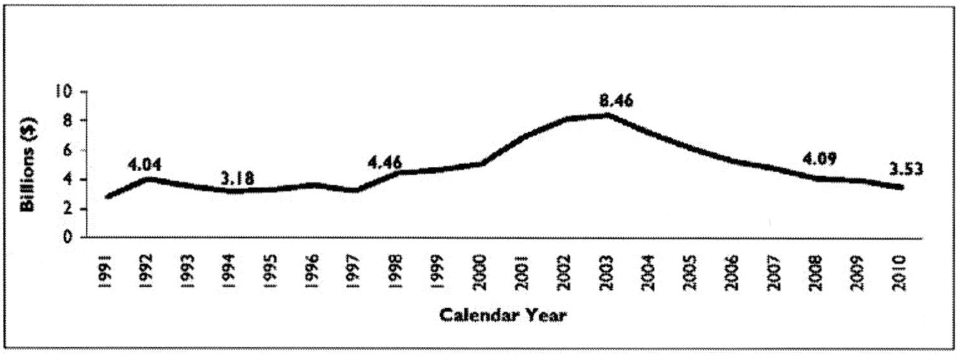

Source: National Association of Insurance Commissioners.

Figure 1. Nationwide Direct Losses Incurred.

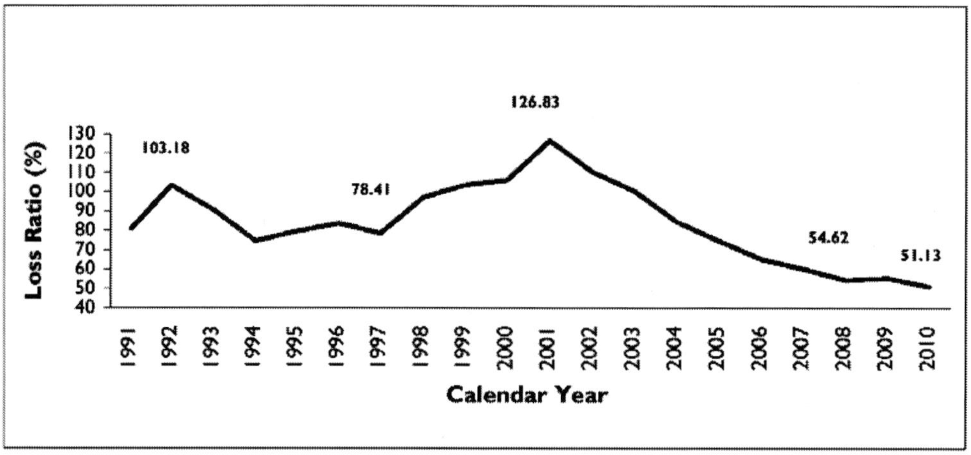

Source: National Association of Insurance Commissioners.

Notes: Loss Ratio = (Direct Losses + Direct Defense and Cost Containment Expenses Incurred)/Direct Premiums Earned.

Figure 2. Nationwide Loss Ratio.

Specific aspects of the insurance system can arguably catalyze or magnify crises. Medical malpractice claims tend to play out over an extended period of time, due both to the lag in recognizing that a claim might exist and to deliberations in the court system. Insurance is based on estimating future claims and estimating the investment returns on premium payments from the time premiums are paid until the time claims are paid. The longer time period associated with liability insurance losses increases uncertainty in these estimations (both in terms of the frequency of claims and the dollar amount of awards), with such uncertainty possibly leading to increased volatility in premiums.

Medical malpractice liability insurance is regulated by the individual states under the federal McCarran-Ferguson Act of 1945,[29] which also provides a limited exemption from federal antitrust laws. This system of state regulation has resulted in variations in the structure of the markets as well as in the data generated. NAIC aggregates some insurance data;

however, much potentially useful data is either not collected or not available. For example, data encompassing all the medical malpractice claims closed by insurers can give a broad picture of the situation in medical malpractice insurance; however, only a handful of states either collect such data or make it available to researchers.

RECENT EXPERIENCE

Recent experience in the medical malpractice insurance market, within the states with respect to the number of malpractice law suits and their average settlement amounts, and among providers that have embarked on quality improvement efforts that reduce malpractice exposure and premiums, can be described as encouraging. It is not yet clear whether these trends are long term or whether they reflect the trough of another cycle in the medical liability insurance marketplace.

The Medical Malpractice Insurance Market

The cyclical experience of medical malpractice insurers is reflected in aggregate data about the industry compiled and analyzed by the NAIC (see Figure 1). From 1992 to 1998, direct incurred losses were relatively stable,[30] varying from a low of $3.18 billion in 1994 to a high of $4.46 billion in 1998. However, from 1998 to 2003, losses grew steadily year after year, to a high of $8.46 billion in that last year, coinciding with the last crisis period. Since 2003, losses have fallen every year. In 2010, losses totaled $3.53 billion, the lowest amount in more than a decade. (The loss data are in nominal dollar amounts.)[31]

Malpractice insurance premiums roughly followed losses as those amounts increased.[32] However, premiums have not fallen nearly as much as losses in recent years as the trend reversed. The loss ratio, which compares losses to premiums, reflects this uneven trend (see Figure 2). A high ratio generally implies lower profits for insurers on the insurance portion of their operations. The loss ratio for the industry rose steadily from 78.41% in 1997 to 126.83% in 2001, tracking closely with the losses trend. Since 2001, the loss ratio has rapidly decreased. In 2010, the loss ratio of 1.13% was the lowest one in nearly two decades, and the 2008 and 2009 ratios were the second and third lowest at 54.62% and 55.66%, respectively. This means that over the past three years, the industry experienced its highest profit margin on direct premiums earned in the calendar years analyzed.[33]

Insurers, who are regulated by state insurance regulators, may also profit, or lose, from their investments. In general, with such low loss ratios, theory would suggest increasing competition as other insurers enter the market in search of profits. This, however, may not be happening as quickly as expected in medical malpractice if prospective insurers are wary due to past variations in medical malpractice losses, or if prospective insurers' capital has been depleted due to losses incurred during the recent financial crisis.

Table 1. Percentage Change in the Number of Paid Medical Malpractice Claims (2003 – 2009) and Claims Per 100,000 Population (2009)

State	% Change in Number of Claims (2003-2009)	Claims Per 100,000 (2009)	State	% Change in Number of Claims (2003- 2009)	Claims Per 100,000 (2009)
AL	-37.5	0.650	MT	-37.9	3.759
AK	-36.8	1.770	NE	-41.5	2.723
AZ	-43.6	2.630	NV	-35.0	2.490
AR	-29.4	1.694	NH	0.00	3.591
CA	-30.7	2.499	NJ	-19.9	5.441
CO	-23.0	2.515	NM	13.7	4.201
CT	-51.9	2.980	NY	-26.5	6.712
DE	-71.9	2.070	NC	-47.8	1.191
DC	-52.4	3.393	ND	-45.5	2.857
FL	-38.7	4.232	OH	-65.4	1.744
GA	-35.6	2.116	OK	0.00	3.677
H1	-35.4	2.517	OR	-34.2	1.931
ID	-28.1	1.513	PA	-38.3	6.203
IL	-42.4	2.225	RI	-40.8	4.057
IN	-56.4	2.913	SC	-28.3	2.559
IA	-39.7	2.367	SD	-35.1	3.027
KS	-29.4	2.612	TN	-12.3	2.182
KY	-53.2	2.414	TX	-56.5	1.910
LA	-02.9	6.080	UT	-08.8	3.012
ME	-16.7	2.306	VT	-34.6	2.763
MD	-36.0	3.184	VA	-35.5	1.544
MA	23.7	4.741	WA	-37.3	1.848
MI	-40.2	3.477	WV	-23.8	4.462
MN	-40.4	1.078	WI	-42.0	1.168
MS	-34.0	2.361	WY	-45.8	2.436
MO	-26.9	2.776			

Source: CRS analysis of Kaiser Family Foundation data, http://www.statehealthfacts.org/comparemaptable.jsp? ind=436&cat=8.

State Reform Efforts

Over the past 35 years, many states have adopted various tort reform proposals, including, among other things, caps on non-economic damages, caps on punitive damages, reform of the collateral source rule,[34] and changes in statutes of limitations. These reforms were designed in part to reduce the number of claims, the dollar amount of claims, or both.

In 2009, there were 10,739 paid medical malpractice claims in the United States—27.6% fewer than in 2003.[35] Some of these claims were paid without a trial. Paid claims represent only a part of total claims and a majority of claims were either dropped or settled through litigation in which the defendant provider was not found liable. At least one study found that in roughly 80% of the cases that went to trial, the alleged wrongdoer in a medical malpractice case has been exonerated.[36] Table 1 shows the percentage change in the number of paid medical malpractice claims between 2003 and 2009. Only two states, Massachusetts and New Mexico, experienced an increase in the number of paid claims over this time period. Six states (Connecticut, Delaware, Indiana, Kentucky, Ohio, and Texas) and the District of Columbia experienced a 50% or greater percentage decline in the number of paid claims.

The average claim paid in the United States in 2009 was $323,273. Although the 2009 figure is up from $289,891 in 2003, the rate of increase over this time period mirrors that found in medical inflation generally. These averages, however, mask considerable variance across states.[37] For instance, in Kansas the average claim paid in 2009 was roughly $155,622 (72 cases) whereas in Wisconsin it was almost $761,000 (65 cases). Figure 3 shows the change in the average total dollars in medical malpractice claims paid from 2003 through 2009.[38] Sixteen states saw a decline in their average medical malpractice claims paid, ranging from roughly 5% to 50%. An additional 17 states saw their average total dollars in medical malpractice claims paid from 2003 through 2009 rise slower than medical inflation. Eighteen states saw their average total dollars in medical malpractice claims paid from 2003 through 2009 rise faster than medical inflation.

These statistics, while illustrative, still lend themselves to different interpretations. Averages may not fully reflect circumstances in particular states or among particular high-risk specialties. Some states appearing to have *sticky* premiums which have not fallen despite a reduction in the number of claims, and some specialties experienced premium increases over the past decade well in excess of medical inflation.

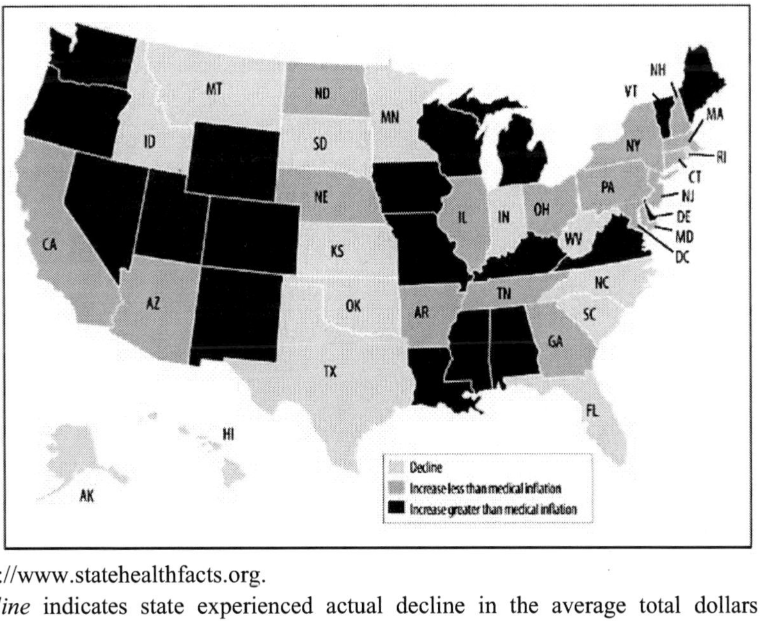

Source: http://www.statehealthfacts.org.

Notes: *Decline* indicates state experienced actual decline in the average total dollars in medical malpractice claims paid. *Increase less than medical inflation* indicates state experienced an increase in the average total dollars in medical malpractice claims paid but the increase was less than the rate of medical inflation during the 2003-2009 period. *Increase less than medical inflation* indicates state experienced an increase in the average total dollars in medical malpractice claims paid and the increase exceeded the rate of medical inflation during the 2003-2009 period.

Figure 3. Change in the Average Paid Medical Malpractice Claim 2003 – 2009.

Recent Experience among Providers

Providers, both physicians and institutional, appear to have been increasingly successful at identifying the causes of medical injuries and reducing them through quality improvement efforts. This appears to have reduced the number of medical malpractice suits and resulted in lower medical malpractice premiums. For instance, the American Society of Anesthesiologists (ASA) reports that the number of anesthesiology deaths declined dramatically, from 1 in 5,000 to less than 1 in 200,000, and real malpractice premiums for anesthesiologists declined more than 40% in real terms since 1985.[39]

The apparent connections between quality improvements and safety, lower premiums, and fewer law suits extend beyond anesthesiology. A recent RAND Corporation study found that "improvements in patient safety reduce malpractice claims." Specifically, the study, conducted at the county level in California, found that a county that "saw a decrease of 10 adverse events (achieved through improvements in the quality of care provided) in a given year would also see a decrease of 3.7 malpractice claims."[40] Similarly, in 2010, Virginia Mason Medical Center, in Seattle, WA, was named Hospital of the Decade by the Leapfrog Group, along with the University of Maryland Medical Center, for "major achievements in reducing medical errors and other innovations in patient safety and quality." Virginia Mason reports that[41]

> with improving quality of care and preventing errors, we have seen a decline in our medical malpractice premiums. We have seen decreases in medical malpractice premiums every year since 2005. As of 2011, our premiums have dropped by 52% since 2005, saving us literally millions of dollars.

Although other medical systems have also achieved similar improvements while pursuing efforts to raise quality and prevent medical errors,[42] some argue that enough is not being done to ensure that hospitals and other providers fully internalize the costs of their errors such that they have a good solid business case for improving quality and reducing errors.[43]

End Notes

[1] E. Thomas et al., "Incidence and Types of Adverse Events and Negligent Care in Utah and Colorado," *Medical Care*, vol. 38, no. 3, (March 2000); T. Brennan et al., "Incidence of Adverse Events and Negligence in Hospitalized Patients," *New England Journal of Medicine*, vol. 324, no. 6, (February 7, 1991).

[2] Michelle M. Mello and Troyen A. Brennan, "Deterrence of Medical Errors: Theory and Evidence for Malpractice Reform," 80 Tex. L. Rev. 1595 (2002).

[3] L. Sato et al., "Legal Liability and Protection of Patient Safety Data," Harvard Risk Management Foundation, 2005.

[4] Prior versions of this bill have been introduced in past Congresses. See H.R. 4600, 107th Cong. (2nd sess., 2002); H.R. 5, 108th Cong. (1st sess., 2003); H.R. 4280, 108th Cong. (2nd sess., 2004); H.R. 5/H.R. 534 (1st sess., 2005); H.R. 2580, 110th Cong. (1st sess., 2007); H.R. 1086, 111th Cong. (1st sess., 2009).

[5] Non-economic damages typically compensate for intangibles, such as pain and suffering and capacity to enjoy life, as opposed to economic damages, which compensate for more tangible elements, such as medical expenses and loss of earnings.

[6] Punitive damages are damages in excess of those needed to compensate an individual for injuries or loss and are designed to punish the alleged wrongdoer for bad behavior.

[7] See also CRS Report R41661, *Medical Malpractice Liability Reform: Legal Issues and 50-State Surveys on Tort Reform Proposals*, by Vivian S. Chu.

[8] Congressional Budget Office, "Cost Estimate for H.R. 5 as ordered reported by the House Committee on the Judiciary on February 16, 2011," March 10, 2011. Available at http://cbo.gov/ftpdocs/120xx/doc12095/hr5.pdf.

[9] Congressional Budget Office, "Cost Estimate for H.R. 5 as ordered reported by the House Committee on Energy and Commerce on May 11, 2011," May 23, 2011. Available at http://www.cbo.gov/ftpdocs/122xx/doc12209/HR5.pdf.

[10] The White House Office of Management and Budget, *Fiscal Year 2012 Budget of the United States Government*, p. 25, http://www.whitehouse.gov/sites/default/files/omb/budget/fy2012/assets/budget.pdf.

[11] The White House Office of Management and Budget, *Fiscal Year 2012 Budget of the United States Government*, p. 737, http://www.whitehouse.gov/sites/default/files/omb/budget/fy2012/assets/jus.pdf.

[12] Emily P. Walker, "Obama's Budget Includes $250M in Malpractice Grants," *MedPage Today*, February 16, 2011, http://www.medpagetoday.com/PracticeManagement/Medicolegal/24904.

[13] NAIC, "Countrywide Summary of Medical Malpractice Insurance, Calendar Years 1991-2009," provided to CRS on December 16, 2010.

[14] Douglas Elmendorf, "Expanding Health Insurance Coverage and Controlling Costs for Health Care," testimony provided to the Senate Budget Committee, February 10, 2009, http://www.cbo.gov/ftpdocs/99xx/doc9982/02-10-HealthVolumes_Testimony.pdf.

[15] See, e.g., Michelle Mello, "Understanding medical malpractice insurance: A primer," Robert Wood Johnson Foundation, Research Synthesis Report No. 8, January 2006, and Office of Technology Assessment, "Defensive Medicine and Medical Malpractice," 1994.

[16] Michelle M. Mello, Amitabh Chandra, and Atul A. Gawande et al., "National Costs Of The Medical Liability System," *Health Affairs*, vol. 29, no. 9 (September 2010), pp. 1569-1577.

[17] See CBO, "Budget Options, Volume 1: Health Care," December 2008.

[18] Congressional Budget Office, "Cost Estimate for H.R. 5 as ordered reported by the House Committee on the Judiciary on February 16, 2011," March 10, 2011. Available at http://cbo.gov/ftpdocs/120xx/doc12095/hr5.pdf. and Congressional Budget Office, "Cost Estimate for H.R. 5 as ordered reported by the House Committee on Energy and Commerce on May 11, 2011," May 23, 2011. Available at http://www.cbo.gov/ftpdocs/122xx/doc12209/HR5.pdf

[19] See P. Danzon, "Liability for Medical Malpractice," *Handbook of Health Economics*, Culyer and Newhouse, eds., 2000; D. Kessler and M. McClellan, "How Liability Law Affects Medical Productivity," Working Paper No. 7533, National Bureau of Economic Research, February 2000, and "Do Doctors Practice Defensive Medicine?," *Quarterly Journal of Economics*, vol. 111, no. 2, May 1996; and F. Hellinger and W. Encinosa, "The Impact of State Laws Limiting Malpractice Damage Awards on Health Care Expenditures," *American Journal of Public Health*, August 2006.

[20] Much of health care consumed in the private sector is provided through employer-sponsored health benefits that are not taxed as income for the employee. The JCT assumed that implementation of tort reforms would lead to lower health care costs, which in turn, would lead to higher wages, which are taxable. Thus, higher taxable income would result in greater revenue.

[21] Congressional Budget Office, "Cost Estimate for H.R. 5 as ordered reported by the House Committee on the Judiciary on February 16, 2011," March 10, 2011. Available at http://cbo.gov/ftpdocs/120xx/doc12095/hr5.pdf and Congressional Budget Office, "Cost Estimate for H.R. 5 as ordered reported by the House Committee on Energy and Commerce on May 11, 2011," May 23, 2011. Available at http://www.cbo.gov/ftpdocs/122xx/doc12209/HR5.pdf.

[22] See, e.g., David Studdert et al., "Negligent Care and Malpractice Claiming Behavior in Utah and Colorado," *Medical Care* (March 2000); Paul Weiler et al., A Measure of Malpractice (1993); T. Brennan et al., "Incidence of Adverse Events and Negligence in Hospitalized Patients: Results of the Harvard Medical Practice Study I," *New England Journal of Medicine*, vol. 324, no. 6 (February 7, 1991).

[23] David Studdert et al., "Negligent Care and Malpractice Claiming Behavior in Utah and Colorado," *Medical Care* (March 2000).

[24] David A. Hyman and Charles Silver, "Medical Malpractice Litigation and Tort Reform: It's the Incentives, Stupid," *Vanderbilt Law Review*, vol. 59, no. 4 (2006), p. 1100. "For instance, one major study of closed insurance claims found that injured (non-injured) individuals were compensated (not compensated) in a total of 73% of the cases. Moreover, it was 1.6 times more likely that an injured individual would not receive compensation than it was that a non-injured individual would receive compensation. Finally, the amount a non-injured individual received when compensated in error was almost half that received by those truly injured."

[25] General Accounting Office, "Medical Malpractice: Implications of Rising Premiums on Access to Health Care," GAO-03-836, August 2003.

[26] Ibid.

[27] See analysis presented by M. Mello and D. Studdert, "The Medical Malpractice System: Structure and Performance," Medical Malpractice and the U.S. Health Care System, W. Sage and R. Kersh, eds., Cambridge University Press, 2006.

[28] "Addressing the New Health Care Crisis: Reforming the Medical Litigation System to Improve the Quality of Health Care," Office of the Assistant Secretary for Planning and Evaluation, U.S. Department of Health and Human Services, March 3, 2003.

[29] 15 U.S.C. §1011 *et seq.*

[30] Incurred losses are payments for claims during a certain time period, in this case during a calendar year. Incurred losses for any given year include payments for claims submitted prior to that year, and account for outstanding claims at the end of the time period. The NAIC loss data is in nominal dollar amounts.

[31] The distinction between nominal vs. real dollars is significant when considered over the longer-time period. For example, while the 2008 loss of $4.09 billion does not seem much more than the 1992 loss of $4.04 billion, because these amounts do not reflect the effects of inflation, the 2008 losses are actually much lower than those in 1992.

[32] This aggregate national data does not include, among other things, the number of policies written or the number of providers covered. As such, other trends such as consolidation of providers within hospitals or changes in the number of providers self-insuring or changes in the level of self insurance can impact the aggregate figures.

[33] Other factors, such as returns on investments and administrative costs, in addition to losses, are likely to impact the total profitability of insurers.

[34] A collateral source rule provides that the benefits received by an injured party from a source wholly independent of the wrongdoer, such as the injured party's insurer, will not operate to lessen the damages recoverable from the wrongdoer.

[35] See http://statehealthfacts.kff.org/comparemaptable.jsp?ind=436&cat=8.

[36] David A. Hyman and Charles Silver, "Medical Malpractice Litigation and Tort Reform: It's the Incentives, Stupid," *Vanderbilt Law Review*, vol. 59, no. 4 (2006), p. 1107.

[37] There are also considerable year-to-year variations for some states both in the numbers of cases and the average dollar amounts of claims paid.

[38] The actual number of cases in some states, particularly those with a small number of cases each year on average, can vary considerably from year to year just as the average dollar amount of claims paid in Figure 3 can be dependant on the nature of the claims settled in any one year.

[39] Karen B. Domino, *Professional Liability Insurance Premiums for Anesthesiologists: Stability Despite the Economic Crisis*, American Society of Anesthesiologists, 2010, http://depts.washington.edu/asaccp/prof/asa73_8_44_45.pdf.

[40] Michael D. Greenberg, Amelia M. Haviland, and J. Scott Ashwood, et al., *Is Better Patient Safety Associated with Less Malpractice Activity? Evidence from California*, Rand Corporation, Santa Monica, CA, 2010, http://www.rand.org/content/dam/rand/pubs/technical_reports/2010/RAND_TR824.pdf.

[41] E-mail from Dr. Craig Blackmore, Virginia Mason Medical Center, January 25, 2011.

[42] One major integrated health care system reported a roughly 70% decline in malpractice costs between 2005 and 2010 and attributes the decline to both the soft insurance market and its quality improvement efforts.

[43] Michelle M. Mellol, David M. Studdert, and Eric J. Thomas, "Who Pays for Medical Errors? An Analysis of Adverse Event Costs, the Medical Liability System, and Incentives for Patient Safety Improvement," *Journal of Empirical Legal Studies*, vol. 4, no. 4 (December 2007), pp. 835-860.

In: Medical Malpractice: Considerations and Proposals ISBN: 978-1-61942-141-7
Editors: Vincent Braswell and Don Mccloud

Chapter 3

MEDICAL MALPRACTICE INSURANCE: AN ECONOMIC INTRODUCTION AND REVIEW OF HISTORICAL EXPERIENCE

Baird Webel

SUMMARY

Insurance is a critical piece of a modern economic system, but it often goes unnoticed until it becomes prohibitively expensive or its availability is curtailed. Such problems occurred in the medical malpractice liability insurance market most recently in the early part of the 2000s. Many physicians experienced substantial increases in insurance premiums, and there were reports of problems with availability of physician services due to doctors retiring or relocating from areas that had seen high premium increases. This was not the first time such a crisis has been proclaimed; similar events occurred in the latter half of both the 1970s and 1980s. In the latter half of this decade, overall losses for medical malpractice insurance have dropped and premiums have moderated. Public discussion of medical malpractice has lessened as well.

The fundamental purpose of insurance is to transfer an indefinite risk from one party to another for a definite premium. The pricing of this premium is critical, but determining this price is uncertain because it depends on estimates of the chance of a future loss, as well as the estimated value of that loss. The premium will also depend on estimates of future investment gains or losses because an insurer also acts as a financial intermediary and invests the capital that is held in reserve against future losses.

The market for medial malpractice liability insurance has been unstable during the past three decades for a variety of reasons. Recurring market problems have provoked various policy reactions in both state legislatures and in Congress. Assessing the effectiveness of particular policy changes is, however, complex and strong conclusions have typically been equally strongly disputed.

Congress has not directly addressed medical malpractice liability insurance since the 109th Congress, when the House passed a bill, H.R. 5, whose centerpiece was a limitation on tort claims for medical malpractice; similar bills passed the House in the previous two Congresses. The Senate, however, did not act on any of these House bills and failed to invoke cloture on the Senate bills addressing medical malpractice. Although the medical malpractice insurance market is not currently in the midst of a crisis, Congress has again focused on medical malpractice as a part of overall healthcare reform.

This report examines the economic issues and historical experience surrounding medical malpractice insurance. It includes an explanation of the fundamentals of insurance and how these fundamentals relate specifically to medical malpractice insurance. It also includes a discussion of the evolution of the medical malpractice insurance market since the 1970s and policy changes over this time.

INTRODUCTION

Insurance is a critical piece of a modern economic system, but it often goes unnoticed until it becomes prohibitively expensive or its availability is curtailed. Such problems occurred in the medical malpractice insurance market in the first half of this decade. Many physicians experienced substantial increases in insurance premiums, and there were reports of problems with the availability of physician services because of doctors retiring or relocating from areas that have seen high premium increases. There were also protests and job actions in some locations, with hospitals finding it necessary to curtail services and send patients to more distant facilities.[1] Crises have been proclaimed in the past as well; similar events occurred in the latter half of both the 1970s and 1980s. Since 2004 or so, overall losses experienced by medical malpractice insurers have dropped significantly and overall premiums have moderated as well, although not nearly to the same extent as losses.

The recurring problems have provoked various reactions in the insurance marketplace and in legislatures both at the state level, where insurance law and tort law are normally shaped, and in Congress. In the 107th (H.R. 4600), the 108th (H.R. 5 and H.R. 4279), and 109th (H.R. 5) Congresses, the House passed bills whose central thrust was to limit damages for medical malpractice tort claims. The Senate, however, did not act on any of these House bills and failed to invoke cloture on the Senate bills addressing medical malpractice (S. 11, S. 2061, and S. 2207 in the 108th Congress; S. 22 and S. 23 in the 109th Congress). The 110th Congress did not consider any bills on the floor to address directly medical malpractice insurance.

The medical liability insurance market is not currently exhibiting widespread crisis symptoms. That is not to say that the affordability and availability of malpractice insurance are no longer issues, but such problems are not as acute as compared with other time periods. According to the latest summary information published by the Medical Liability Monitor, 2008 premiums for malpractice insurance are part of a “downward trend of the past few years.”[2] By extension, physicians and physician groups (primarily the American Medical Association) are not responding to current market conditions in the same manner as during crisis periods, when they engaged in more public displays of dissatisfaction (e.g., participating in “strikes”). However, even during a non-crisis period, the malpractice system is characterized by issues with equity, access, and other problems. For example, the current system performs poorly with respect to compensating patients who have been harmed by malpractice,[3] deterring substandard medical care,[4] and promoting patient safety,[5] among other issues.

CURRENT FOCUS ON MEDICAL MALPRACTICE AND HEALTH REFORM

The current legislative interest in medical malpractice reform differs from the past in that it is largely driven by overall health reform, rather than an immediate crisis in medical malpractice insurance. As such, the focus is likely to be broadened. Beyond asking what can be done to stabilize premiums for medical malpractice, Congress may decide to ask what changes to the medical malpractice system might do for overall health reform? In terms of direct costs, medical malpractice insurance adds relatively little to the cost of health care. Medical malpractice premiums written in 2008 totaled approximately $11.2 billion,[6] whereas health expenditures are estimated by the Congressional Budget Office (CBO) to total $2.6 trillion.[7] Indirect costs, particularly increased utilization of tests and procedures by physicians to protect against future lawsuits or "defensive medicine," have been estimated to be much higher than direct premiums. These conclusions, however, are controversial, particularly in light of synthesis studies that have concluded that national estimates of defensive medicine are unreliable.[8]

CBO has noted that there is no "consistent evidence that changes in the medical malpractice environment would have a measurable impact on health care spending."[9] CBO conducted its own analysis, as well as synthesized and analyzed previous studies on the relationship between medical malpractice and health care costs.[10] These studies differed somewhat in their findings. For example, the studies' estimates for the reduction of health care spending attributable to state tort reforms varied, though they all found relatively little impact (4%-6%). Other studies not analyzed by CBO have found even less of an impact.[11]

To date, of the health reform proposals that have been reported out of the three committees of jurisdiction in the House (Ways and Means, Energy and Commerce, and Education and Labor) and the Senate Health, Education, Labor and Pensions Committee, only the one reported out of House Energy and Commerce includes language addressing issues with the medical malpractice system.[12] The Energy and Commerce version would allow states to receive incentive payments to enact and implement a medical liability law. The state law would be required to provide for an "early offer" system, a "certificate of merit" program, or a combination of both.[13] The Secretary of Health and Human Services would determine that a state law was compliant if she were satisfied that the state had enacted and was currently implementing the law, and if she found the law to be "effective." To determine the effectiveness of a law, the Secretary would consider whether it (1) made the medical liability system more reliable through the prevention of, or prompt and fair resolution of, disputes; (2) encouraged the disclosure of health care errors; and (3) maintained access to affordable liability insurance.

INSURANCE FUNDAMENTALS

Risk Transfer and Financial Intermediation

The most obvious function of insurance is to allow a person or corporation facing some risk, such as the risk that a physician will be sued for medical malpractice, to transfer this risk to another economic entity. Typically the entity accepting the risk will be a company, resulting in this risk then being spread across the owners of the insurer, either the stock holders in a normal incorporated insurance company or other policy holders in the case of a mutual insurance company.[14] Risk is also spread from one insurer to others through reinsurance.

Transferring risk, however, is not the only role that insurance plays. In the course of receiving payment for accepting risk, large amounts of capital are generated. This capital is then invested, allowing for its productive use to generate jobs and economic growth in addition to providing a reserve against future losses. Although the risk transfer and sharing aspect of insurance is the most obvious, the financial intermediation aspect is an equally integral part of the modern operations of insurance companies. The gains from investment of capital typically allow an insurer to offer lower rates to the insured than would be the case if the insured was paying completely for the transfer of risk. This also means, however, that the insured face some of the volatility in premium amounts inherent in relying upon investment returns. This can be seen in the alternating market cycles that are discussed below.

Insurance Operations and Pricing

Insurance involves complex calculations regarding uncertain outcomes of future events, although the basic operations can be explained in simple terms. A company begins with a certain amount of capital, or "policyholders surplus," to allow it to promise credibly to provide insurance in the future, as well as enough to satisfy regulators that it will be able to fulfill this promise. It offers insurance policies against whichever risks it is willing to assume. Money flows into an insurer primarily from two sources: premiums from customers of insurance and investment income from the company's reserves. Money flows out of an insurer primarily to pay for claims made for events for which the insurer has agreed to bear the risk, including costs such as defending against lawsuits in the case of medical liability insurance.[15]

The ability of insurance to fulfill its role as a financial intermediary, as well as the solvency of individual insurers, rests critically on keeping the inflows and outflows balanced over time. This means estimating the future return on investments as well as estimating future losses from claims. The accuracy of these estimates can vary widely and insurers have relatively little direct control over what either actual value will turn out to be. Insurers can affect their returns somewhat by varying the mix of their investments, but this mix is subject to state regulation. In the United States, most investments are relatively stable investments such as bonds, but even bonds are subject to the vagaries of the marketplace. Many insurers also try to minimize claims through sharing information with policy holders on reducing risks and offering incentives to policy holders who take action to minimize risks.

The one variable that an insurer does directly control, subject to the pressures of the marketplace and sometimes state insurance regulators,[16] is the price or premium that it charges for a certain amount of insurance. This price should cover the value in today's dollars (the "present value") of any future loss, multiplied by the expected probability of this loss. If a physician wants to insure against the risk of paying a $1 million malpractice claim today, and the insurance company believes that there is a 1% chance that this claim will occur today, then it will charge approximately $10,000 for this insurance. If the insurance extends for a length of time further into the future, then the future amounts of money to be paid out would be adjusted based on the expected inflation rate, or the expected rate of return, that the insurer foresees over the period of time the insurance is in place.

Because insurance pricing is theoretically based on the risk that is being transferred, this implies charging a different premium to people or companies with different inherent levels of risk. Without the ability to segment different risks into different categories, and charge these different categories different rates, the price charged to everyone will be relatively high reflecting the possibility that the purchaser is in a high risk category. A high price would tend to lead those who believe their own risks are low not to buy insurance or to underinsure, whereas those who believe their risks are high would tend to continue to buy insurance or even to overinsure. This tendency is known as "adverse selection" and usually results from the insured having more information than the insurer regarding their own risk. Adverse selection results in a higher overall level of risk in the pool of those who buy insurance and thus results in higher than expected claims. Higher claims are eventually followed by higher prices, which are then followed by lower risk clients not buying insurance and so on. The extreme result of this would be a situation where an insurance market essentially ceases to exist.

Market Cycles: Hard and Soft Markets

Insurance in general, and property and casualty insurance (of which medical malpractice is a part) in particular, has experienced alternating periods of "soft" markets and "hard" markets. This cycle is usually ascribed to changes in the investment climate, although it may be more accurate to think about it as due to changes in the comparison between insurers' financial inflows and outflows.

A soft market typically occurs when the investment climate is good and insurers make returns on the capital that they are holding in reserve that are high relative to expected insurance payouts. These high investment returns allow insurers to offer lower prices on insurance, sometimes selling insurance at a premium that they know will result in losses, and then offsetting these losses by the gains from investing the premium. Soft markets are usually marked by increases in the number of insurers and by the expansion in the geographic area or types of insurance offered by existing insurers.

A hard market typically occurs when the investment climate worsens and returns drop. Low investment returns imply that the premium paid for insurance must cover more of the actual loss that is expected from this insurance. This means higher premiums and can lead to withdrawals from poorly performing lines of insurance or from particular geographic areas that remain unprofitable. For an insurer offering only one type of coverage in a specific geographic area, such withdrawal is not an option. Such companies must either raise rates or eventually withdraw from the business of insurance if the investment returns do not increase or if costs are not somehow lowered. At the beginning of a hard market, especially when it is preceded by a long soft market, very large increases in premiums occur as the premium level comes closer to the value of the actual losses due to the risk that is being transferred.

Because of high capital mobility and interdependence in financial markets, hard markets might be expected to be a nationwide or even international phenomenon. The experience in the United States, however, has been that periods of market hardening have a disparate impact among the various states. This suggests that when market problems develop, there may be more at work than simply a general hard market due to lower investment returns. If different insurers offer insurance in the various states, it also may be that particular insurers' investment portfolios perform differently.

MEDICAL MALPRACTICE INSURANCE

Different insurance markets have very different characteristics. Life insurance, for example, tends to be stable because the amounts that are to be paid out are known and the estimates that are used for life expectancy are generally reliable. Insuring against hurricane damage is less stable; it is much harder to predict how many hurricanes might hit, where they might hit, and how much damage they might do. With enough historical and other data, however, insurance can operate effectively even in such uncertain environments. Insuring against medical malpractice liability offers some particular difficulties as compared to other lines of insurance and it has proven challenging for companies to operate in this field over time. Among the difficulties are the longer time frames inherent in malpractice claims, high and uncertain claim amounts, and uncertainty in recognizing and segmenting high-risk from low-risk healthcare providers.

Medical Malpractice's Long "Tail"

Medical malpractice liability insurance has what is known in the insurance industry as a long "tail." Liability policies in general are often written to cover the claims arising from a certain period of time. In fire insurance, for example, this is relatively unproblematic; whether a fire has occurred is generally straightforward and uncomplicated. There may be disputes arising about the extent of damage that should be paid or whether there was some sort of malfeasance involved, but, at a minimum, a company will know at the end of the insurance period or shortly thereafter whether a claim will be made. In contrast, injuries from medical malpractice, and thus the claims that arise from them, can take a longer time to manifest themselves, as many as several years in some cases. Even after injuries are noticed, the time before a full amount an insurer must pay is known and actually paid out is often measured in years because litigation can be complex and demand long discovery processes with various medical experts examining the case.

To address the tail problem, many insurers have changed their policies from an "occurrence" policy, which covers claims resulting from an action that occurred during the period that the insurance was in effect, to a "claims made" policy, which covers only claims actually made during the insured period. Such a shift has an immediate impact in reducing the uncertainty for the insurer, but the effect is largely a one time phenomenon. If a claims made policy stays in effect for several years, the total risk to the insurer under this type of policy converges with the risk that the insurer would bear under an occurrence policy.

Impact of Tort System

The claim amounts that medical malpractice insurers pay out are generally determined either through the tort system, or by threats to use the tort system. The details of tort law vary from state to state, but compensatory damages under tort law are often separated into two types: economic damages and noneconomic damages. Economic damages are generally intended to redress direct economic loss, such as lost wages and costs for medical care. Noneconomic damages are not tied to direct out-of-pocket expenses and include damages due to pain and suffering. Another primary type of damages is punitive damages. Punitive damages are noncompensatory damages that are intended to punish a defendant for egregious conduct.[17]

Economic damages generally have the greatest impact on medical malpractice claims through the medical cost component. The damage from medical malpractice usually requires additional medical treatment to repair, sometimes an entire lifetime of medical treatment. As a result, medical costs tend to be a higher component of medical malpractice claims than most other types of insurance claims. Coupled with this is the experience that medical costs have typically risen faster than the general rate of inflation. All other things being equal, this implies that the rates for medical malpractice insurance will rise faster than most other types of insurance.

Although the medical cost component of economic damages tends to drive medical malpractice insurance generally higher than other insurance, noneconomic and punitive damages add another aspect to malpractice claims: unpredictability. By definition, noneconomic and punitive damages are more subjective and difficult to quantify than economic damages. Different juries in the same town or city can and do come to different conclusions as to the monetary value of a plaintiff's pain and suffering or the amount of punitive damages warranted to punish willful misconduct, for example. Jury awards are even more variable when comparisons are made involving different parts of the country.[18] The conclusions reached on such damages can also be difficult to dispute in contrast to damages that are specifically related to concrete economic factors. This unpredictability reduces the accuracy of the estimations of expected losses that are at the heart of insurance pricing.

Risk Segmentation

Risk segmentation and adverse selection in the health care field are particularly problematic because information to judge accurately the quality of a provider, and thus ostensibly to estimate accurately his or her risk of a malpractice claim, is sparse. Some of this is due to past public policy choices, which have resulted in few mechanisms to track the quality of health care, but some is also due to the inherent difficulties in doing this tracking. It can be very difficult to distinguish between a physician with poor skills and one with high skills who takes on sicker patients and more difficult cases. Both may have poor patient outcomes but without a careful examination of the incoming patient population, which is rarely practicable to undertake, an insurer is likely to charge both physicians similar rates. Risk segmentation in medical malpractice insurance is generally based on geographic area and specialty type, but relatively little is based on some measure of provider quality or on malpractice claims history.

One of the particular aspects of the historical evolution of the medical malpractice insurance market, which is discussed in greater detail below, has been the proliferation of small insurers, particularly provider-owned companies. This success runs contrary to one of the theoretical fundamentals of insurance, namely spreading risk across as wide a base as possible. A small, provider-owned company transfers risk away from individual physicians or other health care providers, but still leaves the risk to the company itself more concentrated relative to a bigger, shareholder-owned company.

Smaller companies, however, may do a better job at reducing the risk that they choose to bear, rather than just spreading it. This risk reduction could come, for example, if smaller insurers were more able to persuade physicians to adopt lower risk practices or if they could better identify doctors who are at greater risk for operating in a manner that might invite malpractice claims and either charge them a higher premium or choose not to insure such doctors. One advantage of mutual insurers, particularly small ones, may be reduced moral hazard[19] because the insured are also the owners of the company. Smaller companies can also reduce the concentration of risk that they take on by purchasing reinsurance and this device is used often by insurers.[20]

Historical Experience in Medical Malpractice Insurance

Particular problems in medical malpractice insurance have been observed for many years. As far back as 1969, a report of a Senate subcommittee[21] concluded the following:

1. The number of malpractice suits and claims is rising sharply in certain regions of the country. The size of judgments and settlements is increasing rapidly.
2. Most malpractice suits are the direct result of injuries suffered by patients during medical treatment or surgery. The majority have proved justifiable. These suits are the indirect result of the deterioration of the traditional physician-patient relationship.
3. The publicity given to the higher malpractice judgments and settlements, based frequently on new legal precedents, is likely to trigger increased litigation in other States. The situation threatens to become a national crisis.
4. Already higher judgments and settlements are having the following direct results:
   (a) Companies providing malpractice insurance are increasing the cost of coverage.
   (b) These costs—in the form of higher charges—are being passed on to patients, their health care insurance companies, and Federal health care programs.
5. The rising number of malpractice suits is forcing physicians to practice what they call defensive medicine, viewing each patient as a potential malpractice claimant. Physicians often order excessive diagnostic procedures for patients, thereby

increasing the cost of care. Moreover, they are declining to perform other procedures, which in themselves, may entail some risk of patient injury.

6. At present, it appears no one affected by the rise in malpractice suits and claims has been able to deal with this problem in a manner that promises to alleviate this situation.
7. The lion's share of the total cost to the insurance companies of malpractice suits and claims goes to the legal community.
8. There is a definite Federal role in the malpractice problem.

There is certainly continuing dispute over some of these conclusions, but such a list might very well have been prepared during the recent debate rather than 40 years ago.

Evolution in the Insurance Market

Until the mid-1970s, medical malpractice insurance coverage was dominated by traditional insurers who offered it as one of several different lines of insurance. A list of the top 10 companies in 1976 was composed of primarily diversified shareholder-owned insurers with 61% of the market among them. With the market hardening in the mid- to late 1970s, many of these diversified insurers pulled back from offering medical malpractice insurance, leaving a void in the market. In response to this void, numerous new companies were created specifically focusing on insuring medical malpractice liability. Not only were these companies specialized, they also were largely owned by small groups of medical providers or by the entire group of their policy holders. These companies were also usually focused on a geographic area, often serving only one state. Some were, and still are, affiliated with a particular state's medical society.

With additional capacity in the market, and the aforementioned shift to claims-made policies, the difficulties of the 1970s abated and were replaced by a soft market for the first half of the 1980s. The shift in market structure away from larger, diversified insurers, however, seems to have been permanent. By 1986, six of the top 10 medical malpractice insurers were provider-owned and market concentration was somewhat less, with the top 10 companies holding 56% of the market. One exception to this shift was The St. Paul Companies, Inc. The St. Paul is a diversified shareholder-owned insurance company and grew from 11% of the nationwide market in 1976 to 21% in 1986.[22] Taking this company out of the situation gives a view of a more pronounced splintering of the market. The total market share of numbers two through 10 on the list of top insurers dropped from 51% of the market in 1976 to only 36% of the market in 1986.

The market cycle turned again in 1985-1986 and problems arose that bear many of the hallmarks of the situation in the early 2000s, including reports of physician work stoppages and problems with access to care. This situation was broader than just physicians or healthcare liability insurance and included difficulties in access to many other forms of liability insurance. In healthcare, larger providers, such as hospitals and nursing homes, were more severely affected than individual physicians. The market response was again the formation of new smaller insurance companies. These new companies, however, were not just more traditional mutual insurance companies, but also a large number of captive insurers.[23] Many of these captive insurers were located offshore in such locales as the Cayman Islands and thus operated outside of the U.S. tax and regulatory system. The offshore nature of these entities makes it difficult to ascertain reliably the size and scope of this market, but overall growth has been significant. One of the captives that was not offshore, Health Care Indemnity, a captive of the HCA hospital chain, grew over seven-fold from 1993 to 1994 to become the fourth largest medical malpractice insurer at the time.[24]

The 1990s saw predominantly a soft market with high investment returns fueling low rates and strong competition across various insurance lines. Medical malpractice insurance followed this trend with an increase in competition in many forms. Some traditional shareholder-owned insurers entered or reentered the market whereas some captives and mutuals converted to stock companies or expanded their geographic base into areas beyond their initial ones. This increased competition can be seen in the total number of companies directly underwriting medical malpractice premiums as reported by the National Association of Insurance Commissioners (NAIC).[25] There were 398 of such companies in 1991, but by 1995, the number had jumped to 623 and it reached a high of 666 in 1997.[26]

This soft market began to harden in the late 1990s, a trend exacerbated by the unexpected losses from the September 11, 2001 attacks. Starting in 1999, the malpractice insurance market saw increasing premiums along with both general withdrawals from the market and contractions in the geographical areas covered by companies. The insurance rating firm A.M. Best reports that aggregate medical malpractice premiums increased 15.6 % in 2001,[27] 22.5% in 2002,[28] and 13.5% in 2003.[29] Perhaps the most striking occurrence in this time period was the decision in December 2001 by The St. Paul to withdraw completely from writing medical malpractice insurance as part of an "effort to improve profitability."[30] Withdrawal typically occurs gradually through non-renewal of policies, but because The St. Paul's market share approached 50% in some states, the impact of even gradual withdrawal was significant.

The hard market in medical malpractice insurance seems to have peaked between 2002 and 2004. Statistics from A.M. Best show a 5.5% increase in aggregate premiums in 2004 and only 0.5% in 2005.[31] In 2007, A.M. Best's statistics show aggregate premiums dropping by 6.5%, followed by a drop of 5.3% in 2008.[32] The individual premiums reported in surveys done by *Medical Liability Monitor* (MLM) lag to some degree the aggregate statistics from A.M. Best. In 2003 and 2004, the MLM surveys showed increases of 20.4% and 20.5% respectively, with a 9.5% increase in 2005. Rates increased only 0.7% and 0.4% according to the 2006 and 2007 surveys, with individual rates falling by 4.3% in 2008.[33]

Policy Responses

When problems of availability or affordability of insurance have arisen, the situations have been met with more than just marketplace evolution; various policy changes have been made as well. Some of these changes have been intended to facilitate market supply, such as the creation of alternative sources of insurance, whereas others have addressed the problem from the cost side through various changes in the tort system. In addition, there have been attempts to address the problem through direct regulation of insurance, with California's Proposition 103 being the primary example as discussed below.

Expanding Market Supply

The basic legal structures for the mutual insurers that arose in response to the market difficulties of the 1970s have been in place for some time. Mutual insurers existed essentially as long as insurance has existed. Captives are a newer concept, dating from the 1950s and 1960s, but they also serve many areas outside of medical malpractice. In some cases, however, states went beyond the existing mutual or captive framework to allow for medical malpractice insurance. For example, in Florida, statutes were passed in the 1970s specifically allowing for medical malpractice self-insurance trusts.[34] This statute was amended in 1992 to disallow its future use, but a governor's task force recommended rescinding this action given the difficulties in Florida's medical malpractice market.[35] States also created nonstandard entities, such as joint underwriting associations (JUA). JUAs are nonprofit pooling arrangements intended to provide an "insurer of last resort" for healthcare providers who are unable to find insurance elsewhere.

The federal government, although not the primary regulator in the insurance markets, has also taken an interest in the market supply of liability insurance. The Liability Risk Retention Act of 1986[36] allows for the establishment of risk retention groups and risk purchasing groups. Risk retention groups operate much like a mutual insurer. They are made up of groups of entities involved in a similar business who wish to spread the risk among group participants. Such groups can be formed under state law, but the federal law allowed for reduced regulation because under federal law these groups are regulated only in the state where they are chartered rather than in every state where they write insurance. Risk purchasing groups essentially allow for group purchasing of insurance with the expectation that such purchase will be lower cost than individual purchase.

The initial 1981 act was limited to manufacturers, and was not widely used because of the soft market that prevailed at its time of passage. The 1986 law, however, amended the availability to include nearly all types of liability insurance, including medical malpractice. Companies offering medical malpractice liability insurance under the act began as early as 1987 with the Ophthalmic Mutual Insurance Company. The act's usage has continued in the most recent crisis. For example, at the beginning of 2003, 10 risk retention groups formed in the previous year were offering medical malpractice insurance in Pennsylvania,[37] one of the states then experiencing market difficulties.

Reducing Insurers' Costs

As detailed above, the primary outflow of money from a medical malpractice insurer is driven by the tort system. The tort system has thus been a primary focus of attempts to reduce insurer costs. It is beyond the scope of this report to discuss in detail issues surrounding tort changes,[38] but it should be noted that a cap on noneconomic damages for medical malpractice claims is not the only change that has been implemented at the state level. There have also been limits on other damages, lawyers' fees, and joint and several liability. Some states allow or encourage arbitration in place of litigation to resolve medical malpractice disputes or have implemented patient compensation funds, which limit insurer liability. Some states, such as Florida and Virginia, have implemented very limited "no-fault" systems, bypassing the question of liability altogether.

A frequently cited example of tort reform, as well as the expressed model for the previous bills considered by Congress, such as H.R. 5 in the 109th Congress, was passed by California in 1975: the Medical Injury Compensation Reform Act (MICRA). MICRA placed a $250,000 limit on noneconomic damages, such as pain and suffering, forced disclosure of other sources of payment to injured parties, limited lawyer fees, and strengthened the system that disciplines doctors. After passage in 1975, MICRA was challenged in the courts over several years before finally being upheld in 1984 and 1985.[39]

Strengthening Regulation

The first two policy responses implicitly treat an insurance "crisis" as the result of what might be described as normal market forces. An alternative explanation, however, is that the increasing prices and reduced availability that have marked medical malpractice crises are the result of improper market manipulation rather than a confluence of market forces. This concern has been raised at the federal level where the McCarran-Ferguson Act[40] gives a limited antitrust exemption to the insurance industry. It is not clear what the impact of removing this exemption might be, since some observers believe the information sharing facilitated by the exemption helps the industry operate more efficiently, possibly leading to lower premiums.[41]

In response to difficulties in the medical malpractice insurance market, Senator Patrick Leahy's Medical Malpractice Insurance Antitrust Act of 2003 and of 2005 (108th Congress' S. 352 and 109th Congress' S. 1525) were aimed at the antitrust exemption as it relates to medical malpractice insurance. Broader concerns over the insurance industry prompted bills by Senator Leahy and Representative Peter DeFazio (110th Congress' S. 618/H.R. 1081) to repeal the antitrust exemption for all insurance. Representative DeFazio also introduced this bill, H.R. 1583, in the 111th Congress.

Such federal action would be relatively indirect compared to what individual states have done or might do. The insurance industry is highly regulated at the state level, with many states, for example, requiring prior approval before a company can adjust rates, change policy forms, or even withdraw from writing certain lines of insurance. The most dramatic action taken on the insurance regulatory front since the recurring market problems began was Proposition 103, a ballot initiative approved by California voters in 1988. Proposition 103 was a broad change that was not specifically aimed at medical malpractice insurance but affected all property-casualty insurers in California. It created an elected, not appointed, insurance commissioner, forced insurers to justify their rate increases to the insurance commissioner, required insurance companies to open their books so regulators could determine if they needed rate increases, and allowed citizens to challenge proposed rate increases.

How Effective Have Policy Changes Been?

Assessing the effectiveness of any of the various policy changes over the past three decades is empirically difficult and strong conclusions have often equally been strongly disputed. For example, after the Liability Risk Retention Act of 1986, the U.S. Department of Commerce issued a report concluding that the 1981 and 1986 Acts were effective in reducing problems with the availability of liability insurance, citing among other things the numbers of insured then covered by risk retention groups.[42] In contrast, the NAIC saw no improvement from the formation these groups, indicating that the market cycle would inevitably have turned and that these insureds would have been able to find insurance in the commercial market.[43] As noted before, risk retention groups were still being formed to deal with the medical malpractice market situation at the time, but this alone does not prove conclusively that either of the previous Department of Commerce or NAIC positions were correct. Coming to this or any other conclusion requires assessing both what has happened and what would have happened in the absence of the law.

The most voluminous debate has been over California's experience. California has experienced significantly lower medical malpractice premium growth over the years since the passage of MICRA in 1975. This is cited by some as evidence that tort reforms work and should be more widely adopted.[44] Countering this, others have argued that most of the slow growth, or even declines, in California premiums have come since Proposition 103 in 1988, suggesting the effectiveness of strengthened regulation.[45] A difficulty in economic analysis of the two arguments stems from the relative closeness of the two policy changes, particularly because MICRA was not finally upheld in court until 1985. As was discussed earlier, the pricing of insurance is a long-term economic enterprise fraught with many uncertainties. In such an endeavor, underwriters may wait to see what definite effect a policy change has on their losses before making dramatic changes to insurance pricing. Another difficulty in judging the California experience is the fact that liability insurance in general was experiencing a hard market in the mid-1980s and these market conditions may arguably have temporarily overwhelmed the effect of other policy changes.[46]

End Notes

[1] See, e.g., Joelle Babula, "Desert Springs Hospital: Emergency surgeons unavailable," *Las Vegas Review-Journal*, March 26, 2003, sec. B, p. 1B.

[2] Chad Karls, "Medical Liability Monitor," Vol. 33, No. 10, October 2008, p. 1.

[3] E. Thomas, et al., "Incidence and Types of Adverse Events and Negligent Care in Utah and Colorado," *Medical Care*, Vol. 38, No. 3, Mar. 2000, and T. Brennan, et al., "Incidence of Adverse Events and Negligence in Hospitalized Patients," *New England Journal of Medicine*, Vol. 324, No. 6, Feb. 7, 1991.

[4] M. Mello and T. Brennan, "Deterrence of Medical Errors: Theory and Evidence for Malpractice Reform," *Texas Law Review*, Vol. 80, 2002.

[5] L. Sato, et al., *Legal Liability and Protection of Patient Safety Data*, Harvard Risk Management Foundation, 2005.

[6] NAIC, "Countrywide Summary of Medical Malpractice Insurance, Calendar Years 1991-2008," September 1, 2009.

[7] Douglas Elmendorf, "Expanding Health Insurance Coverage and Controlling Costs for Health Care," testimony provided to the Senate Budget Committee, February 10, 2009.

[8] For example, see Michelle Mello, "Understanding medical malpractice insurance: A primer," Robert Wood Johnson Foundation, Research Synthesis Report No. 8, Jan. 2006, and Office of Technology Assessment, "Defensive Medicine and Medical Malpractice," 1994.

[9] U.S. Congressional Budget Office, *Key Issues in Analyzing Major Health Insurance Proposals*, December 2008, p. 154 available at http://www.cbo.gov/ftpdocs/99xx/doc9924/12-18-KeyIssues.pdf.

[10] CBO, "Budget Options, Volume 1: Health Care, December, 2008; D. Kessler and M. McClellan: "Malpractice Law and Health Reform: Optimal Liability Policy in an Era of Managed Care," *Journal of Public Economics*, Vol. 84, No. 2, May 2002; "How Liability Law Affects Medical Productivity," Working Paper No. 7533, National Bureau of Economic Research, Feb. 2000); and "Do Doctors Practice Defensive Medicine?," *Quarterly Journal of Economics*, Vol. 111, No. 2, May 1996.

[11] See P. Danzon, "Liability for Medical Malpractice," *Handbook of Health Economics*, Culyer and Newhouse, eds., 2000.

[12] The Senate Finance Committee is currently marking up its health reform proposal, "America's Healthy Future Act." The Chairman's mark includes a Sense of Senate statement regarding the opportunity that health reform presents to address concerns with medical malpractice and malpractice insurance.

[13] In general, an early offer system permits a defendant to offer to a claimant within 180 days after a claim is filed, periodic payment of the claimant's economic losses. If an early offer is not made, the injured party can proceed with a normal tort claim for both economic and noneconomic damages. However, if an early offer is

made and the claimant declines the offer, both the standard of misconduct and standard of proof are raised. A certificate of merit program requires claimants, when a medical malpractice suit is first filed, to include testimony from a qualified medical expert that establishes that there is merit to the claim.

[14] A mutual insurance company is a nonprofit insurer owned by the policy holders with ownership shares in proportion to their premium volume.

[15] There are, of course, other substantial payments that an insurer makes, such as operational expenses and profits returned to stockholders, that are critical in differentiating among companies, but not as critical in discussing industry-wide issues.

[16] Laws in many states require preapproval by the state before an insurer can change the rates charged for insurance. The justification for this regulation is generally twofold: (1) to prevent insurance companies from charging too much and gouging their customers, and (2) to prevent insurance companies from charging too little and risking insolvency when their losses are greater then their reserves.

[17] See CRS Report RL31692, *Medical Malpractice Liability Reform: Legal Issues and Fifty-State Survey of Caps on Punitive Damages and Noneconomic Damages*, by Henry Cohen; and CRS Report RL31721, *Punitive Damages in Medical Malpractice Actions: Burden of Proof and Standards for Awards in the 50 States*, by Henry Cohen, for additional discussion of tort law as it relates to medical malpractice.

[18] See, e.g., "Malpractice crisis? Not here!," *Medical Economics*, July 12, 2002, pp. 86-96.

[19] Moral hazard is the term used for the increased chance of a loss actually due to the existence of insurance. For example, those insured against loss from fire may be more careless in fireproofing their property.

[20] The Reinsurance Association of America reports that in 2005, approximately 14% of medical malpractice occurrence policy premiums and 23% of the claims made policy premiums were reinsured. This compares to an average for all P/C lines of approximately 21%, available at http://www.reinsurance.org/i4a/pages/Index.cfm?pageID=3324.

[21] U.S. Congress, Senate Committee on Government Operations, Subcommittee on Executive Reorganization, *Medical Malpractice: The Patient Versus The Physician*, 91st Cong., 1st sess. (Washington: GPO, 1969), pp. 1-2.

[22] Conning & Company, *Medical Malpractice Insurance: A Prescription for Chaos 2001,* pp. 82-85.

[23] A captive insurer is an insurer owned by a parent company for the purpose of insuring this parent company. Such a captive may insure other parties as well.

[24] Conning & Company, *Medical Malpractice Insurance: A Prescription for Chaos 2001,* p. 88.

[25] The NAIC is the national organization collectively representing the insurance commissioners from the 50 states plus the District of Columbia.

[26] Davin Cermak, "Medical Malpractice: The New Health Care Crisis or History Repeated?," *NAIC Research Quarterly*, Fall, 2002.

[27] "Medical Malpractice, Top Writers—2001," *A.M. Best Statistical Study*, August 5, 2002, p. 1.

[28] "Medical Malpractice, Top Writers—2002," *A.M. Best Statistical Study*, November 17, 2003, p. 1.

[29] "Medical Malpractice, Top Writers—2003," *A.M. Best Statistical Study*, November 15, 2004, p. 1.

[30] See The St. Paul Companies, Inc. press release "The St. Paul Announces Fourth-Quarter Actions to Improve Profitability and Business Positioning," December 12, 2001, at http://www.prnewswire.co.uk/cgi/news/release?id= 78106.

[31] "Continued Improvement in 2005 Results as Medical Malpractice Premium Growth Subsides," *A.M. Best Statistical Study*, August 28, 2006, p. 1.

[32] A.M. Best, "U.S. Medical Professional Liability 2008 Market Review," *Best's Special Report*, April 27, 2009, p. 1.

[33] "Overall Average Rate Change by Year," *Medical Liability Monitor*, vol. 33, no. 10, October 2006, p. 4.

[34] Section 627.357, F.S.

[35] "Report and Recommendations," *Governor's Select Task Force on Healthcare Professional Liability Insurance*, Tallahassee, FL, January 2003, p. xv. Available online at http://www.doh.state.fl.us/myflorida/DOH-Large-Final%20Book.pdf.

[36] Formerly the Product Liability Risk Retention Act of 1981 (15 U.S.C. 3901 *et seq*).

[37] "Risk Retention Act Responds to Pennsylvania's Health Care Crisis," *The Risk Retention Reporter*, vol. 17 no. 1, January 2003.

[38] See the aforementioned CRS Report RL31692, *Medical Malpractice Liability Reform: Legal Issues and Fifty-State Survey of Caps on Punitive Damages and Noneconomic Damages*, by Henry Cohen, for a more complete discussion.

[39] *Fein v. Permanente Medical Group*, 38 Cal.3d 137 (1985), *appeal dismissed*, 474 U.S. 892 (1985); *Roa v. Lodi Medical Group, Inc.*, 37 Cal.3d 920 (1985), *appeal dismissed*, 474 U.S. 990 (1985); *Barme v. Wood*, 37 Cal.3d 174 (1984); *American Bank & Trust Co. v. Community Hospital*, 36 Cal.3d 359 (1984).

[40] 15 U.S.C. Sec. 1011 *et seq.*

[41] See CRS Report RS22639, *Impact of the Abolition of McCarran-Ferguson Antitrust Exemption for the "Business of Insurance"*, by Janice E. Rubin and Baird Webel.

[42] U.S. Department of Commerce, *Liability Risk Retention Act of 1986: Operations Report, 1989*, NTIS PB 90-123134, pp. 9-14.

[43] Ibid., Appendix E-4.

[44] See, for example, *California's MICRA Should Go National*, an opinion piece written by a past president of the California Medical Association, available at http://www.calphys.org/html/bb193.asp.

[45] See, for example, *Insurance Regulation, Not Malpractice Caps, Stabilize Doctors' Premiums*, a fact sheet by The Foundation for Taxpayer & Consumer Rights, available at http://www.consumerwatchdog.org/healthcare/fs/fs003013.php3.

[46] Although the general economic analysis regarding California's experience seems inconclusive, there is at least one specific case where the stronger regulatory structure introduced by Proposition 103 resulted in lower medical malpractice premiums. In 2002, an insurer, the SCPIE Companies, filed for a 15.6% rate increase for 2003 that was then approved by the California Department of Insurance. Following the procedures set forth in Proposition 103, this increase was challenged by The Foundation for Taxpayer & Consumer Rights. On July 24, 2003, an administrative law judge reduced the increase to 9.9% in response to this challenge. See http://www.insurance.ca.gov/ADM/DandR/SCPIE_Decision_for_Internet.pdf for the text of the decision. Arguments from the two sides can be found at http://www.scpie.com/publications/medigram/2003_special.pdf and http://www.consumerwatchdog.org/insurance/pr/ pr002904.php3.

In: Medical Malpractice: Considerations and Proposals ISBN: 978-1-61942-141-7
Editors: Vincent Braswell and Don Mccloud

Chapter 4

MEDICAL MALPRACTICE LIABILITY REFORM: LEGAL ISSUES AND 50-STATE SURVEYS ON TORT REFORM PROPOSALS

Vivian S. Chu

SUMMARY

Medical malpractice liability is governed by state law, but Congress has the power, under the Commerce Clause of the U.S. Constitution (Art. I, § 8, cl. 3), to enact tort reform laws that would affect actions for medical malpractice liability brought under state law. In the 112th Congress, H.R. 5, the Help Efficient, Accessible, Low-cost, Timely Healthcare (HEALTH) Act was introduced by Representative Phil Gingrey on January 24, 2011, and was marked up on February 9 and 16, 2011, by the House Committee on the Judiciary. This bill would preempt state law with respect to certain aspects of medical malpractice lawsuits. Past Congresses have considered similar measures.

This report does not examine the effects of medical malpractice litigation or medical malpractice liability reform on the health care system or on the cost of liability insurance premiums; rather, it explains specific tort reform proposals that are commonly included in medical malpractice liability reform bills, and discusses the individual arguments in favor of and against such proposals from a legal perspective. These proposals include imposing caps on noneconomic damages and punitive damages; permitting defendants to be held liable for no more than their share of responsibility for a plaintiff's injuries; requiring that damage awards be reduced by amounts plaintiffs receive from collateral sources such as health insurance; limiting lawyers' contingent fees; creating a federal statute of limitations; and requiring that awards of future damages in some cases be paid periodically rather than in a lump sum. It also includes, where appropriate, a description of H.R. 5's provisions with respect to these categories.

An Appendix to this report includes five tables. The first table (Table A-1) is a 50-state survey of definitions of a medical malpractice action or to whom state medical malpractice statutes apply. The second table (Table A-2) is a 50-state survey of caps on noneconomic and punitive damages. The third table (Table A-3) is a 50-state survey of the burden of proof standards for punitive damages and whether a state requires a separate proceeding to determine such damages. The fourth table (Table A-4) is a 50-state survey of whether the doctrine of joint and several liability applies to malpractice actions in a state and whether periodic payment of damages is to be considered in an award for a medical malpractice action. The fifth table (Table A-5) is a 50-state survey of limits on attorneys' contingency fees. The sixth table (Table A-6) is a 50-state survey of statute of limitation provisions for both medical malpractice and product liability actions.

INTRODUCTION

This report does not examine the merits or possible effects of medical malpractice litigation or medical malpractice liability reform on the health care system or on the cost of liability insurance premiums.[1] Rather, this report explains specific tort reform proposals that are commonly considered in medical malpractice liability reform measures, and discusses their individual arguments in favor of and against such proposals from a legal perspective. These include imposing caps on noneconomic damages and punitive damages; permitting defendants to be held liable for no more than their share of responsibility for a plaintiff's injuries; requiring that damage awards be reduced by amounts plaintiffs receive from collateral sources such as health insurance; limiting lawyers' contingent fees; creating a federal statute of limitations; and requiring that awards of future damages in some cases be paid periodically rather than in a lump sum. Where appropriate, the report includes a brief summary of the tort reform measures included in H.R. 5.

THE TORT OF MEDICAL MALPRACTICE

Medical malpractice is a tort, which is a civil (as distinct from a criminal) wrong, other than a breach of contract, that causes injury for which the victim may sue to recover damages. Actions in tort derive from the common law, which means that the rules that govern them were developed by the courts of the 50 states, and no statute is necessary in order to bring a tort action. Statutes, however, can change the court-made rules that govern tort actions, and many states have enacted tort reform statutes, including medical malpractice reform statutes. Congress also has the power, under the Commerce Clause of the U.S. Constitution (Art. I, § 8, cl. 3), to enact tort reform laws that would affect actions for medical malpractice liability brought under state law.

Medical malpractice liability arises when a health care professional engages in negligence or commits an intentional tort. Negligence has been defined as conduct "which falls below the standard established by law for the protection of others against unreasonable risk of harm."[2] In most instances it arises from a failure to exercise due care, but a defendant may have carefully considered the possible consequences of his conduct and still be found to have imposed an unreasonable risk on others. "Negligence is conduct, and not a state of mind."[3] The following is a traditional description of the standard of care to which doctors are held to avoid liability for medical malpractice:

> This legal duty requires that the physician undertaking the care of a patient possess and exercise that reasonable and ordinary degree of learning, skill, and care commonly possessed and exercised by reputable physicians practicing in the same locality.[4]

Today, however, many jurisdictions utilize some variation of the national standard of care. As one U.S. court of appeals explained:

> The skill, diligence, knowledge, means and methods [required] are not those "ordinarily" or "generally" or "customarily" exercised or applied, but those that are "reasonably" exercised or applied. Negligence cannot be excused on the ground that others practice the same kind of negligence. Medicine is not an exact science and the proper practice cannot be gauged by a fixed rule.[5]

While most medical malpractice actions rely on the theory of negligence, medical malpractice liability, as noted, may arise from an intentional tort as well as from negligence. In such actions, the practitioner is generally alleged to have intentionally acted in a fashion that ultimately caused harm to the patient.[6] The general difference between an action based in negligence and one based in intentional tort is that "a medical procedure poorly performed might constitute negligence, while a medical procedure correctly performed that was not consented to might constitute an intentional tort."[7]

NONECONOMIC DAMAGES

Economic damages refer to monetary losses that result from an injury, such as medical expenses, lost wages, and rehabilitation costs. Noneconomic damages consist primarily of damages for pain and suffering. Determining the amount of noneconomic damages is traditionally subject to broad discretion on the part of juries, which must equate two variables—money and suffering—that are essentially incommensurable. Judges, however, have the authority to reduce damage awards that they find excessive.[8] See Table A-2 for a 50-state survey of caps on noneconomic and punitive damages.

Section 4 of the H.R. 5 would not limit the amount of economic damages a claimant recovers in a health care lawsuit.[9] Economic damages under the bill would be defined as monetary losses incurred, such as past and future medical expenses, loss of past and future earnings, cost of obtaining domestic services, loss of employment, and loss of business or employment opportunities.[10] However, it generally would limit noneconomic damages, if awarded, to $250,000, regardless of the number of parties against whom the action is brought, or the number of separate claims or actions brought with respect to the same injury.[11] Noneconomic damages would be defined as damages for physical and emotional pain, suffering, inconvenience, physical impairment, mental anguish, disfigurement, loss of enjoyment of life, loss of society and companionship, loss of consortium (other than loss of domestic service), hedonic damages, injury to reputation, and all other nonpecuniary losses of any kind of nature.[12]

Arguments for Caps on Noneconomic Damages

Advocates for caps on noneconomic damages argue that a lack of caps guarantees inconsistency and unpredictability in the tort system, and forces insurers to counter this uncertainty by charging higher premiums. Disagreement over the amount of pain and suffering damages is a major obstacle to out-of-court settlement, thus increasing litigation and, as advocates maintain, coercing insurers to overpay on settlements of smaller claims. Further complicating the problem, they argue, is a tendency of juries to inflate pain and suffering awards to cover some or all of the plaintiff's attorney's fees.

Arguments against Caps on Noneconomic Damages

It has been argued that caps on noneconomic damages could have disparate effects on different patient populations.[13] For example, elderly plaintiffs and poorer individuals who are involved in a malpractice case may not be able to claim much in economic damages, such as lost wages. Thus, capping noneconomic damages would leave these types of plaintiffs little in damages from a malpractice suit and therefore decreased incentive for a lawyer to represent them. Furthermore, opponents of a cap assert that the $250,000, included in H.R. 5, was adopted by California in 1975 "at a time when pain-and-suffering awards rarely exceeded that amount," and that more than 30 years later inflation has taken a toll.[14]

Punitive Damages

Punitive damages (also called exemplary damages) are awarded not to compensate plaintiffs but to punish and deter particularly egregious conduct on the part of defendants—generally meaning reckless disregard for the safety of others, and more than negligence or even gross negligence.

Punitive damages are noneconomic by nature, but state statutes that impose caps on punitive damages usually treat them separately from compensatory noneconomic damages.[15]

The mere commission of a tort is generally not sufficient to obtain an award of punitive damages. As one treatise states:

> There must be circumstances of aggravation or outrage, such as spite or "malice," or a fraudulent or evil motive on the part of the defendant, or such a conscious and deliberate disregard of the interests of others that the conduct may be called wilful or wanton. There is general agreement that, because it lacks this element, mere negligence is not enough, even though it is so extreme as to be characterized as "gross," a term of ill-defined content, which occasionally, in a few jurisdictions, has been stretched to include the element of conscious indifference to consequences, and so to justify punitive damages.[16]

Among the restrictions that have been proposed with regard to punitive damages, besides that they be capped, are (1) that the circumstances in which they may be awarded be narrowed, (2) that plaintiffs be required to prove by "clear and convincing" evidence that they are entitled to them (instead of having to prove it by a mere "preponderance of the evidence."), (3) that liability for punitive damages be determined in a separate proceeding from liability for compensatory damages, and (4) that punitive damages be paid in part to the government or to a fund that serves a public purpose instead of to the plaintiff.[17] See Table A-3 for a 50-state survey of the burden of proof standards for punitive damages and whether a state requires a separate proceeding to determine such damages.

Section 7 of H.R. 5 would limit punitive damages to the greater of $250,000 or two times the amount of economic damages awarded, although a jury would not be informed of the limitation.[18] Punitive damages would not be awarded in a health care lawsuit where a judgment for compensatory (i.e., economic and noneconomic) damages is not rendered.[19]

Under the bill, a claimant would not be permitted to make a demand for punitive damages when initially filing the health care lawsuit. Upon a motion by the claimant, a court would be permitted to allow the claimant to amend his or her pleading only after a hearing and a finding by the court that the claimant has established by a substantial probability that he or she will prevail on the claim for punitive damages.[20] H.R. 5 provides that punitive damages only would be awarded if it is proven by clear and convincing evidence that the defendant acted with malicious intent to injure or that the defendant deliberately failed to avoid unnecessary injury that he or she knew the claimant would suffer.[21] Malicious intent to injure would be defined as intentionally causing or attempting to cause physical injury other than providing health care goods or services.[22]

After the claimant is permitted to amend his pleading to make a demand for punitive damages, either party would be allowed to request that the trier of fact consider (1) whether punitive damages are to be awarded and the amount of such award, and (2) the amount of punitive damages following a determination of punitive liability. If there is a separate proceeding, then no evidence relevant to the claim for punitive damages would be admissible in any proceeding to determine whether compensatory damages, which cover both economic and noneconomic damages, are to be awarded.[23] In determining the amount of punitive damages, the trier of fact would be required to consider only the following: (1) the severity of the harm caused by the conduct of such party; (2) the duration of the conduct or any concealment of it by such party; (3) the profitability of the conduct to such party; (4) the number of products sold or medical procedures rendered for compensation, as the case may be, that caused the harm complained of by the claimant; (5) any criminal penalties imposed on such party as a result of the conduct complained of; and (6) the amount of any civil fines assessed against such party as a result of the conduct complained of by the claimant.[24]

Arguments for Caps on Punitive Damages

Similar to the arguments for capping noneconomic damages, advocates argue that a lack of cap on punitive damages contributes to instability in the insurance system, among other things.[25] Critics charge that punitive damage awards in medical malpractice cases "are often unfair, arbitrary and unpredictable, and result in overkill.... [and] that reform is needed because there has been an outpouring of 'the most outrageous punitive damage awards' in medical malpractice."[26] Although it has been acknowledged that punitive damage awards occur in a small number of cases, "they can have a devastating impact on individual defendants and can impose big costs on the economy as a whole."[27]

Arguments against Caps on Punitive Damages

Some argue that a cap on punitive damages does not lead to a reduction in medical malpractice insurance premiums[28] and that awards are not "multimillion dollar jackpots," because of skewed data.[29] Because punitive damages are meant to deter others, it has been said that they "must be allowed to fill the gaps the criminal law leaves open."[30] Finally, plaintiffs often do not recover the amounts that juries award, because trial judges often reduce punitive damages awards that they find excessive. Furthermore, a recent Supreme Court decision "makes it easier for appellate courts to reduce punitive damages."[31] It has been reported that "[s]ometimes, even before a jury rules, a plaintiff has signed an agreement that limits how much money actually changes hands."[32]

PERIODIC PAYMENT OF DAMAGES

Traditionally, damages are paid in a lump sum, even if they are for future medical care or future lost wages. In recent years, however, "attorneys for both parties in damages actions have occasionally foregone lump-sum settlements in favor of structured settlements, which give the plaintiff a steady series of payments over a period of time through the purchase of an annuity or through self-funding by an institutional defendant."[33] Many forms of periodic payment statutes exist throughout the United States, and they can involve complicated calculations, "creating barriers for those who use the periodic payment process."[34]

Proposals concerning the periodic payment of damages have been applied to future damages as well as to all damages. An issue that may arise in connection with awards of future damages is whether such awards should be converted to present value. Not to require such conversion "could be a very major change, significantly reducing awards, if it is intended to allow a defendant to pay, for example, a $1 million award over a 10-year period at $100,000 a year."[35] Yet, if a jury is required to convert an award—an annuity with a present value of $1 million—into its present value, then the reform doesn't mean that much. As a practical matter, the defendant would be paying the same amount as before, because it would have to spend $1 million for an annuity that, as it earned interest over the years of its distribution, would yield the plaintiff more than $1 million. Had the defendant paid the plaintiff a lump sum of $1 million, then the plaintiff could have purchased that same annuity.[36]

If Congress addresses periodic payment of future damages, it may consider utilizing the Uniform Periodic Payment of Judgments Act for guidance. For example, the uniform act includes sections that would account for inflation and for the effect of the plaintiff's death on unpaid amounts. Section 5(a) of the uniform act provides that, in a trial, "evidence of future changes in the purchasing power of the dollar is admissible on the issue of future damages." Section 13 provides that "liability to a claimant for periodic payments not yet due for medical expenses terminates upon the claimant's death." Damages for other economic losses, however, except in actions for wrongful death, must be paid to the plaintiff's estate. See Table A-4 for a 50-state survey of whether periodic payment of damages is to be considered in an award for a medical malpractice action.

Section 8 of the bill would permit any party to request to the court that future damages be paid by period payment, if an award of future damages is made that equals or exceeds $50,000, without a reduction to a present value. This would be permitted so long as the party against whom the judgment was made has sufficient insurance or other assets to fund a periodic payment of such judgment. H.R. 5 provides that "the court may be guided by the Uniform Periodic Payment of Judgments Act promulgated by the National Conference of Commissioners on Uniform State Laws."[37]

Arguments for the Periodic Payment of Damages

Advocates argue that generally, both parties are benefitted by a period payment scheme because the defendant need not immediately pay out a large sum of money, and the plaintiff is prevented from dissipating a recovery and is provided a secure, tax-free income for a long period, without having to assume the costs and risks of managing an investment portfolio.[38] Periodic payments are not very different than the structured settlements that lawyers utilize in other transactions. "Periodic payment of malpractice awards is nothing more than what lawyers have been doing for years in structured settlements. It is workable and often the only means of providing full compensation for an injured claimant when resources are otherwise unavailable."[39]

Arguments against the Periodic Payment of Damages

Some argue that if periodic payments will in fact benefit plaintiffs, then they will agree to them, as they sometimes do, without the need for legislation. Some plaintiffs may prefer to invest their awards themselves and not risk the insolvency of the defendant or the company from which the defendant purchases an annuity.

LIMITING JOINT AND SEVERAL LIABILITY

Joint and several liability is the common-law rule that, if more than one defendant is found liable for a plaintiff's injuries, then each defendant may be held 100% liable. A plaintiff may not recover more than once, but he may recover all his damages from fewer than all liable defendants. Any defendant who pays more than its share of the damages is entitled to seek contribution from other liable defendants.

Some states have eliminated joint and several liability, making each defendant liable only for its share of responsibility for the plaintiff's injury. Other states have adopted compromise positions such as eliminating joint and several liability only for noneconomic damages, presumably with the view that it is more important for the plaintiff to recover all his economic damages than all his noneconomic damages; or, eliminating joint and several liability only for defendants responsible for less than a specified percentage (e.g., 50%) of the plaintiff's harm, presumably with the view that it is especially unfair for such defendants to be held liable for up to 100% of the damages. See Table A-4 for a 50-state survey of whether the doctrine of joint and several liability applies to malpractice actions in a state.

Section 4 of the bill, which primarily addresses a cap on noneconomic damages, also provides that where there are multiple defendants, the bill would make each party responsible for an amount of damages that is in direct proportion to its individual percentage of fault, and it would not make an individual liable for the share of any other person. The trier of fact would determine the responsibility of each party for the claimant's harm.[40]

Arguments for Limiting Joint and Several Liability

Advocates of abolishing or limiting joint and several liability argue that it

> frequently operates in a highly inequitable manner—sometimes making defendants with only a small or even *de minimis* percentage of fault liable for 100% of plaintiff's damage. Accordingly, joint and several liability in the absence of concerted action has led to the inclusion of many 'deep pocket' defendants such as governments, larger corporations, and insured entities whose involvement is only tangential and who probably would not be joined except for the existence of joint and several liability.[41]

Arguments against Limiting Joint and Several Liability

Advocates of joint and several liability cite the reason that the common law adopted it: it is preferable for a wrongdoer to pay more than its share of the damages than for an injured plaintiff to recover less than the full compensation to which he is entitled.

ABOLISHING THE COLLATERAL SOURCE RULE

The collateral source rule is the common-law rule that allows an injured party to recover damages from the defendant even if he is also entitled to receive them from a third party. Common third parties, that is, collateral sources, include a health insurance company, an employer, or the government. To abolish the collateral source rule would be to allow or require courts to reduce damages by amounts a plaintiff receives or is entitled to receive from collateral sources.

Often a collateral source, such as a health insurer or the government, has a right of subrogation against the tortfeasor (the person responsible for the injury).[42] This means that the collateral source takes over the injured party's right to sue the tortfeasor, for up to the amount the collateral source owes or has paid the injured party. Though the collateral source rule may enable the plaintiff to recover from both his insurer and the defendant, if there is subrogation, the plaintiff must reimburse his insurer the amount it paid him. If the collateral source rule were eliminated, then the defendant would not have to pay the portion of damages covered by a collateral source, and the collateral source would apparently not be able to recover the amount it paid the plaintiff through subrogation. In the medical malpractice context, therefore, eliminating the collateral source rule would benefit liability insurers at the expense of health insurers.

Some jurisdictions, however, have abolished the collateral source rule only in cases in which there is no right of subrogation. In jurisdictions where there is no right of subrogation, the collateral source would be unaffected by elimination of the collateral source rule (i.e., the health insurer would still not recover its money), and the defendant would benefit by not having to pay the plaintiff.[43]

Some proposals to abolish the collateral source rule have taken into account that the plaintiff may have paid insurance premiums for his collateral source benefit. Such proposals, instead of allowing a damage award to be reduced by the full amount of a collateral source benefit, allow it to be reduced by the full amount of a collateral source benefit minus the amount the plaintiff paid to secure that benefit. Other proposals would allow the defendant to introduce evidence of collateral source payments, but do not specify whether the jury must reduce economic damages awards by the amount of such payments.

Eliminating the collateral source rule could also indirectly reduce noneconomic damages awards, because juries often set such awards as a multiple of economic damages. If the collateral source rule were abolished, then the plaintiff could disclose to the jury only her out-of-pocket expenses, or she could disclose her total economic damages before collateral source payments are deducted. If the former, then the plaintiff might receive a lesser award of noneconomic damages.

H.R. 5 included a provision on collateral source benefits and introduction of evidence. An amendment that was adopted during the House Committee on the Judiciary mark-up eliminated this provision from the bill.[44]

Arguments for Abolishing the Collateral Source Rule

Advocates of abolishing the collateral source rule object to the fact that it "permits the plaintiff to obtain double recovery for certain components of his damages award," unless the collateral source is subrogated to the plaintiff's claim against the defendants.[45] Abolishing the collateral source rule will reduce damage awards without denying plaintiffs full recovery of their damages.

Arguments against Abolishing the Collateral Source Rule

Advocates of the collateral source rule cite the reason that the common law adopted it: it is preferable for the victim rather than the wrongdoer to profit from the victim's prudence (as in buying health insurance) or good fortune (in having some other collateral source available). One commentator has also noted that, when the collateral source is the government, and the benefit it provides are future services, such as physical therapy, there is no guarantee that it will provide such services for as long as they are needed, as government programs may be cut back.[46]

LIMITING ATTORNEYS' CONTINGENT FEES

A contingent fee is one in which a lawyer, instead of charging an hourly fee for his services, agrees, in exchange for representing a plaintiff in a tort suit, to accept a percentage of the recovery if the plaintiff wins or settles, but to receive nothing if the plaintiff loses. Payment is thus contingent upon there being a recovery. Plaintiffs agree to this arrangement in order to afford representation without paying anything out-of-pocket, and lawyers agree to it because the percentage they receive—usually from 33⅓% to 40%—generally amounts to more than an hourly fee would. Many states regulate contingent fees in medical malpractice cases in one or more of the following ways: "(1) establishment of a sliding scale for the attorney fees; (2) establishment of a maximum percentage of the award that may be paid for attorney fees; and (3) provision for court review of the reasonableness of the attorney fees."[47]

Legislation to limit contingency fees might consider specifying whether plaintiffs' attorneys would be allowed to add costs, including expert-witness fees, travel, and photocopying on top of the cap, or whether costs would only be recovered from the amount the attorney recoups under the cap. In medical malpractice cases, where costs can skyrocket, the difference is significant. See Table A-5 for a 50-state survey of limits on attorneys' contingency fees.

Section 5 of the H.R. 5 would empower the court to supervise the arrangements for the payment of damages to protect against conflicts of interest (e.g., a claimant's attorney having a financial stake in the outcome by virtue of a contingency fee). The court would have the power to restrict the payment of a claimant's damage recovery to such attorney, and to redirect the damages to the claimant.

The bill would impose a sliding scale for attorney fees. In any health care lawsuit, the total of all contingency fees for representing all claimants would not exceed (1) 40% of the first $50,000 recovered by the claimant(s); (2) 33 % of the next $50,000 recovered by the claimant(s); (3) 25% of the next $500,000 recovered by the claimant(s); and (4) 15% of any amount where the recovery is in excess of $600,000. The sliding scale would be applicable regardless of whether the recovery is by judgment, settlement, mediation, arbitration, or any other form of alternative dispute resolution.[48]

Arguments for Limiting Attorneys' Contingent Fees

Advocates of limiting contingent fees argue that such fees cause juries to inflate verdicts, result in windfalls for lawyers, and prompt lawyers to file frivolous suits in the hope of settling. They also argue that, where there is no dispute as to liability, but only as to damages, there is no contingency and therefore no justification for contingent fees. One study proposed that, if a defendant makes a prompt settlement offer, then counsel fees be "limited to hourly rate charges and capped at 10% of the first $100,000 of the offer and 5% of any greater amounts.... When plaintiffs reject defendants' early offers, contingency fees may only be charged against net recoveries in excess of such offers."[49]

Arguments against Limiting Attorneys' Contingent Fees

Opponents of limiting contingent fees argue that such fees enable injured persons, faced with medical bills and lost wages, to finance lawsuits that they otherwise could not afford—especially if their injuries have disabled them from working. They argue that lawyers are unlikely to file frivolous lawsuits if they stand to recover nothing if they lose,[50] and that studies have shown that contingent fees do not encourage frivolous lawsuits.[51] Finally, they note, "[a]n hourly fee arrangement [such as defendants' lawyers use] can encourage delay, inefficiency, and unnecessary action," whereas "[a] contingent fee is an added inducement for a lawyer to be efficient and expeditious."[52]

Creating a Federal Statute of Limitations

The statute of limitations—the period within which a lawsuit must be filed—for medical malpractice suits under state law is typically two or three years, starting on the date of injury. Sometimes, however, the symptoms of an injury do not appear immediately, or even for years after, malpractice occurs. Many states therefore have adopted a "discovery" rule, under which the statute of limitations starts to run only when the plaintiff discovers, or in the exercise of reasonable diligence, should have discovered, his injury—or, sometimes, his injury and its cause. Plaintiffs would favor allowing a statute of limitations to run only upon discovery of an injury and its cause because it may take additional time after symptoms become manifest to discover that an injury was caused by medical malpractice. See Table A-6 for a 50-state survey on general statute of limitation provisions for both medical malpractice and product liability actions, as some tort reform proposals' provisions would affect the statute of limitations for both types of actions.

Section 3 of H.R. 5 would require a health care lawsuit to be brought within either three years after the date of manifestation of the injury, or within one year after the claimant discovers, or through the use of reasonable diligence should have discovered, the injury, whichever occurs first. No lawsuit could be brought after three years of the date of manifestation of the injury, but such a limitation could be extended upon a showing of (1) proof of fraud; (2) intentional concealment; or (3) the presence of a foreign body, which has no therapeutic or diagnostic purpose or effect, in the person of the injured party. For minors, the action must be commenced within three years from the date of the manifestation of injury, except that actions by a minor under the full age of six must be commenced within three years of the manifestation of the injury or prior to the minor's eighth birthday, whichever provides a longer period. In the event of fraud, the statute of limitations for a minor could be tolled.[53]

Appendix. Fifty-State Surveys

Table A-1 sets forth the definition of a medical malpractice action in the 50 states. As not all states use the words "medical malpractice action" in their statutes, this table was compiled by using variations and combinations of the terms *medical, health care, liability, malpractice, negligence, injury,* and *claim*. This table does not cover the definition of malpractice actions

where a state had a separate statutory scheme for other medical specialties, for example, dentistry. Where possible, this table provides state definitions of medical malpractice or health care liability action and to whom such provisions apply. Where a state had provisions on medical liability tort reform but no explicit definition of a medical malpractice action, the table reflects to which groups these provisions apply to give a sense of the scope of the parties that are covered under the medical malpractice statutes. For example, if the state had a specific statute of limitation on actions for medical malpractice, the table provides the definition of "health care provider" as used applicable to that statute. Where "no statute found" is entered means that there may have been state statutes governing medical malpractice actions, but that CRS could not identify a specific provision that defines an action for medical malpractice, or similar phrases, or a specific definition of the individuals to whom the provisions apply.

Table A-1. State Definitions of Medical Malpractice or Health Care Lawsuit

State	Definition
Alabama	**Ala. Code § 6-5-481 (2011) Medical Liability Actions: Definitions.** "Medical liability" means a finding by a judge, jury, or arbitration panel that a physician, dentist, medical institution, or other health care provider did not meet the applicable standard of care, and that such failure was the proximate cause of the injury complained of, resulting in damage to the patient.
Alaska	**Alaska Stat. § 09.55.560 (2011) Medical Malpractice Actions: Definitions.** "Professional negligence" means a negligent act or omission by a health care provider in rendering professional services. "Health care provider" means an acupuncturist licensed under AS 08.06; an audiologist or speech-language path-ologist licensed under AS 08.11; a chiropractor licensed under AS 08.20; a dental hygienist licensed under AS 08.32; a dentist licensed under AS 08.36; a nurse licensed under AS 08.68; a dispensing optician licensed under AS 08.71; a naturopath licensed under AS 08.45; an optometrist licensed under AS 08.72; a pharmacist licensed under AS 08.80; a physical therapist or occupational therapist licensed under AS 08.84; a physician or physician assistant licensed under AS 08.64; a podiatrist; a psychologist and a psychological associate licensed under AS 08.86; a hospital as defined in AS 47.32.900, including a governmentally owned or operated hospital; an employee of a health care provider acting within the course and scope of employment; an ambulatory surgical facility and other organizations whose primary purpose is the delivery of health care, including a health maintenance organization, individual practice association, integrated delivery system, pre-ferred provider organization or arrangement, and a physical hospital organization.
Arizona	**Ariz. Rev. Stat. § 12-561 (2011) Actions Relating To Health Care: Definitions.** "Medical malpractice action" or "cause of action for medical malpractice" means an action for injury or death against a licensed health care provider based upon such provider's alleged negligence, misconduct, errors or omissions, or breach of contract in the rendering of health care, medical services, nursing services or other health-related services or for the rendering of such health care, medical services, nursing services or other health-related services, without express or implied consent including an action based upon the alleged negligence, misconduct, errors or omissions or breach of contract in collecting, processing or distributing whole human blood, blood components, plasma, blood fractions or

State	Definition
	blood derivatives. "Licensed health care provider" means both: (a) a person, corporation or institution or certified by the state health care, medical services or health-related services and includes the officers, employees and agents thereof working under the supervision of such person, corporation or institution in providing such health care, medical services,nursing services or other health-related services; (b) a federally licensed, regulated or registered blood bank, blood center or plasma center collecting, processing or distributing whole human blood, blood components, plasma, blood fractions or derivatives for use by licensed health care provider and includes officers, employees, agents working under the supervision of the blood bank, blood center or plasma center.
Arkansas	**Ark. Code Ann. § 16-114-201 (2010) Actions for Medical Injury: Definitions.** As used in this subchapter, unless the context otherwise requires: "Action for medical injury" means any action against a medical care provider, whether based in tort, contract, or otherwise, to recover damages on account of medical injury; "Medical care provider" means a physician, certified registered nurse anesthetist, physician's assistant, nurse, optometrist, chiropractor, physical therapist, dentist, podiatrist, pharmacist, veterinarian, hospital, nursing home, community mental health center, psychologist, clinic, or not-for-profit home health care agency licensed by the state or otherwise lawfully providing professional medical care or services, or an officer, employee or agent thereof acting in the course and scope of employment in the providing of such medical care or medical services; and "Medical injury" or "injury" means any adverse consequences arising out of or sustained in the course of the professional services being rendered by a medical care provider, whether resulting from negligence, error, or omission in the performance of such services; or from rendition of such services without informed consent or in breach of warranty or in viola-tion of contract; or from failure to diagnose; or from premature abandonment of a patient or of a course of treatment; or from failure to properly main-tain equipment or appliances necessary to the rendition of such services; or otherwise arising out of or sustained in the course of such services.
California	**Cal. Civ. Code §§ 3333.1, 3333.2 (2010) Collateral Benefits and Noneconomic Losses in Medical Malpractice Actions.** "Professional negligence" means a negligent act or omission to act by a health care provider in the rendering of professional services, which act or omission is the proximate cause of a personal injury or wrongful death, provided that such services are within the scope of services for which the provider is licensed and which are not within any restriction imposed by the licensing agency or licensed hospital. "Health care provider" means any person licensed or certified pursuant to Division 2 (commencing with Section 500) of the Business and Professions Code, or licensed pursuant to the Osteopathic Initiative Act, or the Chiropractor Initiative Act, or licensed to Chapter 2.5 (commencing with Section 1440) of Division 2 of the Health and Safety Code; and any clinic, health dispensary, or health facility, licensed pursuant to Division 2 (commencing with Section 1200) of the Health and Safety Code. Health care provider includes the legal representatives of a health care provider. ***See also* Cal. Civ. Proc. Code §§ 340.5, 364, 667.7, 1295 (2010)**
Colorado	No statute found.

Table A-1. (Continued)

State	Definition
Connecticut	**Conn. Gen. Stat. § 52-184c (2010) Standard of Care in Negligence Action Against Health Care Provider. Qualifications of Expert Witness.** In any civil action to recover damages resulting from personal injury or wrongful death occurring on or after October 1, 1987, in which it is alleged that such injury or death resulted from the negligence of a health care provider, as defined in section 52-184b, the claimant shall have the burden of proving by the preponderance of the evidence that the alleged actions of the health care provider represented a breach of the prevailing professional standard of care for that health care provider. The prevailing professional standard of care for a given health care provider shall be that level of care, skill and treatment which, in light of all relevant surrounding circumstances, is recognized as acceptable and appropriate by reasonably prudent similar health care providers. **Conn. Gen. Stat. § 52-184b (2010) Failure to bill and advance payments inadmissible in malpractice cases.** For the purposes of this section, "health care provider" means any person, corporation, facility or institution licensed by this state to provide health care or professional services, or an officer, employee or agent thereof acting in the course and scope of his employment.
Delaware	**Del. Code Ann. tit. 18, § 6801 (2011) Health Care Medical Negligence Insurance Litigation: Definitions.** "Medical negligence" means any tort or breach of contract based on health care or professional services rendered, or which should have been renderd, by a health care provider to a patient. The standard of skill and care required of every health care provider in rendering professional services or health care to a patient shall be that degree of skill and care ordinarily employed in the same or similar field of medicine as defendant, and the use of reasonable care and diligence.
District of Columbia	No statute found.
Florida	**Fla. Stat. Ann. § 766.102 (2011) Medical Negligence; Standards of Recovery; Expert Witness.** In any action for recovery of damages based on the death or personal injury of any person in which it is alleged that such death or injury resulted from the negligence of a health care provider as defined in s. 766.202(4), the claimant shall have the burden of proving by the greater weight of evidence that the alleged actions of the health care provider represented a breach of the prevailing professional standard of care for that health care provider. The prevailing professional standard of care for a given health care provider shall be that level of care, skill, and treatment which, in light of all relevant surrounding circumstances, is recognized as acceptable and appropriate by reasonably prudent similar health care providers. **Fla. Stat. Stat. § 766.202 (2011) Medical Malpractice And Related Matters: Definitions.** "Health care provider" means any hospital, ambulatory surgical center, or mobile surgical facility as defined and licensed under chapter 395; a birth center licensed under chapter 383; any person licensed under chapter 458, chapter 459, chapter 460, chapter 461, chapter 462, chapter 463, part I of chapter 464, chapter 466, chapter 467, or chapter 486; a clinical lab licensed under chapter 483; a health maintenance organization certificated under part I of chapter 641; a blood bank; a plasma center; an industrial clinic; a renal dialysis facility; or a professional association partnership, corporation, joint venture, or other association for professional activity by health care providers.

State	Definition
Georgia	**Ga. Code Ann. § 9-3-70 (2011) Action for Medical Malpractice Defined.** As used in this article, the term "action for medical malpractice" means any claim for damages resulting from the death of or injury to any person arising out of: (1) Health, medical, dental, or surgical service, diagnosis, prescription, treatment, or care rendered by a person authorized by law to perform such service or by any person acting under the supervision and control of the lawfully authorized person; or (2) Care or service rendered by any public or private hospital, nursing home, clinic, hospital authority, facility, or institution, or by any officer, agent, or employee thereof acting within the scope of his employment. **Ga. Code Ann. § 9-9-60 (2011) Arbitration: "Medical malpractice claim" defined.** For the purposes of this article, the term "medical malpractice claim" means any claim for damages resulting from the death of or injury to any person arising out of: (1) Health, medical, dental, or surgical service, diagnosis, prescription, treatment, or care, rendered by a person authorized by law to perform such service or by any person acting under the supervision and control of a lawfully authorized person; or (2) Care or service rendered by any public or private hospital, nursing home, clinic, hospital authority, facility, or institution, or by any officer, agent, or employee thereof acting within the scope of his employment. ***See also* Ga. Code Ann. §§ 9-11-8, 9-11-54 (2011)**
Hawaii	**Haw. Rev. Stat. Ann. § 671-1 (2011) Medical Torts: Definitions.** "Medical tort" means professional negligence, the rendering of professional service without informed consent, or an error or omission in professional practice, by a health care provider, which proximately causes death, injury, or other damage to a patient. "Health care provider" means physician, osteopathic physician, surgeon, or physician assistant licensed under chapter 453, a podiatrist licensed under 463E, a health care facility as defined in section 323D-2, and the employees of any of them. Health care provider shall not mean any nursing institution, nursing service conducted by and for those who rely upon treatment by spiritual means through prayer alone, or employees of the institution or service.
Idaho	**Idaho Code Ann. § 6-1012 (2011) Medical Malpractice: Proof of Community Standard of Health Care Practice in Malpractice Case.** In any case, claim or action for damages due to injury to or death of any person, brought against any physician and surgeon or other provider of health care, including, without limitation, any dentist, physicians' assistant, nurse practitioner, registered nurse, licensed practical nurse, nurse anesthetist, medical technologist, physical therapist, hospital or nursing home, or any person vicariously liable for the negligence of them or any of them, on account of the provision of or failure to provide health care or on account of any matter incidental or related thereto, such claimant or plaintiff must, as an essential part of his or her case in chief, affirmatively prove by direct expert testimony and by a preponderance of all the competent evidence, that such defendant then and there negligently failed to meet the applicable standard of health care practice of the community in which such care allegedly was or should have been provided, as such standard existed at the time and place of the alleged negligence of such physician and surgeon, hospital or other such health care provider and as such

Table A-1. (Continued)

State	Definition
	standard then and there existed with respect to the class of health care provider that such defendant then and there belonged to and in which capacity he, she or it was functioning. Such individual providers of health care shall be judged in such cases in comparison with similarly trained and qualified providers of the same class in the same community, taking into account his or her training, experience, and fields of medical specialization, if any. If there be no other like provider in the community and the standard of practice is therefore indeterminable, evidence of such standard in similar Idaho communities at said time may be considered. As used in this act, the term "community" refers to that geographical area ordinarily served by the licensed general hospital at or nearest to which such care was or allegedly should have been provided.
Illinois	**735 Ill. Comp. Stat. Ann. § 5/2-1704 (2011) Medical Malpractice Action.** As used in this Part, "medical malpractice action" means any action, whether in tort, contract or otherwise, in which the plaintiff seeks damages for injuries or death by reason of medical, hospital, or other healing art malpractice. The term "healing art" shall not include care and treatment by spiritual means through prayer in accord with the tenets and practices of a recognized church or religious denomination.
Indiana	**Ind. Code Ann. § 34-18-2-18 (2011) Malpractice.** "Malpractice" means a tort or breach of contract based on health care or professional services that were provided, or that should have been provided, by a health care provider, to a patient. **Ind. Code Ann. § 34-18-2-14 (2011) Health Care Provider.** "Health care provider" means an individual, a partnership, a limited liability company, a corporation, a professional corporation, a facility, or an institution licensed or legally authorized by this state to provide health care or professional services as a physician, psychiatric hospital, hospital, health facility, emergency ambulance service (IC 16-18-2-107), dentist, registered or licensed practical nurse, physician assistant, midwife, optometrist, podiatrist, chiropractor, physical therapist, respiratory care practitioner, occupational therapist, psychologist, paramedic, emergency medical technician-intermediate, emergency medical technician-basic advanced, or emergency medical technician, or a person who is an officer, employee, or agent of the individual, partnership, corporation, professional corporation, facility, or institution acting in the course and scope of the person's employment It also includes: college, university, or junior college that provides health care to a student, faculty member, or employee, and the governing board or a person who is an officer, employee, or agent of the college, university, or junior college acting in the course and scope of the person's employment; a blood bank, community mental health center, community mental retardation center, community health center, or migrant health center; a home health agency (as defined in IC 16-27-1-2); a health maintenance organization (as defined in IC 27-13-1-19)'; a health care organization whose members, shareholders, or partners are health care providers under subdivision (1); a corporation, limited liability company, partnership, or professional corporation not otherwise qualified under this section that, as one its functions, provides health care, or is organized or registered under state law, and is determined to be eligible for coverage as a health care provider under this article for its health care function.
Iowa	**Iowa Code Ann. § 614.1 (2010) Limitations on Actions. Period.** Limitation on time for "malpractice" which is an action founded on injuries to persons for wrongful death against any physician and surgeon, osteopathic

State	Definition
	physician and surgeon, dentist, podiatrist, physician, optometrist, pharmacist, chiropractor, physician assistant, or nurse, licensed under chapter 147, or hospital licensed under chapter 135B, arising out of patient care.
Kansas	No statute found.
Kentucky	**Ky. Rev. Stat. Ann. § 304.40-260 (2010) Health Care Malpractice Insurance Claims: Definitions.** As used in KRS 304.40-250 to 304.40-320, the following words and terms shall be defined as follows: "Malpractice" means any tort or breach of contract based on health care or professional services rendered, or which should have been rendered, by a health care provider to the patient, "Health care" means any act, or treatment performed or furnished, or which should have been performed or furnished, by any health care provider to a patient during that patient's care, treatment, or confinement for a physical or mental condition.
Louisiana	**La. Rev. Stat. Ann. 40:1299.41 (2011) Medical Malpractice: Definitions and general applications.** "Malpractice" means any unintentional tort or any breach of contract based on health care or professional services rendered, or which should have been rendered, by a health care provider, to a patient, including failure to render services timely and the handling of a patient, including loading and unloading of a patient, and also includes all legal responsibility of a health care provider arising from acts or omissions during the procurement of blood or blood components, in the training or supervision of health care providers, or from defects in blood, tissue, transplants, drugs, and medicines, or from defects in or failures of prosthetic devices implanted in or used on or in the person of a patient.
Maine	No statute found.
Maryland	**Md. Code Cts. & Jud. Proc. Code Ann. § 3-2A-01 (2011) Health Care Malpractice Claims: Definitions**
	"Medical injury" means injury arising or resulting from the rendering or failure to render health care. "Health care provider" means a hospital, a related institution as defined in § 19-301 of the Health - General Article, a medical day care center, a hospice care program, an assisted living program, a freestanding ambulatory care facility as defined in § 19-3B-01 of the Health -General Article, a physician, an osteopath, an optometrist, a chiropractor, a registered or licensed practical nurse, a dentist, a podiatrist, a psychologist, a licensed certified social worker-clinical, and a physical therapist, licensed or authorized to provide one or more health care services in Maryland. "Health care provider" does not include any nursing institution conducted by and for those who rely upon treatment by spiritual means through prayer alone in accordance with the tenets and practices of a recognized church or religious denomination.
Massachusetts	**Mass. Ann. Laws, ch. 231, § 60B (2010) Tribunal for Screening of Medical Malpractice Claims; Evidence Considered; Subpoena Power; Witnesses; Bond Requirements; Provider of Health Care Defined.** Every action for malpractice, error or mistake against a provider of health care shall be heard by a tribunal consisting of a single justice of the superior court, a physician licensed to practice medicine in the commonwealth under the provisions of section two of chapter one hundred and twelve and an attorney authorized to practice law in the commonwealth, at which hearing the plaintiff

Table A-1. (Continued)

State	Definition
	shall present an offer of proof and said tribunal shall determine if the evidence presented if properly substantiated is sufficient to raise a legitimate question of liability appropriate for judicial inquiry or whether the plaintiff's case is merely an unfortunate medical result. For the purposes of this section, a provider of health care shall mean a person, corporation, facility or institution licensed by the commonwealth to provide health care or professional services as a physician, hospital, clinic or nursing home, dentist, registered or licensed nurse, optometrist, podiatrist, chiropractor, physical therapist, psychologist, social worker, or acupuncturist, or an officer, employee or agent thereof acting in the course and scope of his employment.
Michigan	**Mich. Comp. Laws. Serv. § 600.2912a (2011) Action alleging malpractice; Burden of Proof.** In an action alleging malpractice, the plaintiff has the burden of proving that in light of the state of the art existing at the time of the alleged malpractice: (a) The defendant, if a general practitioner, failed to provide the plaintiff the recognized standard of acceptable professional practice or care in the community in which the defendant practices or in a similar community, and that as a proximate result of the defendant failing to provide that standard, the plaintiff suffered an injury. (b) The defendant, if a specialist, failed to provide the recognized standard of practice or care within that specialty as reasonably applied in light of the facilities available in the community or other facilities reasonably available under the circumstances, and as a proximate result of the defendant failing to provide that standard, the plaintiff suffered an injury.
Minnesota	**Minn. Stat. Ann. § 541.076 (2010) Health Care Provider Action: Limitation of Time.** For purposes of this section, "health care provider" means a physician, surgeon, dentist, occupational therapist, or other health care professionals as defined in section 145.61, hospital, treatment or facility.
Mississippi	**Mississippi Code Ann. § 15-1-36 (2010) Actions for Medical Malpractice: Limitation of Time.** Specific time limitation for an action against a licensed physician, osteopath, dentist, hospital, nurse, pharmacist, podiatrist, optometrist or chiropractor for injuries or wrongful death arising out of course of medical, surgical, or other professional services.
Missouri	**Missouri § 516.015 (2011) Statute of Limitations: Actions against health care providers (medical malpractice).** Actions against physicians, hospitals, dentists, registered or licensed practical nurses, optometrists, podiatrists, pharmacists, chiropractors, professional physical therapists, and any other entity providing health care services and all employees of any of the foregoing acting in the course and scope of their employment, for damages for malpractice, negligence, error or mistake related to health care. **Missouri § 538.205 (2011) Tort Actions Based on Improper Health Care. Definitions.** "Health care provider" means any physician, hospital, health maintenance organization, ambulatory surgical center, long-term facility, dentist, registered or licensed practical nurse, optometrist, podiatrist, pharmacist, chiropractor, professional physical therapist, psychologist, physician-in-training, and any other entity that provides health care services under the authority of a license or certificate.

State	Definition
	"Health care services" means any services rendered by a health care provider in the ordinary course of the health care provider's profession, or, if the health care provider is an institution, in the ordinary course of furthering the purposes for which is organized. Professional services shall include, but are not limited to, transfer to a patient of goods or services incidental to or pursuant to the practice of the health care provider's profession.
Montana	**Mont. Code Ann. § 25-9-411 (2010) (Temporary)Medical malpractice Noneconomic Damages Limitation.** "Malpractice claim" means a claim based on a negligent act or omission by a health care provider in the rendering of professional services that is the proximate cause of a personal injury or wrongful death. **Mont. Code Ann. § 27-6-103 (2010) Montana Medical Legal Panel Act: Definitions.** "Malpractice claim" means a claim or potential claim of a claimant against a health care provider for medical or dental treatment, lack of medical or dental treatment, or other alleged departure from accepted standards of health care that proximately results in damage to the claimant, whether the claimant's claim or potential claim sounds in tort or contract, and includes but is not limited to allegations of battery or wrongful death.
Nebraska	**Neb. Rev. Stat. Ann. § 44-2810 (2010) Nebraska Hospital-Medical Liability Act: Malpractice or Professional Negligence, Defined.** Malpractice or professional negligence shall mean that, in rendering professional services, a health care provider has failed to use the ordinary and reasonable care, skill, and knowledge ordinarily possessed and used under like circumstances by members of his profession engaged in a similar practice in his or in similar localities. In determining what constitutes reasonable and ordinary care, skill, diligence on the part of a health care provider in a particular community, the test shall be that which health care providers, in the same community or similar communities and engaged in the same or similar lines of work, would ordinarily exercise and devote to the benefit of their patients under like circumstances. **Neb. Rev. Stat. Ann. § 44-2803 (2010) Nebraska Hospital-Medical Liability Act; Health Care Provider, Defined.** Health care provider means: (1) a physician; (2) a certified registered nurse anesthetist; (3) an individual, partnership, limited liability company, corporation, association, facility, institution, or other entity authorized by law to provide professional medical services by physicians or certified nurse anesthetists; (4) a hospital; or (5) a personal representative as defined in section 30-2209 who is successor or assignee of any health care provider designated in subdivisions (1)-(4).
Nevada	**Nev. Rev. Stat. Ann. § 41A.009 (2010) Actions for Medical or Dental Malpractice: "Medical malpractice" Defined.** "Medical malpractice" means the failure of a physician, hospital or employee of a hospital, in rendering services, to use the reasonable care, skill or knowledge ordinarily used under similar circumstances. **Nev. Rev. Stat. Ann. § 630A.060 (2010) Homeopathic Medicine: "Malpractice" Defined.** "Malpractice" means failure on the part of a homeopathic physician to exercise the degree of care, diligence and skill ordinarily exercised by homeopathic physicians in good standing in the community in which he or she practices. As used in this section, "community" embraces the entire area customarily served by homeopathic physicians among whom a patient may reasonably choose, not

Table A-1. (Continued)

State	Definition
	merely the particular area inhabited by the patients of that individual physician or the particular city or place where the homeopathic physician has an office. **Nev. Rev. Stat. Ann. § 633.071 (2010) Osteopathic Medicine: "Malpractice" Defined.** "Malpractice" means failure on the part of an osteopathic physician to exercise the degree of care, diligence and skill ordinarily exercised by osteopathic physicians in good standing in the community in which he or she practices.
New Hampshire	**N.H. Rev. Stat. Ann. § 507-C:1 (2011) Actions for Medical Injury: Definitions.** "Action for medical injury" means any action against a medical care provider, whether based in tort, contract, or otherwise, to recover damages on account of medical injury. "Medical care provider" means a physician's assistant, registered or licensed practical nurse, hospital, clinic or not-for-profit home health care agency licensed by the state or otherwise lawfully providing medical care or services, or an officer, employee or agent thereof acting in the course and scope of employment. "Medical injury" or "injury" means any adverse, untoward or undesired consequences arising out of or sustained in the course of professional services rendered by a medical care provider, whether resulting from negligence, error or omission in the performance of such services; from rendition of such services without informed consent or in breach of warranty or in violation of contract; from failure to diagnose; from premature abandonment of a patient or of a course of treatment; from failure properly to maintain equipment or appliances necessary to the rendition of such services; or otherwise arising out of sustained in the course of such service. ***See also*** **N.H. Rev. Stat. Ann. § 507-E: 1 (2011) Medical Injury Actions Definitions.**
New Jersey	No statute found.
New Mexico	**N.M. Stat. Ann. § 41-5-3 (2010) Medical Malpractice Act: Definitions.** "Malpractice claim" includes any cause of action arising in this state against a health care provider for medical treatment, lack of medical treatment or other claimed departure from accepted standards of health care which proximately results in injury to the patient, whether the patient's claim or cause of action sounds in tort or contract, and includes but is not limited to actions based on battery or wrongful death; "malpractice claim" does not include a cause of action arising out of the driving, flying or nonmedical acts involved in the operation, use or maintenance of a vehicular or aircraft ambulance. "Health care provider" means a person, corporation, organization, facility or institution licensed or certified by this state to provide health care or professional services as a doctor of medicine, hospital, outpatient health care facility, doctor of osteopathy, chiropractor, podiatrist, nurse anesthetist or physician's assistant.
New York	No statute found.
North Carolina	**N.C. Gen. Stat. § 90-21.11 (2010) Medical Malpractice Actions: Definitions.** As used in this Article, the term "medical malpractice action" means a civil action for damages for personal injury or death arising out of the furnishing or failure to furnish professional services in the performance of medical, dental, or other health care by a health care provider. As used in this Article, the term "health care provider" means without limitation any person who pursuant to the provisions of Chapter 90 of the General Statutes is licensed, or is otherwise registered or certified to engage in the practice of or otherwise performs duties associated with any of the following: medicine,

State	Definition
	surgery, dentistry, pharmacy, optometry, midwifery, osteopathy, podiatry, chiropractic, radiology, nursing, physiotherapy, pathology, anesthesiology, anesthesia, laboratory analysis, rendering assistance to a physician, dental hygiene, psychiatry, psychology; or a hospital or a nursing home; or any other person who is legally responsible for the negligence of such person, hospital or nursing home; or any other person acting at the direction or under the supervision of any of the foregoing persons, hospital, or nursing home.
North Dakota	**N.D. Cent. Code § 32-42-01 (2011) Alternative Dispute Resolution: Definitions.** "Health care malpractice action" means a claim for relief brought against a health care provider, or other defendant joined in the action, regardless of the theory of liability on which the claim is based, in which the claimant alleges a health care malpractice claim. "Health care malpractice claim" means a claim brought against a health care provider or other defendant joined in a claim alleging that an injury was suffered by the claimant as a result of health care negligence or gross negligence, breach of express or implied warranty or contract, failure to discharge a duty to warn, or failure to obtain consent arising from the provision of or failure to provide health care services. "Health care negligence" means an act or omission by a health care provider which deviates from the applicable standard of care and causes an injury.
Ohio	**Ohio Rev. Code Ann. § 2305.113 (2011) Time Limitations for Bringing Medical, Dental, Optometric, or Chiropractic Claims.** "Medical claim" means any claim that is asserted in any civil action against a physician, podiatrist, hospital, home, or residential facility, against any employee or agent of a physician, podiatrist, hospital, home, or residential facility, or against a licensed practical nurse, registered nurse, advanced practice nurse, physical therapist, physician assistant, emergency medical technician-basic, emergency medical technician-intermediate, or emergency medical technician-paramedic, and that arises out of the medical diagnosis, care, or treatment of any person.
Oklahoma	**Okla. Stat. tit. 63, § 1-1708.1C (2010) Affordable Access To Health Care Act: Definitions.** "Medical liability action" means any civil action involving, or contingent upon, personal injury or wrongful death brought against a health care provider based on professional negligence. "Health care provider" means any person or other entity who is licensed pursuant to provision Title 59 or Title 63 of the Oklahoma Statutes, or pursuant to the laws of another state, to render health care services in the practice of a profession or in the ordinary course of business. "Health care services" means any services provided by a health care provider, or by an individual working under the supervision of a health care provider, that relate to diagnosis, assessment, prevention, treatment or care of any human illness, disease, injury or condition.
Oregon	No statute found.
Pennsylvania	**42 Pa. Cons. Stat. § 5101.1, 40 (2010) Venue in Medical Professional Liability Actions. 40 Pa. Cons. Stat. § 1303.103 (2010) Medical Care Availability and Reduction of Error Act.** "Medical professional liability action" means any proceeding in which a medical professional liability claim is asserted, including an action in a court of law or an arbitration proceeding.

Table A-1. (Continued)

State	Definition
	”Medical professional liability claim” means any claim seeking the recovery of damages or loss from a health care provider arising out of any tort or breach of contract causing injury or death resulting from the furnishing of health care services which were or should have been provided. “Health care provider” means any primary health care center, a personal care home licensed by the Department of Public Welfare, or a person including a corporation, university or other education institution licensed or approved by the Commonwealth to provide health care or professional medical services as a physician, certified nurse midwife, a podiatrist, hospital, nursing home, birth center, and an officer, employee or agent of any of them acting in the course and scope of employment.
Rhode Island	**R.I. Gen. Laws § 5-37-1 (2011) Board Of Medical Licensure And Discipline: Definitions.** “Medical malpractice” or “malpractice” means any tort, or breach of contract based on health care or professional services rendered, or which should have been rendered, by a physician, dentist, hospital, clinic, health maintenance organization or professional service corporation providing health care services and organized under chapter 5.1 of title 7, to a patient or the rendering of medically unnecessary services except at the informed request of the patient.
South Carolina	**S.C. Code Ann. § 15-79-110 (2010) Medical Malpractice Actions: Definitions.** “Medical malpractice” means doing that which the reasonably prudent health care provider or health care institution would not do or not doing that which the reasonably prudent health care provider or health care institution would do in the same or similar circumstances. “Health care institution” means an ambulatory surgical facility, a hospital, an institutional general infirmary, a nursing home, and a renal dialysis facility. “Health care provider” means a physician, surgeon, osteopath, nurse, oral surgeon, dentist, pharmacist, chiropractor, optometrist, podiatrist, or any similar category of licensed health care provider, including health care practice, association, partnership, or other legal entity.
South Dakota	**S.D. Codified Laws § 15-2-14.1 (2010) Medical Malpractice Action: Two-year limitation.** An action against a physician, surgeon, dentist, hospital, sanitarium, registered nurse, licensed practice nurse, chiropractor, or other practitioner of the health arts for malpractice, error, mistake or failure to cure, whether based upon tort or contract, can be commenced only within two years after the alleged malpractice.
Tennessee	**Tenn. Code Ann. § 56-54-103 (2011) Tennessee Medical Malpractice Reporting Act: Chapter Definitions.** “Medical malpractice” means an actual or alleged negligent act, error, or omission in providing or failing to provide health care services. “Health care provider” means (A) a person licensed in either title 63, except chapter 12, or title 68 to provide health care or related services, including, but not limited to, an acupuncturist, a physician, a surgeon, an osteopathic physician, a dentist, a nurse, an optometrist, a podiatrist, a chiropractor, a physical therapist, a psychologist, a pharmacist, an optician, a physician assistant, a certified professional midwife, an orthopedic physician assistant, or a nurse practitioner.
Texas	**Tex. Civ. Prac. & Rem. Code § 74.001 (2010) Medical Liability: Definitions.** “Health care liability claim” means a cause of action against a health care provider or physician for treatment, lack of treatment, or other claimed departure from accepted standards of medical care, or health care, or safety or professional or administrative services directly related to health care, which proximately

State	Definition
	results in injury to death of a claimant, whether the claimant's claim or cause of actions sounds in tort or contract. "Health care provider" means any person, partnership, professional association, corporation, facility, or institution duly licensed, certified, registered, or chartered by the State of Texas to provide health care, including: a registered nurse; a dentist; a podiatrist; a pharmacist; a chiropractor; an optometrist; or health care institution. (B) The term includes: (i) an officer, director, shareholder, member, partner, manager,owner, or affiliate of a health care provider or physician; and (ii) an employee, independent contractor, or agent of a health care provider or physician acting in the course and scope of the employment or contractual relationship.
Utah	**Utah Code Ann. § 78B-3-403 (2011) Utah Health Care Malpractice Act: Definitions.** "Malpractice action against a health care provider" means any action against a health care provider, whether in contract, tort, breach of warranty, wrongful death, or otherwise, based upon alleged personal injuries relating to or arising out of health care rendered or which should have been rendered by the health care provider. "Health care provider" includes any person, partnership, association, corporation, or other facility or institution who causes to be rendered or who renders health care or professional services as a hospital, health care facility, physician, registered nurse, licensed practical nurse, nurse-midwife, licensed Direct-entry midwife, dentist, dental hygienist, optometrist, clinical laboratory technologist, pharmacist, physical therapist, physical therapist assistant, podiatric physician, psychologist, chiropractic physician, naturopathic physician, osteopathic physician, osteopathic physician and surgeon, audiologist, speech-language pathologist, clinical social worker, certified social worker, social service worker, marriage and family counselor, practitioner of obstetrics, or others rendering similar care and services relating to or arising out of the health needs of persons or groups of persons and officers, employees, or agents of any of the above acting in the course and scope of their employment.
Vermont	**Vt. Stat. Ann. tit. 12, § 1908 (2011) Conduct of Trial: Burden of proof.** For the purpose of this section, malpractice shall mean professional medical negligence comprised of the elements listed herein. In a malpractice action based on the negligence of the personnel of a hospital, a physician licensed under chapter 23 of Title 26, a dentist licensed under chapter 13 of Title 26, a podiatrist licensed under chapter 7 of Title 26, a chiropractor licensed under chapter 9 of Title 26, a nurse licensed under chapter 27 of Title 26, or an osteopathic physician licensed under chapter 33 of Title 26.
Virginia	**Va. Code Ann. § 8.01-581.1 (2011) Medical Malpractice Review Panels; Arbitration Of Malpractice Claims: Definitions.** "Malpractice" means any tort action or breach of contract action for personal injuries or wrongful death, based on health care or professional services rendered, or which should have been rendered, by a health care provider, to a patient. "Health care provider" means (i) a person, corporation, facility or instit-ution licensed by this Commonwealth to provide health care or professi-onal services as a physician or hospital, dentist, pharmacist, registered nurse or licensed practical nurse or a person who holds a multistate privilege to practice such nursing under the Nurse Licensure Compact, optometrist, podiatrist, chiropractor, physical therapist, physical therapy assistant, clinical psychologist, clinical social worker, professional counselor, licensed marriage and family therapist, licensed dental hygienist, health maintenance organization, or emergency medical care

Table A-1. (Continued)

State	Definition
	attendant or technician who provides services on a fee basis; (ii) a professional corporation, all of whose shareholders or members are so licensed; (iii) a partnership, all of whose partners are so licensed; (iv) a nursing home as defined in § 54.1-3100 except those nursing institutions conducted by and for those who rely upon treatment by spiritual means alone through prayer in accordance with a recognized church or religious denomination; (v) a professional limited liability company comprised of members as described in subdivision A 2 of § 13.1-1102; (vi) a corporation, partnership, limited liability company or any other entity, except a state-operated facility, which employs or engages a licensed health care provider and which primarily renders health care services; or (vii) a director, officer, employee, independent contractor, or agent of the persons or entities referenced herein, acting within the course and scope of his employment or engagement as related to health care or professional services.
Washington	**Wash. Rev. Code Ann. § 48.140.010 (2011) Medical Malpractice Closed Claim Reporting: Definitions.** "Medical malpractice" means an actual or alleged negligent act, error, or omission in providing or failing to provide health care services that is actionable under chapter 7.70 RCW. **Was. Rev. Code Ann. § 7.70.020 (2011) Actions For Injuries Resulting from Health Care: Definitions.** In this chapter, "health care provider" means either: (1) A person licensed by this state to provide health care or related services including, but not limited to, an East Asian medicine practitioner, a physician, osteopathic physician, dentist, nurse, optometrist, podiatric physician and surgeon, chiropractor, physical therapist, psychologist, pharmacist, optician, physician assistant, midwife, osteopathic physician's assistant, nurse practitioner, or physician's trained mobile intensive care paramedic, including, in the event such person is deceased, his or her estate or personal representative; (2) An employee or agent of a person described in part (1) above, acting in the course and scope of his employment, including, in the event such employee or agent is deceased, his or her estate or personal representative; or (3) An entity, whether or not incorporated, facility, or institution employing one or more persons described in part (1) above, including, but not limited to, a hospital, clinic, health maintenance organization, or nursing home; or an officer, director, employee, or agent thereof acting in the course and scope of his or her employment, including in the event such officer, director, employee, or agent is deceased, his or her estate or personal representative.
West Virginia	**W. Va. Code Ann. § 55-7B-2 (2011) Medical Professional Liability: Definitions.** "Medical professional liability" means any liability for damages resulting from the death or injury of a person for any tort or breach of contract based on health care services rendered, or which should have been rendered, by a health care provider or health care facility to a patient. "Health care" means any act or treatment performed or furnished, or which should have been performed or furnished, by any health care provider for, to or on behalf of a patient during the patient's medical care, treatment or confinement. "Medical injury" means injury or death to a patient arising or resulting from the rendering of or failure to render health care.
Wisconsin	**Wis. Stat. § 655.001 (2010) Health Care Liability and Injured Patients And Families Compensation: Definitions.** Chapter 655 of the Wisconsin statutes covers health care liability actions. This applies to: "Health care practitioner"

State	Definition
	means a health care professional, as defined in s. 180.1901 (1m), who is an employee of a health care provider described in s. 655.002 (1) (d), (e), (em), or (f) and who has the authority to provide health care services that are not in collaboration with a physician under s. 441.15 (2) (b) or under the direction and supervision of a physician or nurse anesthetist. "Health care provider" means a person to whom this chapter applies under s. 655.002 (1) or a person who elects to be subject to this chapter under s. 655.002 (2).
Wyoming	**Wyo. Stat. Ann. § 1-1-130 (2011) Actions Against Health Care Providers; Admissibility of Evidence.** In any civil action or arbitration brought by an alleged victim of an unanticipated outcome of medical care against a health care provider. For purposes of this section: "Health care provider" means a person who is licensed, certified or otherwise authorized or permitted by the laws of this state to administer health care in the ordinary course of business or practice of a profession "Unanticipated outcome" means the result of a medical treatment or procedure that differs from an expected result. **Wyo. Stat. Ann. § 9-2-1515 (2011). Medical Review Panel: Definitions.** As used in this act: "Malpractice claim" or "claim" means any claim against a health care provider for alleged medical treatment, alleged lack of medical treatment, or other alleged departure from accepted standards of health care which results in damage to the patient.

Source: LexisNexis State Statutes database.

Notes: The statutory language included is from the current version of the state's code which may not reflect very recent legislative enactments yet to be codified. CRS did not search state regulations that may provide additional definitions.

Table A-2 summarizes state laws that impose caps on punitive damages and noneconomic damages in medical malpractice cases. Where "no statute found" is entered, this indicates that the state apparently imposes no cap in medical malpractice suits, either because the state constitution prohibits caps or because the state legislature has chosen not to enact a cap. This table quotes some, but not necessarily all, state constitutional provisions that prohibit caps.

Table A-2. State Caps on Noneconomic and Punitive Damages in Medical Malpractice Lawsuits

State	Noneconomic Damages	Punitive Damages
Alabama	**Ala. Code § 6-5-544 (2011)** Imposes a $400,000 cap on noneconomic losses, including punitive damages. Held unconstitutional. Moore v. Mobile Infirmary Ass'n, 592 So. 2d 156 (Ala. 1991). **Ala. Code § 6-5-547 (2011)** $1,000,000 total cap in wrongful death actions against a health care provider. This provision was held to violate state constitution. Smith v. Schulte, 671 So. 2d 1334 (Ala.1995), cert. denied, 517 U.S. 1220 (1996).	**Ala. Code § 6-11-21 (2011)** The greater of three times compensatory damages or $500,000 ($1.5 million if physical injury), with exceptions.

Table A-2. (Continued)

State	Noneconomic Damages	Punitive Damages
Alaska	**Alaska Stat. § 09.17.010 (2011)** Imposes a $400,000 cap or the injured person's life expectancy in years multiplied by $8,000, whichever is greater, but $1,000,000 or the person's life expectancy in years multiplied by $25,000, whichever is greater, when the damages are awarded for severe permanent physical impairment or severe disfigurement.	**Alaska Stat. § 09.17.020 (2011)** The greater of three times compensatory damages or $500,000, except if defendant was motivated by financial gain and actually knew the adverse consequences, then the greatest of four times compensatory damages, four times financial gain, or $7,000,000.
Arizona	**Ariz. Const. Art. II, § 31 (2011)** No law shall be enacted in this State limiting the amount of damages to be recovered for causing the death or injury of any person.	**Ariz. Const. Art. II, § 31 (2011)** No law shall be enacted in this State limiting the amount of damages to be recovered for causing the death or injury of any person.
Arkansas	**Ark. Const. Art. 5, § 32 (2010)** No law shall be enacted limiting the amount to be recovered for injuries resulting in death or for injuries to persons or property.	**Ark. Code Ann. § 16-55-208 (2010)** The greater of $250,000 or three times compensatory damages, not to exceed $1,000,000, to be adjusted as of January 1, 2006 and at three-year intervals thereafter, in accordance with the Consumer Price Index. No cap if defendant intentionally caused injury or damage.
California	**Cal. Civ. Code § 3333.2 (2010)** $250,000.	No statute found.
Colorado	**Colo. Rev. Stat. §§ 13-21-102.5, 13-64-302 (2010)** $250,000 noneconomic cap, but $500,000 cap if court finds justification for more than $250,000. Both caps adjusted for inflation. $1,000,000 total cap in suits against health care providers.	**Colo. Rev. Stat. § 13-21-102 (2010)** The amount of actual damages awarded, but three times that amount if the defendant continues to act in a willful and wanton manner during the pendency of the case.
Connecticut	**Conn. Gen. Stat. § 52-228c (2010)** Whenever, the jury renders a verdict specifying noneconomic damages in an amount exceeding one million dollars, the court shall review the evidence prese-nted to the jury to determine if the amount is excessive as a matter of law.	No statute found.
Delaware	No statute found.	No statute found.
District of Columbia	No statute found.	No statute found.

State	Noneconomic Damages	Punitive Damages
Florida	**Fla. Stat. Ann. § 766.118(2) (2011)** $500,000, except $1 million cap on all practitioners in the aggre-gate if permanent vegetative state or death, or if, because of special circumstances, noneco-nomic harm is particularly severe and injury was catastrophic. For non-practitioners, above caps are $750,000 and $1.5 million, respectively. For emergency services, caps are $150,000 for practitioners, $750,000 for non-practitioners, with maximum damages recoverable by all claimants $300,000 and $1.5 million, respectively.	**Fla. Stat. Ann. § 768.73(1) (2011)** The greater of three times compensatory damages or $500,000, except, if wrongful conduct was motivated solely by unreasonable financial gain, and unreasonably dangerous nature of the conduct and high likelihood of injury were known, then the greater of four times compensatory damages or $2 million. No cap where specific intent to harm plaintiff. **Fla. Stat. Ann. § 766.207(7)(d) (2011)** Punitive damages prohibited in voluntary binding arbitration.
Georgia	**Ga. Code Ann. § 51-13-1 (2011)** Health care providers or medical facility: $350,000. Medical facilities: $750,000. The aggregate amount of noneconomic damages recoverable under such subsections shall in no event exceed $1,050,000.00. This provision held unconstitutional. Atlanta Oculoplastic Surgery, P.C. v. Nestlehutt, 691 S.E.2d 218 (Ga. 2010).	**Ga. Code Ann. § 51-12-5.1 (2011)** $250,000. If it is found that the defendant acted, or failed to act, with the specific intent to cause harm, or that the defendant acted or failed to act while under the influence of alcohol, drugs other than lawfully prescribed drugs administered in accordance with prescription, or any intentionally consumed glue, aerosol, or other toxic vapor to that degree that his or her judgment is substantially impaired, there shall be no limitation regarding the amo-unt which may be awarded.
Hawaii	**Haw. Rev. Stat. Ann. § 663-8.7 (2011)** $375,000 (cap does not apply to intentional torts).	No statute found.
Idaho	**Idaho Code Ann. § 6-1603 (2011)** For actions accruing after July 1, 2003, $250,000 subject to increase or decrease in accordance with the average annual wage.	**Idaho Code Ann. § 6-1604 (2011)** For actions accruing after July 1, 2003, the greater of 250,000 or three times compensatory damages.
Illinois	**735 Ill. Comp. Stat. Ann. 5/2-1706.5 (2011)** Hospital and its personnel or hospital affiliates: $1 million.	**735 Ill. Comp. Stat. Ann. 5/2-1115 (2011)** Punitive damages are not recoverable in healing

Table A-2. (Continued)

State	Noneconomic Damages	Punitive Damages
	Physician and the physician's business or corporate entity and personnel or health care professional: $500,000. This provision held unconstitutional. Lebron v. Gottlieb Mem. Hosp., 930 N.E.2d 895 (Ill. 2010).	art and legal malpractice cases.
Indiana	**Ind. Code Ann. § 34-18-14-3 (2011)** $1,250,000., total cap. Qualified health care provider: $250,000 total cap.	**Ind. Code Ann. § 34-51-3-4 (2011)** Greater of three times compensatory damages or $50,000.
Iowa	No statute found.	No statute found.
Kansas	**Kan. Stat. Ann. § 60-19a02(b) (2009)** $250,000 by each party from all defendants.	**Kan. Stat. Ann. § 60-3702(e), (f) (2009)** The lesser of the defendant's annual gross income or $5,000,000, but if the profitability of the misconduct exceeds such amount, the cap is 1.5 times the profit.
Kentucky	**Ky. Const. § 54 (2010)** The General Assembly shall have no power to limit the amount to be recovered for injuries resulting in death, or for injuries to person or property.	**Ky. Const. § 54 (2010)** The General Assembly shall have no power to limit the amount to be recovered for injuries resulting in death, or for injuries to person or property.
Louisiana	**La. Rev. Stat. Ann. § 40:1299.42 (2011)** $500,000 total cap, exclusive of future medical care and related benefits. Qualified health care provider: $100,000 total cap per patient.	Punitive damages prohibited at common law.
Maine	**Me. Rev. Stat. tit. 18-A, § 2-804(b) (2011)** Wrongful death actions: $500,000 for the loss of comfort, society and companionship of the deceased, including any damages for emotional distress arising from the same facts.	**Me. Rev. Stat. tit. 18-A, § 2-804(b) (2011)** Wrongful death actions: $250,000.
Maryland	**Md. Code Ann., Cts. & Jud. Proc. § 3-2A-09 (2011)** 1) (i) Except as provided in paragraph (2)(ii), a cause of action arising between January 1, 2005, and December 31, 2008, inclusive, may not exceed $650,000. (ii) The limitation increase by $15,000 on January 1 of each year beginning January 1, 2009. The increased amount shall apply to causes of action arising between January 1 and December 31 of that year, inclusive. (2) (i) Except as provided in subparagraph (ii) of this paragraph, the limitation under paragraph	No statute found

State	Noneconomic Damages	Punitive Damages
	(1) shall apply in the aggregate to all claims for personal injury and wrongful death arising from the same medical injury, regardless of the number of claims, claimants, plaintiffs, beneficiaries, or defendants. (ii) If there is a wro-ngful death action in which there are two or more claimants or beneficiaries, whether or not there is a personal injury action arising from the same medical injury, the total amount awarded for noneconomic damages for all actions may not exceed 125% of the limitation established under paragraph (1) of this subsection, regardless of the number of claims, claimants, plaintiffs, beneficiaries, or defendants. **Md. Code Ann., Cts. & Jud. Proc. § 11-108 (2011)** $500,000 if cause of action arises on or after October 1, 1994, increased by $15,000 on October 1 of each succeeding year for causes of action that arise on or after the date of the increase.	
Massachusetts	**Mass. Ann. Laws, ch. 231, § 60H (2010)** $500,000, unless death resulted or "special circumstances" are found. **Mass. Ann. Laws, ch. 231, § 85K (2010)** Charitable institution: $20,000 total cap.	**Mass. Ann. Laws, ch. 229, § 2 (2010)** In wrongful death cases, not less than $5,000 where decedent's death was caused by the malicious, willful, wanton or reckless conduct of the defendant or by the gross negligence of the defendant. Punitive damages otherwise prohibited at common law.
Michigan	**Mich. Comp. Laws. Serv. § 600.1483 (2011)** $280,000, recoverable by all plaintiffs, resulting from the negligence of all defendants, but $500,000 if a serious injury enumerated in the statute occurred.	No statute found.
Minnesota	No statute found.	No statute found.
Mississippi	**Miss. Code Ann. § 11-1-60 (2010)** $500,000 cap for injury based on malpractice or breach of standard of care against a provider of health care, including institutions for aged or infirm.	**Miss. Code Ann. § 11-1-65 (2010)** $20 million if defendant's net worth exceeds $1 billion; $15 million if it exceeds $750 million but is not more than $1 billion; $10 million if it exc-eeds $500 million but is not more than $750 million; $7½ million if it exceeds $100 million but is not more than $500 million; $5 million if it exceeds $50 million but is not

Table A-2. (Continued)

State	Noneconomic Damages	Punitive Damages
		more than $100 million; 4% of defendant's net worth if defendant's net worth is $50 million or less.
Missouri	**Mo. Rev. Stat. § 538.210 (2011)** Not to exceed $350,000 irrespective of the number of defendants.	No statute found.
Montana	**Mont. Code Ann. § 25-9-411 (2010)** $250,000 cap on noneconomic damages for actions based on the same act or series of acts that allegedly caused the injury, injuries, death or deaths; or regardless the number of defendant health care providers.	**Mont. Code Ann. § 27-1-220 (2010)** $10 million or 3% of a defendant's net worth, whichever is less.
Nebraska	**Neb. Rev. Stat. Ann. § 44-2825 (2010)** Healthcare provider and the Excess Liability Fund: $1,750,000, total cap. Healthcare provider: $500,000.	Punitive damages prohibited at common law.
Nevada	**Nev. Rev. Stat. Ann. § 41A.035 (2010)** Not to exceed $350,000.	**Nev. Rev. Stat. Ann. § 42.005 (2010)** Three times compensatory damages if compensatory damages are $100,000 or more; $300,000 if the compensatory damages are less than $100,000.
New Hampshire	**N.H. Rev. Stat Ann. § 507-C:7 (2011)** Not to exceed $250,000. This provision held unconstitutional. Carson v. Maurer, 424 A.2d 825 (N.H. 1980).	**N.H. Rev. Stat Ann. § 507:16 (2011)** No punitive damages shall be awarded in any action, unless otherwise provided by statute. No statute provides for punitive damages in medical malpractice actions.
New Jersey	No statute found.	**N.J. Rev. Stat. 2A:15-5.14 (2011)** Greater of five times compensatory damages or $350,000.
New Mexico	**N.M. Stat. Ann. § 41-5-6 (2010)** $600,000 total cap. Monetary damages shall not be awarded for future medical expenses in malpractice claims.	**N.M. Stat. Ann. § 41-5-6 (2010)** Punitive damages and medical care and related benefits are not subject to the $600,000 cap.
New York	No statute found.	No statute found
North Carolina	No statute found.	**N.C. Gen. Stat. § 1D-25 (2010)** Greater of three times the amount of compensatory damages or $250,000.

State	Noneconomic Damages	Punitive Damages
North Dakota	**N.D. Cent. Code § 32-42-02 (2011)** Not to exceed $500,000 cap on noneconomic damages regardless the number of health care providers.	**N.D. Cent. Code § 32-03.2-11(4) (2011)** Greater of two times compensatory damages or $250,000.
Ohio	**Ohio Rev. Code Ann. § 2323.43 (2011)** The greater of $250,000 or three times plaintiff's economic loss, to a maximum of $350,000 for each plaintiff or a maximum of $500,000 for each occurrence. But, if specified serious injuries occur, cap is $500,000 for each plaintiff or $1 million for each occurrence.	**Ohio Rev. Code Ann. § 2315.21 (2011)** Punitive or exemplary damages in excess of two times the amount of the compensatory damages; Small employer or individual: lesser of two times the amount of the compensatory damages or 10% of the employer's or individual's net worth, up to $350,000. Except where the alleged injury, death, or loss to person or property resulted from the defendant acting with one or more of the culpable mental states described in statute.
Oklahoma	**Okla. Stat. tit., 23, § 61.2 (2010)** $400,000.00, regardless of the number of parties against whom the action is brought or the number of actions brought. No limit on noneconomic damages arising from a claimed bodily injury resulting from professional negligence against a physician if the judge and jury finds, by clear and convincing evidence, that: 1. The plaintiff or injured person has suffered permanent and substantial physical abnormality or disfigurement, loss of use of a limb, or loss of, or substantial impairment to, a major body organ or system; or 2. The plaintiff or injured person has suffered permanent physical functional injury which prevents them from being able to independently care for themselves and perform life sustaining activities; or 3. The defendant's acts or failures to act were: a. in reckless disregard for the rights of others, b. grossly negligent, c. fraudulent, or d. intentional or with malice.	**Okla. Stat. tit., 23, § 9.1 (2010)** Where reckless disregard, greater of $100,000 or actual damages awarded. Where intentional and with malice, greatest of $500,000, twice actual damages awarded, or financial benefit derived by defendant. If court finds beyond a reasonable doubt that defendant engaged in conduct life-threatening to humans, then no cap.
Oregon	**Or. Rev. Stat. § 31.710 (2010)** Not to exceed $500,000. This provision held unconstitutional where damages are recoverable under common law. Lakin v. Senko Products, Inc., 987 P.2d 463 (Ore. 1999).	**Or. Rev. Stat. § 31.740 (2010)** Prohibited against specified health practitioners.

Table A-2. (Continued)

State	Noneconomic Damages	Punitive Damages
Pennsylvania	**Pa. Const. Art. 3, § 18 (2010)** The General Assembly may enact laws requiring the pay-ment by employers, or employ-yers and employees jointly, of reasonable compensation for injuries to employees arising in the course of their employment, and for occupational diseases of employees, whether or not such injuries or diseases result in death, and regardless of fault of employer or employee, and fixing the basis of ascertainment of such compensation and the maximum and minimum limits thereof, and providing special or general remedies for the collection thereof; but in no other cases shall the General Assembly limit the amount to be recovered for injuries resulting in death, or for injuries to persons or property, and in case of death from such injuries, the right of action shall survive, and the General Assembly shall prescribe for whose benefit such actions shall be prosecuted. **40 Pa. Cons. Stat. § 1303.712(c)(2)(i) (2010)** Caps total liability of the Medical Professional Liability Catastrophe Loss Fund at $500,000 for each occurrence and $1,500,000 per annual aggregate.	**40 Pa. Cons. Stat. § 1303.505(d) (2010)** Except in cases alleging intentional misconduct, punitive damages against an individual physician shall not exceed 200% of the compens-atory damages awarded. Punitive damages, when awarded, shall not less than $100,000 unless a lower verdict amount is returned by the trier of fact.
Rhode Island	No statute found.	No statute found.
South Carolina	**S.C. Code Ann. § 15-32-220 (2010)** A single health care provider or a single health care institution: $350,000 for each claimant, regardless of the number of separate causes of action. One health care institution, or more than one health care provider, or any combination thereof, the limit of civil liability for noneconomic damages for each health care institution and each health care provider is limited to an amount not to exceed $350,000 for each claimant, and the limit of civil liability for oneconomic damages for all health care institutions and health care providers is limited to an amount not to exceed $1,050,000 for each claimant. (E) The limitations for nonecon-omic damages rendered against any health care provider or health care institution do not apply if the jury or court determines that the defendant was grossly negligent, willful, wanton, or reckless, and such conduct was the proximate cause of the claimant's noneconomic damages, or if the defendant has engaged in fraud or	**S.C. Code Ann. § 15-32-220 (2010)** This section does not limit the amount of punitive damages in cases where the plaintiff is able to prove an entitlement to an award of punitive damages as required by law.

State	Noneconomic Damages	Punitive Damages
	misrepresentation related to the claim, or if the defendant altered or destroyed medical records with the purpose of avoiding a claim or liability to the claimant.	
South Dakota	**S.D. Codified Laws § 21-3-11 (2011)** The total general damages which may be awarded may not exceed the sum of five hundred thousand dollars. There is no limitation on the amount of special damages which may be awarded.	No statute found.
Tennessee	No statute found.	No statute found.
Texas	**Tex. Civ. Prac. & Rem. §§ 74.301, 302 (2010)** $250,000 per claimant against a physician or health care provider and $250,000 per claimant against a health care institution. If more than one health care institution is liable, cap against them all is $500,000 per claimant. **Tex. Civ. Prac. & Rem. § 74.303 (2010)** In a wrongful death or survival action on a health care liability claim where final judgment is rendered against a physician or health care provider, the limit of civil liability for all damages, including exemplary damages, shall be limited to an amount not to exceed $500,000 for each claimant, regardless of the number of defendant physicians or health care providers against whom the claim is asserted or the number of separate causes of action on which the claim is based, subject to increase or decrease in accordance with consumer price index.	**Tex. Civ. Prac. & Rem. § 41.008 (2010)** Greater of (1) two times the amount of economic damages plus the amount of noneconomic damages up to $750,000; or (2) $200,000. **Tex. Civ. Prac. & Rem. § 74.303 (2010)** In a wrongful death or survival action on a health care liability claim where final judgment is rendered against a physician or health care provider, the limit of civil liability for all damages, including exemplary damages, shall be limited to an amount not to exceed $500,000 for each claimant, regardless of the number of defendant physicians or health care providers against whom the claim is asserted or the number of separate causes of action on which the claim is based, subject to increase or decrease in accordance with consumer price index.
Utah	**Utah Code Ann. § 78B-3-410 (2011)** (1)(a) for a cause of action arising before July 1, 2001, $250,000; (b) for a cause of action arising on or after July 1, 2001 and before July 1, 2002, the limitation is adjusted for inflation to $400,000; (c) for a cause of action arising on or after July 1, 2002, and before May 15, 2010 the $400,000 limitation described in Subsection (1)(b) shall be adjusted for inflation as provided in Subsection (2); and (d) for a cause of action arising on or after May 15, 2010, $450,000.	**Utah Code Ann. § 78B-3-410 (2011)** The limitations provided in this section do not apply to punitive damages.

Table A-2. (Continued)

State	Noneconomic Damages	Punitive Damages
	(2) (a) Beginning July 1, 2002 and each July 1 thereafter until July 1, 2009, the limit for damages under Subsection (1)(c) shall be adjusted for inflation by the state treasurer.	
Vermont	No statute found.	No statute found.
Virginia	**Va. Code Ann. § 8.01-581.15 (2011)** $1.5 million total cap, to increase by $50,000 every July 1 from 2000 through 2006, and by $75,000 on July 1, 2007 and 2008. The July 1, 2008, increase shall be the final annualincrease.	**Va. Code Ann. § 8.01-38.1 (2011)** Not to exceed $350,000 cap.
Washington	**Wash. Rev. Code Ann. § 4.56.250 (2011)** Amount determined by multi-plying 0.43 by the average annual wage and by the life expectancy of the person incurring noneconomic damages, as the life expectancy is determined by the life expectancy tables adopted by the insurance commissioner. This provision held unconstitutional. Sofie v. Fibreboard Corp., 771 P.2d 711 (Wash. 1989).	Punitive damages prohibited at common law.
West Virginia	**W. Va. Code Ann. § 55-7B-8 (2011)** $250,000 per occurrence, regardless of the number of plaintiffs or defendants, except cap is $500,000 if (1) Wrongful death; (2) permanent and substantial physical deformity, loss of use of a limb or loss of a bodily organ system; or (3) permanent physical or mental functional injury that perman-ently prevents the injured person from being able to independ-ently care for himself or herself and perform life sustaining activities. Annual increases based on Consumer Price Index. Caps apply only if defendant has insurance of at least $1 million per occurrence.	No statute found.
Wisconsin	**Wis. Stat. §§ 655.017, 893.55(4)(d)(1) (2010)** $750,000 for each occurrence under on or after April 6, 2006. A $350,000 cap was held unconstitutional in Ferdon ex rel. Petrucelli v. Wisconsin Patients Compensation Fund, 701 N.W.2d 440 (2005).	**Wis. Stat. § 895.043(6) (2011)- 2011 Wis. Act 2, enacted on 1/27/2011** Not to exceed twice the amount of any compensatory damages recovered by the plaintiff or $ 200,000, whichever is greater.
Wyoming	**Wyo. Const. Art. 10, § 4 (2011)** No law shall be enacted limiting the amount of damages to be recovered for causing the injury or death of any person.	**Wyo. Const. Art. 10, § 4 (2011)** No law shall be enacted limi-ting the amount of damages to be recovered for causing the injury or death of any person.

Source: LexisNexis State Statutes database.

Notes: The statutory language included is from the current version of the state's code which may not reflect very recent legislative enactments yet to be codified.

As discussed in "Noneconomic Damages," the term "economic damages" refers to past and future monetary expenses of an injured party, such as medical bills, rehabilitation expenses, and lost wages. "Noneconomic damages" refers primarily to damages for pain and suffering. Economic and noneconomic damages are both compensatory damages; that is, they are intended to compensate the injured party. As mentioned earlier, punitive damages are awarded not to compensate plaintiffs but to punish and deter particularly egregious conduct on the part of defendants. Though noneconomic by nature, punitive damages are usually treated separately from noneconomic damages.

The dollar amount in the right-hand column refers to the cap on compensatory noneconomic damages, except that "total cap" means a cap on all damages—economic, noneconomic, and punitive damages—combined. We have attempted to note where a state's highest court has declared the cap to violate the state's constitution.

The caps listed in the chart, as well as the entry "punitive damages prohibited," do not necessarily apply to tort actions other than for medical malpractice, though in many cases they do.

Table A-3 sets forth the burden of proof and standards for awards of punitive damages in medical malpractice suits in the 50 states, as well as whether the state requires or permits a separate hearing to determine punitive damages. The burden of proof refers to the plaintiff's duty to present evidence to prove his case. Although the lowest burden, which usually applies in civil cases, is "preponderance of the evidence," many states impose a higher burden of proof to recover punitive damages—proof by "clear and convincing evidence." One state—Colorado—however, requires proof "beyond a reasonable doubt," which is the highest standard—usually the burden that the government must meet in criminal prosecutions.[54]

Table A-3. Punitive Damages—Burden of Proof, Standard, and Separate Proceeding

State and Citation	Burden of Proof	Standard	Separate Proceeding
Alabama	**Ala. Code § 6-11-20 (2011)** Clear and convincing evidence.	**Ala. Code § 6-11-20 (2011)** "[T]he defendant consciously or deliberately engaged in oppression, fraud, wantonness, or malice."	**Ala. Code § 6-11-23 (2011)** Available.
Alaska	**Alaska Stat. § 09.17.020 (2011)** Clear and convincing evidence.	**Alaska Stat. § 09.17.020 (2011)** "[D]efendant's conduct (1) was outrageous, including acts done with malice or bad motives; or (2) evidenced reckless indifference to the interest of another person."	**Alaska Stat. § 09.17.020 (2011)** Mandatory.
Arizona	Clear and convincing evidence. *Linthicum v. Nationwide Life Ins.Co.*, 723 P.2d 675, 681 (1986).	Defendant engaged in "reprehensible conduct" and acted "with an evil mind." *Linthicum v. Natio-nwide Life Ins. Co.*, 723 P.2d 675, 680 (1986).	N/A.

Table A-3. (Continued)

State and Citation	Burden of Proof	Standard	Separate Proceeding
Arkansas	**Ark. Code Ann. § 16-55-207 (2010)** Clear and convincing evidence.	**Ark. Code Ann. § 16-55-206 (2010)** "[D]efendant knew or ought to have known ... that his or her conduct would naturally and probably result in injury or damage and that he or she continued the conduct with malice or in reckless disregard of the consequences ..." or "defendant intentionally pursued a course of conduct for the purpose of causing injury or damages."	**Ark. Code Ann. § 16-55-211 (2010)** Available.
California	**Cal. Civ. Code § 3294 (2010)**Clear and convincing evidence.	**Cal. Civ. Code § 3294 (2010)** "[O]ppression, fraud, or malice."	N/A.
Colorado	**Colo. Rev. Stat. §13-25-127(2) (2010)** Beyond a reasonable doubt.	**Colo. Rev. Stat. § 13-21-102 (2010)** "[F]raud, malice, or willful and wanton conduct."	N/A.
Connecticut	Preponderance of the evidence. *Freeman v. Alamo Management Co.*, 607 A.2d 370, 373 (Conn. 1992).	"{A] reckless indifference to the rights of others or an intentional and wanton violation of those rights." *Sorrentino v. All Seasons Servs.*, 717 A.2d 150, 161 (Conn. 1998).	N/A.
Delaware	Undefined, but likely preponderance of the evidence.	**Del. Code Ann. tit. 18, §6855 (2011)** "[I]njury complained of was maliciously intended or was the result of wilful or wanton misconduct by the health care provider."	N/A.
District of Columbia	Clear and convincing evidence. *Croley v. Republican Nat'l Comm.*, 759 A.2d 682, 695 (D.C. 2000).	"[E]gregious conduct." *Railan v. Katyal*, 766 A.2d 998, 1012 (D.C. 2001). "[M]alice or its equivalent." *Croley v. Republican Nat'l Comm.*, 759 A.2d 682, 695 (D.C. 2000).	N/A.
Florida	**Fla. Stat. Ann. § 768.72(2) (2011)** Clear and convincing evidence.	**Fla. Stat. Ann. § 768.72 (2)(2011)** "[I]ntentional misconduct or gross negligence."	N/A.

State and Citation	Burden of Proof	Standard	Separate Proceeding
Georgia	**Ga. Code Ann. § 51-12-5.1(b) (2011)** Clear and convincing evidence.	**Ga. Code Ann. § 51-12-5.1(b) (2011)** "[W]illful misconduct, malice, fraud, wantonness, oppression, or that entire want of care which would raise the presumption of conscious indifference to consequences."	**Ga. Code Ann. § 51-12-5.1(d)(2) (2011)** Mandatory.
Hawaii	Clear and convincing evidence. *Amfac, Inc. v. Waikiki Beachcomber Inv. Co.*, 839 P.2d 10, 37 (1992)	"[D]efendant has acted wantonly or oppressively or with such malice as implies a spirit of mischief or criminal indifference to civil obligations, or where there has been some wilful misconduct or that entire want of care which would raise the presumeption of conscious indifference to the consequences." *Amfac, Inc. v. Waikiki Beachcomber Inv. Co.*, 839 P.2d 10, 37 (1992)	N/A.
Idaho	**Idaho Code Ann. § 6-1604 (2011)** Clear and convincing evidence.	**Idaho Code Ann. § 6-1604(2011)** "[O]ppressive, fraudulent, malicious or outrageous onduct."	N/A.
Illinois	**735 Ill. Comp. Stat. Ann. 5/2-1115 (2011)** Punitive damages prohibited in medical malpractice cases.		
Indiana	**Ind. Code Ann. § 34-51-3- 2 (2011)** Clear and convincing evidence.	"[A]ct[ing] with malice, fraud, gross negligence, or oppressiveness which was not the result of a mistake of fact or law, honest error or judgment, overzealousness, mere negligence, or other human failing." *USA Life One Ins. Co. of Indiana v. Nuckolls*, 682 N.E.2d 534, 541 (Ind. 1997).	N/A.
Iowa	**Iowa Code Ann. § 668A.1 (2010)** "[P]reponderance of	**Iowa Code Ann. § 668A.1 (2010)** "[W]illful and wanton disregard	N/A.

Table A-3. (Continued)

State and Citation	Burden of Proof	Standard	Separate Proceeding
	clear, convincing, and satisfactory evidence."	for the rights or safety of another."	
Kansas	**Kan. Stat. Ann. § 60-3701 (2009)** Clear and convincing evidence.	**Kan. Stat. Ann. § 60-3701 (2009)** "[W]illful conduct, wanton conduct, fraud or malice."	**Kan. Stat. Ann. § 60-3701 (2009)** Mandatory.
Kentucky	**Ky. Rev. Stat. Ann. § 411.184 (2010)** Clear and convincing evidence.	**Ky. Rev. Stat. Ann. § 411.184 (2010)** "[O]ppression, fraud or malice."	N/A.
Louisiana	Punitive damages unavailable in medical malpractice claims. *See Naquin v. Fluor Daniel Services Corp.*, 935 F. Supp. 847, 849) (E.D. La. 1996) (noting that punitive damages are only available under Louisiana law if specifically permitted by a statute).		
Maine	Clear and convincing evidence. *St. Francis de Sales Federal Credit Union v. Sun Insurance Company of New York*, 818 A.2d 995, 1001 (Me. 2002, revised 2003).	Malice, either express (where the defendant "is motivated by ill will toward the plaintiff"), or implied (defendant's conduct "is so outrageous that malice toward a person injured as a result of that conduct can be implied.") Implied malice is not established "by the defendant's mere reckless disregard of the circumstances." *St. Francis de Sales Fed-eral Credit Union v. Sun Insurance Company of New York*, 818 A.2d 995, 1001 (Me. 2002, revised 2003).	N/A
Maryland	Clear and convincing evidence. *Owens-Illinois, Inc. v. Zenobia*, 601 A.2d 633, 657 (Md.1992).	"[E]vil motive, intent to injure, ill will, or fraud." *Owens-Illinois, Inc. v. Zenobia*, 601 A.2d 633, 652 (Md. 1992).	N/A.

State and Citation	Burden of Proof	Standard	Separate Proceeding
Massachusetts	**Mass. Ann. Laws, ch. 229, § 2 (2010)** Preponderance of the evidence in wrongful death cases. But, punitive damages for medical malpractice otherwise prohibited.	**Mass. Ann. Laws, ch. 229, § 2 (2010)** In wrongful death cases, "malicious, willful, wanton or reckless conduct ... or gross negligence." But, punitive damages for medical malpractice otherwise prohibited.	N/A.
Michigan	Undefined, but likely preponderance of the evidence.	Conduct that "inspires feelings of humiliation, outrage and indignity" and is "malicious or so willful and wanton as to demonstrate a reckless disregard of plaintiff's rights." *Veselenak v. Smith*, 327 N.W.2d 261, 264(1982).	N/A.
Minnesota	**Minn. Stat. Ann. § 549.20 (2010)** Clear and convincing evidence.	**Minn. Stat. Ann. § 549.20 (2010)** "[D]eliberate disregard for the rights or safety of others."	**Minn. Stat. Ann. § 549.20 (2010)** Mandatory.
Mississippi	**Miss. Code Ann. § 11-1-65(1)(a)(2010)** Clear and convincing evidence. **Miss. Code Ann. § 11-1-65(1)(a)(2010)** Clear and convincing evidence.	**Miss. Code Ann. § 11-1-65(1)(a)(2010)** "[A]ctual malice, gross negligence which evidences a willful, wanton or reckless disregard for the safety of others, or committed actual fraud."	**Miss. Code Ann. § 11-1-65(1)(e)(2010)** Mandatory.
Missouri	Clear and convincing evidence. *Rodriguez v. Suzuki Motor Corp.*, 936 S.W.2d 104, 111 (Mo. 1996).	**Mo. Rev. Stat. § 538.210.5 (2011)** For medical malpractice actions, "willful, wanton, or malicious misconduct." § 538.210.5 (2010).	**Mo. Rev. Stat. § 510.263 (2011)** Available.
Montana	**Mont. Code Ann. § 27-1-221 (2010)** Clear and convincing evidence.	**Mont. Code Ann. § 27-1-221 (2010)** "[A]ctual fraud or actual malice."	**Mont. Code Ann. § 27-1-221 (2010)** Mandatory.
Nebraska	Punitive damages prohibited. *Miller v. Kingsley*, 230 N.W.2d 472, 474 (Neb. 1975).		
Nevada	**Nev. Rev. Stat. Ann. § 42.005 (2010)** Clear and convincing evidence.	**Nev. Rev. Stat. Ann.§ 42.005 (2010)** "[O]ppression, fraud or malice, express or implied."	**Nev. Rev. Stat. Ann. § 42.005 (2010)** Mandatory.

Table A-3. (Continued)

State and Citation	Burden of Proof	Standard	Separate Proceeding
New Hampshire	**N.H. Rev. Stat. Ann. § 507:16 (2011)** Punitive damages prohibited.		
New Jersey	**N.J. Rev. Stat. § 2A:15-5.12 (2011)** Clear and convincing evidence.	**N.J. Rev. Stat. § 2A:15-5.12 (2011)** "[A]ctuated by actual malice or accomp-anied by a wanton and willful disregard of persons who foreseeably might be harmed."	N/A.
New Mexico	Preponderance of the evidence. *United Nuclear Corp. v. Allendale Mut. Ins. Co.*, 709 P.2d 649, 654 (N.M. 1985).	"[M]alicious, fraudulent, oppressive, or committed recklessly with a wanton disregard for the plaintiff'srights." *Albuquerque Concrete Coring Co., Inc. v. Pan Am World Services, Inc.*, 879 P.2d 772, 775 (1994).	N/A.
New York	Undefined, but likely preponderance of the evidence.	"[I]ntentional or deliberate wrongdoing, aggravating or outrageous circumstances, fraudulent or evil motive, or conscious act in willful and wanton disregard of another's rights" *Pearlman v. Friedman, Alpern & Green, LLP*, 750 N.Y.S.2d 869 (2002).	Recommended. *Rupert v Sellers*, 368 N.Y.S.2d 904, 912 (N.Y. App. Div. 1975).
North Carolina	**N.C. Gen. Stat. § 1D-15 (2010)** Clear and convincing evidence.	**N.C. Gen. Stat. § 1D-15 (2010)** "(1) Fraud. (2) Malice. (3) Willful or wanton conduct."	**N.C. Gen. Stat. § 1D-30 (2010)** Available.
North Dakota	**N.D. Cent. Code § 32-03.2-11 (2011)** Clear and convincing evidence.	**N.D. Cent. Code § 32-03.2-11 (2011)** "[O]ppression, fraud, or actual malice."	**N.D. Cent. Code § 32-03.2-11 (2011)** Available.
Ohio	**Ohio Rev. Code Ann. §2315.21 (2011)** Clear and convincing evidence.	**Ohio Rev. Code Ann. § 2315.21 (2011)** "[M]alice or aggravated or egregious fraud."	**Mandatory. Ohio Rev. Code Ann. § 2315.21 (2011),** *overruled by Havel v. Villa St.Joseph*, No. 94677, (Ohio Ct. App. Oct. 28, 2010).

State and Citation	Burden of Proof	Standard	Separate Proceeding
Oklahoma	**Okla. Stat. tit., 23, § 9.1 (2010)** Clear and convincing evidence.	**Okla. Stat. tit., 23, § 9.1 (2010)** Lower cap on punitive damages for "reckless disregard," but a higher cap for "intentionally and with malice toward others."	N/A.
Oregon	**Or. Rev. Stat. § 31.730(2010)** Clear and convincing evidence.	**Or. Rev. Stat. § 31.740 (2010)** "Malice" for medical malpractice cases.	N/A.
Pennsylvania	Preponderance of the evidence. *DiSalle v. P.G. Pub. Co.*, 544 A.2d 1345, 1371 n. 24 (Pa. Super. Ct. 1988) (*citing Martin v. Johns-Manville Corp.*, 494 A.2d 1088, 1098 (Pa. 1985)).	**40 Pa. Const. Stat. § 1303.505 (2010)** "[W]illful or wanton conduct or reckless indifference to the rights of others."	N/A.
Rhode Island	Preponderance of the evidence	"[E]vidence of such willfulness, recklessness, or wickedness, ... as amounts to criminality." *Palmisano v. Toth*, 624 A.2d,314 (1993).	N/A
South Carolina	**S.C. Code Ann. § 15-33-135 (2010)** Clear and convincing evidence.	"[W]illful, wanton, or in reckless disregard of the plaintiff's rights." *Mellen v. Lane*, 377 S.C. 261 (2008).	N/A
South Dakota	**S.D. Codified Laws § 21-1-4.1 (2011)** Before one can submit a claim for punitive damages, "the court shall find, after a hearing based upon clear and convincing evidence, that there is reasonable basis to believe that there has been willful, wanton, or malicious conduct on the part of the party claimed against."	**S.D. Codified Laws § 21-3-2 (2011)** Preponderance of the evidence "[W]here defendant has been guilty of oppression, fraud, or malice, actual or presumed." *See also Flockhart v. Wyant*, 467 N.W.2d 473 (1991) (upheld trial court decision to instruct jury to decide an award of punitive damages based on the preponderance of the evidence standard).	N/A.
Tennessee	Clear and convincing evidence.	"[I]ntentional, fraudulent, malicious, or reckless conduct."	Available. *Hodges v. S.C.*

Table A-3. (Continued)

State and Citation	Burden of Proof	Standard	Separate Proceeding
	Hodges v. S.C. Toof & Co., 833 S.W.2d 896 (Tenn. 1992).	*Hodges v. S.C. Toof & Co.*, 833 S.W.2d 896 (Tenn. 1992)	*Toof & Co.*, 833 S.W.2d 896 (Tenn. 1992) ("[T]he court, upon motion of the defendant , shall bifurcate the trial.").
Texas	**Tex. Civ. Prac. & Rem. §41.003 (2010)** Clear and convincing evidence.	**Tex. Civ. Prac. & Rem. §41.003 (2010)** "[D]amages result from: (1) fraud; (2) malice; or (3) willful act or omission or gross neglect in wrongful death actions."	Tex. Civ. Prac. & Rem. § 41.009 (2010) Available.
Utah	**Utah Code Ann. § 78B-8-201 (2011).** Clear and convincing evidence.	**Utah Code Ann. § 78B-8-201 (2011).** "[W]illful and malicious or intentionally fraudulent conduct, or conduct that manifests a knowing and reckless indifference toward, and a disregard of, the rights of others."	N/A.
Vermont	Undefined but likely preponderance of the evidence. *McCormick v. McCormick*, 621 A.2d 238 (Vt. 1993).	"[C]onduct manifesting personal ill will, evidencing insult or oppression, or showing a reckless or wanton disregard of [a party's] rights." *McCormick v. McCormick*, 621 A.2d 238 (Vt. 1993).	N/A.
Virginia	Undefined but likely preponderance of the evidence. *Woods v. Mendez*, 574 S.E.2d 263 (2003).	"[D]efendant's conduct was willful or wanton. Willful and wanton negligence is action undertaken in conscious disregard of another's rights or with reckless indifference to consequences with the defendant aware, from his knowledge of existing circumstances and conditions, that his conduct probably would cause injury to another." *Woods v. Mendez*, 574 S.E.2d 263 (2003).	N/A.
Washington	Punitive damages not allowed unless		

State and Citation	Burden of Proof	Standard	Separate Proceeding
	authorized by state legislature. *Barr v. Interbay Citizens Bank*, 635 P.2d 441 (1981).		
West Virginia	Undefined, but likely preponderance of the evidence. *TXO Prod. Corp. v. Alliance Resources Corp.*, 419 S.E.2d 870 (1992).	"[N]ot only mean-spirited conduct, but also extremely negligent conduct that is likely to cause serious harm" *TXO Prod. Corp. v. Alliance Resources Corp.*, 419 S.E.2d 870 (1992). *See also Mayer v. Frobe*, 22 S.E. 58 (1895) ("[D]efendant has acted wantonly or oppressively, or with such malice as implies a spirit of mischief or criminal indifference to civil obligations.").	N/A.
Wisconsin	Unclear after recodification of punitive damages statute, but likely clear and convincing evidence. *See City of W. Allis v. Wisc. Elec. Power Co.*, 635 N.W.2d 873 (Wisc. App. 2001) ("Before the que-stion of punitive damages can be submitted to a jury, the circuit court must determine ... that to a reas-onable certainty the cond-uct was 'outrageous.' ... The evidence must also be 'clear and convincing.'").	**Wis. Stat. § 895.043(3) (2010)** "The plaintiff may receive punitive damages if evidence is submitted showing that the defendant acted maliciously toward the plaintiff or in an intentional disregard of the rights of the plaintiff." *See also Groshek v. Trewin,* 784 N.W.2d 163 (2010).	N/A.
Wyoming	Preponderance of the evidence.	"Outrageous conduct, malice, and willful and wanton mis-conduct" *Alexander v. Meduna*, 47 P.3d 206 (Wyo. 2002).	N/A.

Source: LexisNexis State Statutes database.

Notes: The statutory language included is from the current version of the state's code which may not reflect very recent legislative enactments yet to be codified.

Standards for awards of punitive damages refer to what the plaintiff must prove to receive an award of punitive damages. To recover compensatory damages in a medical malpractice case, the plaintiff typically must prove negligence. To recover punitive damages, the plaintiff must prove that the defendant's conduct was more egregious than negligence, and usually more egregious than gross negligence.

Separate proceedings for punitive damages refer to whether the computation and award of punitive damages occurs during the initial trial or in a subsequent trial. Such punitive damages proceedings usually include the same jury as in the original trial, but additional discovery can occur and additional evidence can be presented (such as evidence related to the financial condition of the defendant). This report sets forth the specific availability of this bifurcated trial process, noting whether the process is available on the motion of one of the parties, or is mandatory in all proceedings resulting in the award of punitive damages. Where "N/A" is entered does not mean that bifurcation of a punitive damages claim is prohibited or non-existent. Rather, it means that the state (1) may not have a specific statute that addresses bifurcation with respect to punitive damages, or (2) that the its civil procedure rules grants the courts the discretion to have a separate trial on any claim if it would be conducive to expedition or economy. For example, Rule 42 of West Virginia Civil Procedure states that the court may have separate trials on any claim if it would be conducive or expeditious to do so.

Most of the provisions listed in the chart apply to punitive damages not only in medical malpractice cases, but in other tort cases as well. Where "punitive damages prohibited" appears, the prohibition may be limited to medical malpractice cases, or it may apply to other tort cases as well.

Table A-4 sets forth the doctrine of joint and several liability and provisions for periodic payment for damages in the 50 states.

As discussed in "Limiting Joint and Several Liability," the doctrine of joint and several liability is the common-law rule that, if more than one defendant is found liable for a plaintiff's injuries, then each defendant may be held 100% liable. Any defendant who pays for more than its share of the damages is entitled to seek contribution from other liable defendants. In this 50-state survey of joint and several liability, we note whether the doctrine of joint and several liability applies in the state, whether there is some modified version, or whether the doctrine has been abolished and only several liability applies, making each defendant liable only for its share of responsibility for the plaintiff's injury.

How one characterizes a statute as modified joint and several liability or several liability will vary. In this table, we use the term "modified joint and several liability" to refer to instances where the statute tends to find defendants jointly and severally liable for certain types of damages but not others. For example, in Hawaii joint and several liability applies when recovering economic damages, but several liability applies when recovering noneconomic damages if a defendant's negligence is found to be more than 25% or more of the total fault.[55] We use the term "modified joint and several liability" where joint and several liability is triggered once a defendant is found to be negligent by a certain percentage of fault or where joint, or where joint and several liability applies to recover certain damages but not others. For example, in Iowa the rule of joint and several liability does not apply to a defendant who is found to bear less than 50% of the total fault assigned to all parties, but the doctrine will apply where a defendant is found to bear more than 50% and only in the recovery for economic damages.[56] The term "several liability" is used where statutes generally abolished joint and several liability, though in some instances joint and several liability still applies where the tort-feasors acted in concert or with intent to commit the tort. For example, in Idaho the doctrine of joint and several liability is abolished except where joint tort-feasors acted in concert or when a person was acting as an agent or servant of another party.[57]

As discussed in "Periodic Payment of Damages," damages are traditionally paid in lump sum, even if they are for future medical care of future lost wages. With respect to malpractice actions, some states mandate that courts, upon the request of a party, enter a judgment for periodic payment of future damages that exceed a certain amount. Most states have general provisions that govern structured settlements, which usually includes an award for damages in a tort suit. For example, Massachusetts ch. 231C, §§1 *et seq.* governs structured settlement contracts generally; in Hawaii, the Hawaii Revised Statutes §§ 676-1 *et seq.* is the state's Structured Settlement Protection Act; and in New Jersey, N.J. Stat. Ann. §§ 2A:16-63 *et seq.* governs structured settlements. These types of general structured settlement statutes are not captured in this table. Where "no statute found" is entered means that CRS could not locate a statute specific to medical malpractice actions on periodic payment.

Table A-4. State Provisions on Joint and Several Liability and Periodic Payment of Damages

State	Joint and Several Liability	Periodic Payment of Damages
Alabama	Joint and several liability. Where the actions of two or more tort-feasors combine to produce an indivisible injury, each tort-feasor's act is considered to be proximate cause of the injury, and each tort-feasor is jointly and severally liable for the entire injury and judgment. *See General Motors Corp., v. Edwards*, 482 So.2d 1176 (Ala. 1985).	**Ala. Code § 6-5-543 (2011)** If the future damages assessed, is greater than $150,000, the court shall require payment of future damages by periodic payments. Held unconstitutional. *Lloyd Noland Hosp. v. Durham*, 906 So.2d 157 (Ala. 2005).
Alaska	**Alaska Stat. § 9.17.080 (2011)** Several liability. The court shall enter judgment against each party on the basis of several liability in accordance with that party's percentage of fault.	**Alaska Stat. § 9.55.548(a) (2011)** The court may enter a judgment that future damages be paid in whole or in part by periodic payments rather than by lump-sum payment . **Alaska Stat. § 9.17.040 (2011)** At the request of an injured party, the court shall enter judgment ordering that amounts awarded a judgment creditor for future damages be paid to the maximum extent feasibly by periodic payments rather than lump-sum payment.
Arizona	**Ariz. Rev. Stat. § 12-2506 (2011)** Several liability. The liability of each defendant for damages is several only and is not joint, except as for otherwise provided.	**Ariz. Rev. Stat. § 12-581 *et seq* (2011)** Any party may elect to receive or pay future damages for economic loss in periodic installments. Held unconstitutional. *Smith v. Meyers*, 887 P.2d 541 (Ariz. 1994).
Arkansas	**Ark. Code Ann. § 16-55-201 (2010)** Several liability. In action for personal injury, medical injury, the liability of each defendant for	**Ark. Code Ann. § 16-114-208 (2010)** If the future damages assessed is greater than $100,000, the court, at the request of either party, shall order the payment

Table A-4. (Continued)

State	Joint and Several Liability	Periodic Payment of Damages
	compensatory and punitive damages shall be several only and shall not be joint.	to be paid in whole or in part by periodicpayments.
California	**Cal. Civ. Code § 1431.2 (2010)** Modified joint and several liability. The liability of each defendant for noneconomic damages shall be several only and not joint. Each defendant shall be liable in direct proportion to that defendant's percentage of fault.	**Cal. Civ. Code § 667.7 (2010)** If the future damages assessed is greater than $50,000, a superior court, at the request of either party, shall enter a judgment ordering the payment to be paid in whole or in part by periodic payments.
Colorado	**Colo. Rev. Stat. § 13-21-111.5 (2010)** Modified joint and several liability. No defendant shall be liable for an amount greater than that represented by the degree or percentage of the negligence or fault attributable to such defendant that produced the claimed injury, death, damage, or loss, except where two or more defendants consciously conspire and deliberately pursue a common plan or design to commit a tortious act.	**Colo. Rev. Stat. § 13-64-203 (2010)** If the award for future damages is greater than $150,000, the trial judge shall enter a judgment ordering payment by periodic payments. If the award for future damages is less than $150,000, the trial judge may order that such awards be paid by periodic payments.
Connecticut	**Conn. Gen. Stat. § 52-572h (2010)** Modified joint and several liability. Each party against whom recovery is allowed shall be liable to the claimant only for such party's proportionate share of the recoverable damages, with exception.	**Conn. Gen. Stat. § 52-225d (2010)** If the amount of economic damages exceeds $200,000, the court must afford the parties 60 days to negotiate to agree to a periodic payment of damages.
Delaware	**Del. Code Ann. tit. 10, § 6301 (2011)** Joint and several liability.	**Del. Code Ann. tit 18, § 6864 (2011)** The court may fix payment of damages in periodic installments.
District of Columbia	No statute found.	No statute found.
Florida	**Fla. Stat. Ann. § 768.81 (2011)** Several liability. The court shall enter judgment against each party on the basis of such party's percentage of fault and not on the basis of joint and several liability.	**Fla. Stat. Ann. § 768.78 (2011)** If an award of future economic losses exceeds $250,000, the court shall, at the request of either party, enter a judgment ordering payment in whole or in part by periodic payments.
Georgia	**Ga. Code Ann. § 51-12-33 (2011)** Several liability. For claims after February 2005, damages apportioned shall be for liability of each person against each person whom they area awarded, shall not be a joint liability among the persons liable, and shall not be subject to any right of contribution.	**Ga. Code Ann. § 51-13-1(f) (2011)** If an award for future damages is greater than $350,000, the trial court shall, upon the request of either party, issue an order providing that such damages be paid in periodic payments.
Hawaii	**Haw. Rev. Stat. Ann. § 663-10.9 (2011)** Modified joint and several liability. For economic damages, joint and several liability applies in actions involving injury or death. For noneconomic damages, Joint and several liability for applies where joint tort-feasor's negligence is found to be 25% or more, in actions involving injury or death.	No statute found.

State	Joint and Several Liability	Periodic Payment of Damages
Idaho	**Idaho Code Ann. § 6-803 (2011)** Several liability. Doctrine of joint and several liability generally abolished except where joint tort-feasors are acting in concert or when a person was acting as an agent or servant of another party.	**Idaho Code Ann. § 6-1602 (2011)** If the award for future damages exceeds $100,000, the court, at the request of either party, may enter a judgment providing for the periodic payment of such damages.
Illinois	**735 Ill. Comp. Stat. Ann. 5/2-1118 (2011)** Joint and several liability. Defendants in any medical malpractice action based upon negligence are jointly and severally liable for all damages.	**735 Ill. Comp. Stat. Ann. 5/2-1705 (2011)** A party may seek periodic payment of future damages if the amount is in excess of $250,000 and it can show certain requirements.
Indiana	**Ind. Code Ann. § 34-51-2-1 (2011)** Doctrine of joint and several liability seems to apply to medical malpractice actions, as these are not covered by the statute on comparative fault.	**Ind. Code Ann. §§ 34-18-14-1 *et seq*; 34-18-15-1 *et seq* (2011)** Sections provide for method of periodic payment in exchange for discharge from liability.
Iowa	**Iowa Code Ann. § 668.4 (2010)** Modified joint and several liability. The rule of joint and several liability shall not apply to defendants who are found to bear less than 50% of the total fault assigned to all parties. A defendant found to bear more than 50% shall only be jointly and severally liable for economic damages and not for any noneconomic damages.	No statute found.
Kansas	**Kan. Stat. Ann. § 60-258a (2009)** Several liability. The concept of joint and several liability no longer applies in comparative negligence actions. The individual liability of each defendant for payment of damages is to be based on proportionate fault, and contribution among joint judgment debtors is no longer to be required in such cases. *See Brown v. Kelli*, 580 P.2d 867 (Kan. 1978).	**Kan. Stat. Ann. § 60-2609 (2009)** The court may include in its judg-ment a requirement that damages awarded be paid in whole or in part by installment or periodic payment.
Kentucky	**Ky. Rev. Stat. Ann. § 304.40-290 (2010)** Several liability. In action for medical malpra-ctice, the jury shall be instru-cted that it may apportion damages in different percent-tages against the defendants or it may return a verdict of joint and several liability against two or more defendants. Generally joint and several liability abolished. Ky. Rev. Stat. Ann. § 411.182; *See Radcliff Homes Inc. v. Jackson*, 766 S.W.2d 63 (Ky. Ct. App. 1989).	No statute found.
Louisiana	**La. Civ. Code Ann. art. 2324 (2011)** Several liability. A joint tort-feasor shall not be liable for more than his degree of fault and shall not be solidarily liable with any other person for	**La. Rev. Stat. Ann. § 40:1299.43 (2011)** If the patient is in need of future medical care, the amount of future medical care that will be incurred after a certain date

Table A-4. (Continued)

State	Joint and Several Liability	Periodic Payment of Damages
	damages attributable to the fault of such other person.	will be paid, as incurred, from the patient's compensation fund.
Maine	**Me. Rev. Stat. Ann. tit. 14, § 156 (2011)** Joint and several liability. Each defendant is jointly and severally liable. However, any defendant has the right to req-uest of the jury the percent-tage of fault contributed by each defendant. The defendant may be released by the plai-ntiff under which the plaintiff is precluded from collecting against the remaining parties that portion of the damages attributable to the released defendant.	**Me. Rev. Stat. Ann. tit. 24, § 2451 (2011)** If an award for future damages exceeds $250,000, the court, at the request of either party, enter a judgment ordering for periodic payment of future damages.
Maryland	**Md. Code Ann., Cts. & Jud. Proc. § 3-1403 (2011)** Joint and several liability. The recovery of a judgment against one joint does not discharge the other joint tort-feasor.	**Md. Code Ann., Cts. & Jud. Proc. § 11-109 (2011)** The court may order that all or part of future economic damages be paid in periodic installments consistent with the need of the plaintiff.
Massach-usetts	**Mass. Ann. Laws, ch. 231B, § 1 (2010)** Joint and several liability. Language of this section providing that when two or more persons become jointly and severally liable in tort for the same injury to person, there shall be a right of contribution among them that requires that potential contributor be directly liable to plaintiff. *See Liberty Mut. Ins. Co. v. Westerlind*, 373 N.E.2d 957 (Mass. 1978).	No statute found.
Michigan	**Mich. Comp. Laws. Serv. § 600.6304(5) (2011)** Modified joint and several liability. If the plaintiff is determined to have no fault in an action for medical malpractice, the liability of each defendant is joint and several. If the plaintiff is determined to have a percentage of fault, the court shall determine whether all or a part of a party's share of the obligations is uncollectible from that party, and shall reallocate any uncollectible amount among the other parties. The party whose liab-ility is reallocated continues to be subject to contribution and to any continuing liability to the plaintiff on judgment.	**Mich. Comp. Laws. Serv. §§ 600.6307, 600.6309 (2011)** If a judgment of future damages exceeds $250,000, the court shall enter an order that the defendant shall satisfy the amount of the judgment by the purchase of an annuity contract. If the plaintiff and defendant agree to a plan for the structured payment of future damages within 35 days of the judgment, the court shall order that payments be made pursuant to that plan.
Minnesota	**Minn. Stat. Ann. § 604.02 (2010)** Modified joint and several liability. When two or more persons are severally liable, contributions to awards shall be in propo-rtion to the percentage of fault attributable to each, except the following people shall be jointly and severally liable for the whole award: a person whose fault is greater than 50%; two or more persons	**Minn. Stat. Ann. § 549.25 (2010)** If a claimant is awarded future damages in excess of $100,000, the court shall hold a hearing to allow claimant to determine if payment over time would be in best interest of claimant. Claimant may inform court that he does not wish to enter a structured settlement.

State	Joint and Several Liability	Periodic Payment of Damages
	who act in a common scheme or plan that result in injury.	
Mississippi	**Miss. Code Ann. § 85-5-7 (2010)** Several liability. The liability for two or more defendants shall be several only, and not joint and several, and a joint tort-feasor shall be liable only for the amount of damages allocated to him in direct proportion to his percentage of fault.	No statute found.
Missouri	**Mo. Rev. Stat. § 537.067 (2011)** Modified joint and several liability. If a defendant is found to bear 51% ormore of the fault, defendant shall be jointly and severally liable for the amount of damages rendered against the other defendants. If a defendant is found to bear less than 51% of the fault, then defendant shall be responsible only for his percentage of fault.	**Mo. Rev. Stat. § 538.220 (2011)** Past damages are payable in a lump sum. But if the total award of damages exceeds $100,000, the court, upon the request of any party, shall include in the judgment arequirement that future damages be paid in whole or in part in periodic installments.
Montana	**Mont. Code Ann. §§ 27-1-703; 27-1-705 (2010)** Modified joint and several liability. In an action brought as a result of death orinjury to a person, the liability of a defendant is several only and not joint A party's whose negligence is determined to be 50% or less of the combined negligence is severally liable unless acting in concert or as an agent of another. The remaining parties are jointly and severally liable for the total less the percentage attributable to claimant and to any person with whom the claimant has already settledor released from liability.	**Mont. Code Ann. § 25-9-412 (2010)** If an award of $50,000 or more is made in an action for medical malpractice, a party may request the court to enter a judgment ordering future damages to be paid in whole or in part by periodic payment rather than lump sum payment.
Nebraska	**Neb. Rev. Stat. Ann. § 25-21,185.10 (2010)** Modified joint and several liability. Except when part of a common enterprise or plan, the liability for each defendant for economic damages shall be joint and several and the liability for each defendant for noneconomic damages shall be several only and not joint.	No statute found.
Nevada	**Nev. Rev. Stat. Ann. § 41A.045 (2010)** Several liability. In an action against a health care provider based upon professional negligence, each defendant is liable to the plaintiff for economic and noneconomic damages severally only and not jointly, for their percentage of fault.	**Nev. Rev. Stat. Ann. § 42.021 (2010)** If an award for future damages exceeds $50,000, a court shall, at the request of either party, enter a judgment ordering that money damages or its equivalent for future damages be paid in whole or in part by periodic payments rather than a lump sum payment.
New Hampshire	**N.H. Rev. Stat Ann. § 507:+7-e (2011)** Modified joint and several liability. Damages shall be awarded to each defendant in accordance with proportion of fault, and	No statute found.

Table A-4. (Continued)

State	Joint and Several Liability	Periodic Payment of Damages
	each party shall be jointly and severally liable, except if any party shall be less than 50% at fault, then that party's liability shall be several and not joint.	
New Jersey	**N.J. Rev. Stat. § 2A:15-5.3 (2011)** Modified joint and several liability. If a defendant is determined to be 60% or more responsible for the total damages, the claimant may recover the full amount ofdamages from such party. If a defendant is determined to be less than 60% responsible, the claimant may recover only such amount that directly attributable to that defendant.	No statute found.
New Mexico	**N.M. Stat. Ann. § 41-3A-1 (2010)** Several liability. In any cause of action to which the doctrine of compa-rative fault applies, the doctr-ine imposing joint and several liability upon two or more wrongdoers is abolished exc-ept as otherwise provided. The defendants shall be several.	**N.M. Stat. Ann. § 41-5-7 (2010)** if a judgment is made that patient is in need of future medical expenses, such payment for those expenses shall be made as expenses are incurred.
New York	**N.Y. C.P.L.R. § 1601 (2011)** Modified joint and several liability. New York statutory scheme governing limited liability of persons jointly liable modifies the common law rule of joint and several liability by limiting tort-feasor's liability in certain circumstances. *See Rangolan v. County of Nassau,* 749 N.E.2d 178 (N.Y. 2001).	**N.Y. C.P.L.R. § 5031 (2011)** In any award of damages for future pain and suffering in excess of $500,000, the court shall determine the greater of 35% of such damages or $500,000 and such amount shall be paid in a lump sum. The remaining amount of the award for future damages for future pain and suffering, shall be paid in a stream of payments over time over the period determined by trier of fact or eight years, whichever is less.
North Carolina	**N.C. Gen. Stat. § 1B-1(2010)** Joint and several liability. Except as otherwise provided, where two or more persons become jointly or severally liable in tort for the same injury to a person or for the same wrongful death, there is a right of contribution among them.	No statute found.
North Dakota	**N.D. Cent. Code § 32-03.2-02 (2011)** Several liability. When two or more parties are found to have contributed to the injury, the liability of each person is several only, and is not joint, and each party is liable only for the amount of damages attributable to that percentage of fault of that party.	**N.D. Cent. Code § 32-03.2-09 (2011)** If an injured party claims future economic damages for continuing institutional or custodial care that will be required for a period of more than two years, then any party may make periodic payments for this care if the court directs the trier of fact, upon request of a party, to make a special finding for this amount, separate from other future economic damages.

State	Joint and Several Liability	Periodic Payment of Damages
Ohio	**Ohio Rev. Code Ann. § 2307.22 (2011)** Modified joint and several liability. If more than 50% of the tortious conduct is attributable to one defendant, that defendant shall be jointly and severally liable in tort for all compensatory damages that represent economic loss. If less than 50% of the tortious conduct is attributable to a defendant, that defendant shall be liable only to the plai-ntiff only for that defendant's proportionate share of comp-ensatory damages that represent economic loss.	**Ohio Rev. Code Ann. § 2323.55 (2011)** The court shall determine, in its discretion, whether all or part of future damages recoverable by plaintiff shall be received by plaintiff in a series of periodic payments rather than in a lump sum. If a court determines that plaintiff shall receive future damages in a series of periodic payments, it may order the payments only as to the amounts of future damages that exceed $50,000.
Oklahoma	**Okla. Stat. tit., 23, § 15 (2010)** Modified joint and several liability. The liability for damages cause by two or more persons shall be several only in proportion to their fault, except that a defendant shall be jointly and severally liable for damages if the percentage of responsibility attributed to the defendant is greater than 50%.	No statute found.
Oregon	**Or. Rev. Stat. § 31.610 (2009)** Several liability. In any civil action arising out of bodily injury, death or property damage, the liability of each defendant to plaintiff shall be several only and shall not be joint.	No statute found.
Pennsyl-vania	**42 Pa. Cons. Stat. § 7102 (2010)** Joint and several liability. The doctrine of joint and several liability applies against all defendants whom plaintiff is not barred from recovery.	**40 Pa. Cons. Stat. § 1303.509 (2010)** Future damage for medical and other related expenses shall be paid as periodic payments except if claimant objects andstipulates that the total amount of future damages, without reduction to the present value, does not exceed $100,000, payment of such damages shall not be made in periodic installments.
Rhode Island	**R.I. Gen. Laws § 10-6-2 (2010)** Joint and several liability. "Joint tortfeasors" means two or more persons jointly or severally liable in tort for the same injury to person or property whether or not judgment has been recovered against some or all of them.	**R.I. Gen. Laws § 9-21-13 (2010)** In any action to recover for personal injury in which damages, if liability is proved, are likely to exceed $150,000 the parties shall consider the use of periodic payments as a means of settlement.
South Carolina	**S.C. Code Ann. §§ 15-38-15; 15-38-20 (2010)** Modified joint and several liability. If indivisible damages are determined to be proximately caused by more than one defendant, joint and several liability to any defendant whose conduct is determined to be less than 50% of the total conduct. where two or more people become jointly or severally liable in tort for the same injury,	No statute found.

Table A-4. (Continued)

State	Joint and Several Liability	Periodic Payment of Damages
	there is a right of contribution among them. The right of contribution exists only in favor of a tort-feasor who has paid more than his pro rata share of the common liability.	
South Dakota	**S.D. Codified Laws § 15-8-15.1 (2011)** Modified joint and several liability. If court enters judgment on basis of joint and several liability, any party who is allocated less than 50% of the total fault allocated to all parties may not be jointly liable for more than twice his percentage of the fault. Otherwise, the right of contribution exists among joint-tortfeasors.	**S.D. Codified Laws § 21-3A-1 *et seq* (2011)** Provides for periodic payments of only for claims against a physician, surgeon, dentist, hospital, sanitarium, registered nurse, licensed practical nurse, chiropractor or other practitioner of healing arts for malpractice error, mistake, or failure to cure.
Tennessee	**Tenn. Code Ann. § 29-11-101 (2011)** Several liability. *See McIntyre v. Ballentine*, 833 S.W.2d 52 (Tenn 1992).	No statute found.
Texas	**Tex. Civ. Prac. & Rem. § 33.013 (2010)** Modified joint and several liability. Each defendant is liable to claimant only for the percen-tage of fault apportioned to him, except that a defendant may be jointly and severally liable if the percentage of fault attributed to the defendant is greater than 50%.	**Tex. Civ. Prac. & Rem. § 74.503 (2010)** If an award for future damages exceeds $100,000, the court shall, at the request of the defendant, order that medical, health care, or custodial services, or future damages in those respective areas be paid in whole or in part rather than by lump sum payment.
Utah	**Utah Code Ann. § 78B-5-820 (2011)** Several liability. The maximum amount for which a defendant may be liable to any person seeking recovery is that percentage or proportion of the damages equivalent to the percentage or proportion of fault attributed to that defendant.	**Utah Code Ann. § 78B-3-414 (2011)** In any malpractice action against a health care provider, the court shall, at the request of any party, order that future damages which exceed or equal $100,000 be paid by periodic payments rather than lump sum payment.
Vermont	**Vt. Stat. Ann. tit. 12, § 1036 (2011)** Several liability. Where recovery is allowed against more than one defendant, each defendant shall be liable for that proportion of the total dollar amount awarded as damages in the ratio of the amount of his causal negligence to the amount of causal negligence attributed to all defendants against whom recovery is allowed	No statute found.
Virginia	**Va. Code Ann. § 8.01-443 (2011)** Joint and several liability. The claimant may bring separate actions against all joint wrongdoers and proceed to judgment in each, or, if sued jointly, the claimant may proceed to judgment against them successively until judgment has been rendered against, or otherwise disposed of as	No statute found.

State	Joint and Several Liability	Periodic Payment of Damages
	to, all defendants, and no bar shall arise as to any of them by reason of a judgment against another, or others, until the judgment has been satisfied.	
Washington	**Wash. Rev. Code Ann. § 4.22.070 (2011)** Modified joint and several liability. The liability of each defendant shall be several only and shall not be joint except where the trier of fact determines that the claimant was not at fault, then such defendants shall be jointly and severally liable for the sum of their proportionate shares of the claimant's total damages.	**Wash. Rev. Code Ann. § 4.56.260 (2011)** If an award of future damages is $100,000or more, the court shall, at the request of a party, enter a judgment which provides for the periodic payment in whole or in part of the future economic damages.
West Virginia	**W. Va. Code Ann. § 55-7B-9 (2011)** Modified joint and several liability. If the trier of fact renders a verdict for the plaintiff, the court shall enter judgment of several, but not joint, liability against each defendant in accordance with the percenttage of fault attributed to the defendant by the trier of fact.	No statute found.
Wisconsin	**Wis. Stat. § 895.045 (2010)** Modified joint and several liability. The liability of each person found to be causally negligent whose percentage of causal negligence is les than 51% is limited to the percentage of total causal negligence attributed to that person. A person found to be causally negligent whose percentage of causal negligence is 51% or more shall be jointly and severally liable for the damages allowed.	**Wis. Stat. § 655.27 (2010)** Regarding the Injured Patients and Families Compensation Fund, in the event the fund incurs liability for future payments exceeding $1,000,000 to any person under a single claim as a result of a settlement of judgment after May 25, 1995, the fund shall pay after deductions full medical expenses each year, plus an amount not to exceed $500,000 per year that will pay the remaining liability over the person's anticipated lifetime, or until the liability is paid in full.
Wyoming	**Wyo. Stat. Ann. § 1-1-109 (2011)** Several liability. Each defendant is liable only to the extentof the defendant's proportion of the total fault determined.	No statute found.

Source: Westlaw State Statutes database.

Notes: The statutory language included is from the current version of the state's code which may not reflect very recent legislative enactments yet to be codified.

Table A-5 sets forth limits on attorneys' contingency fees in the 50 states. Most statutes have a sliding scale, which limits the amount an attorney can collect to a certain percentage of the award recovered. This table does include provisions that address how attorneys' fees are to be calculated in light of an award for damages or how they are to be considered by the court. For example, the states of Arizona, Kansas, and Washington each have a statutory provisions on how a court shall, upon the request of a party, review the reasonableness of attorneys' fees in a health care action. It mandates that the court take into consideration factors such as (1) the time and labor required, the novelty and difficulty of the questions involved, and the skill requisite to perform the legal services properly; (2) the likelihood, if apparent to the client, that the acceptance of the particular employment will preclude other employment by the lawyer; (3) the fee customarily charged in the locality for similar legal services; (4) the amount involved and the results obtained; and (5) the time limitations imposed by the client or by the circumstances.[58] Another example is Alaska, which directs when an attorney's contingency fee is to be calculated when punitive damages are awarded.[59] This table also does not capture provisions on attorneys' fees like that of North Dakota, which declares that "the amount of the agreement in civil actions must be left to the agreement, express or implied, of the parties."[60] In states where only these types of statutory provisions were identified with respect to attorneys' fees, we have entered "no statute found."

Table A-5. State Limits on Attorneys' Contingency Fees

State	Limits on Attorneys' Fees
Alabama	No statute found.
Alaska	No statute found.
Arizona	No statute found.
Arkansas	No statute found.
California	**Cal. Bus. & Prof. Code § 6146 (2010) Attorneys Fee Agreement: Limitations in amount.** (a) An attorney shall not contract for or collect a contingency fee for representing any person seeking damages in connection with an action for injury or damage against a health care provider based upon such person's alleged professional negligence in excess of the following limits: (1) 40% of the first fifty thousand dollars ($50,000) recovered. (2) 33⅓ % of the next fifty thousand dollars ($50,000) recovered. (3) 25% of the next five hundred thousand dollars ($500,000) recovered. (4) 15% of any amount on which the recovery exceeds six hundred thousand dollars ($600,000). The limitations shall apply regardless of whether the recovery is by settle-ment, arbitration, or judgment, or whether the person for whom the recovery is made is a responsible adult, an infant, or a person of unsound mind.
Colorado	No statute found.
Connecticut	**Conn. Gen. Stat. § 52-251c (2010) Limitation on attorney contingency fees in personal injury, wrongful death and property damage actions. Waiver of limitation by claimant.** (a) In any claim or civil action to recover damages resulting from personal injury, wrongful death or damage to property occurring on or after October 1, 1987, the attorney and the claimant may provide by contract, which contract shall comply with all applicable provisions of the rules of professional conduct governing attorneys adopted by the judges of the Superior Court, that the fee for the attorney shall be paid contingent upon, and as a percentage of: (1) Damages awarded and received by the claimant; or (2) the settlement amount received pursuant to a settlement agreement. (b) In any such contingency fee agreement such fee shall be the exclusive method for payment of the attorney by the claimant and shall not exceed an amount equal to a percentage of the damages awarded and received by the claimant or of the settlement amount received by the claimant as follows: (1) Thirty-three and one-third per cent of the first three hundred thousand dollars; (2) twenty-five per cent of the next three hundred thousand dollars; (3) twenty per cent of the next three hundred thousand dollars; (4) fifteen per cent of the next three hundred thousand dollars; and (5) ten per cent of any amount which exceeds one million two hundred thousand dollars.

State	Limits on Attorneys' Fees
	(c) Notwithstanding the provisions of subsection (b) of this section, a claimant may waive the percentage limitations of said subsection if the claim or civil action is so substantially complex, unique or different from other wrongful death, personal injury or property damage claims or civil actions as to warrant a deviation from such percentage limitations. (f) If a claimant waives the percentage limitations of subsection (b) of this section pursuant to this section, in no event shall (1) the total fee under the contingency fee agreement exceed thirty-three and one-third per cent of the damages awarded and received by the claimant or of the settlement amount received by the claimant, and (2) the claimant be required to repay any costs that the attorney incurred in investigating and prosecuting the claim or civil action if there is no recovery. (g) No fee shall be payable to any attorney who seeks a fee that exceeds the percentage limitations of subsection (b) of this section unless the claimant has waived such limitations pursuant to this section and the contingency fee agreement complies with the requirements of subsection (e) of this section.
Delaware	**Del. Code Ann. tit. 18, § 06865 (2011) Compensation for Health Care Injuries:Limitation on attorney's fees.** (a) The amount of the claimant's attorney's fees may not exceed the amounts in the following schedule: (1) 35% of the first $100,000 of damages; (2) 25% of the next $100,000 of damages; (3) 10% of the balance of any awarded damages.
District of Columbia	No statute found.
Florida	**Fla. Const. Art. 1, § 26 (2011) Claimant's right to fair compensation.** In any medical liability claim involving a contingency fee, the claimant is entitled to receive no less than 70% of the first $250,000.00 in all damages received by the claimant, exclusive of reasonable and customary costs, whether received by judgment, settlement, or otherwise, and regardless of the number of defendants. The claimant is entitled to 90% of all damages in excess of $250,000.00, exclusive of reasonable and customary costs and regardless of the number of defendants. This provision is self-executing and does not require implementing legislation.
Georgia	No statute found.
Hawaii	**Haw. Rev. Stat. Ann. § 607-15.5 (2011) Attorneys' fees in tort actions.** In all tort actions in which a judgment is entered by a court of competent jurisdiction, attorneys' fees for both the plaintiff and the defendant shall be limited to a reasonable amount as approved by the court having jurisdiction of the action. In any tort action in which a settlement is effected, the plaintiff or the defendant may request that the amount of their respective attorneys' fees be subject to approval of the court having jurisdiction of the action.
Idaho	**Idaho Code Ann. § 12-120 (2011) Attorney's fees in civil actions.** (4) In actions for personal injury, where the amount of plaintiff's claim for damages does not exceed twenty-five thousand dollars ($25,000), there shall be taxed and allowed to the claimant, as part of the costs of the action, a reasonable amount to be fixed by the court as attorney's fees. For the plaintiff to be awarded attorney's fees for the prosecution of the action, written demand for payment of the claim and a statement of claim must have been served on the defendant's insurer, if known, or if there is no known insurer, then on the defendant, not less than sixty (60) days before the commencement of the action; provided that no attorney's fees shall be allowed to the plaintiff if the court finds

Table A-5. (Continued)

State	Limits on Attorneys' Fees
	that the defendant tendered to the plaintiff, prior to the commencement of the action, an amount at least equal to 90% of the amount awarded to the plaintiff.
Illinois	**735 Ill. Comp. Stat. Ann. 5/2-1114 (2011) Contingent fees for attorneys in medical malpractice actions.** (a) In all medical malpractice actions the total contingent fee for plaintiff's attorney or attorneys shall not exceed the following amounts: 33⅓ % of the first $150,000 of the sum recovered; 25% of the next $850,000 of the sum recovered; and 20% of any amount recovered over $1,000,000 of the sum recovered. (c) The court may review contingent fee agreements for fairness. In special circumstances, where an attorney performs extraordinary services involving more than usual participation in time and effort the attorney may apply to the court for approval of additional compensation.
Indiana	**Ind. Code Ann. § 34-18-18-1 (2011) Medical Malpractice: Limitation on plaintiff's attorney's fees.** When a plaintiff is represented by an attorney in the prosecution of the plaintiff's claim, the plaintiff's attorney's fees from any award made from the patient's compensation fund may not exceed 15% of any recovery from the fund.
Iowa	**Iowa Code Ann. § 147.138 (2010) Health Related Professions Malpractice: Contingent fee of attorney reviewed by court.** In any action for personal injury or wrongful death against any physician and surgeon,osteopathic physician and surgeon, dentist, podiatric physician, optometrist, pharmacist, chiropractor or nurse licensed under this chapter or against any hospital licensed under chapter 135B, based upon the alleged negligence of the licensee in the practice of that profession or occupation, or upon the alle-ged negligence of the hospital in patient care, the court shall determine the reasonableness of any contingent fee arrangement between the plaintiff and the plaintiff's attorney.
Kansas	No statute found.
Kentucky	No statute found.
Louisiana	No statute found.
Maine	**Me. Rev. Stat. tit. 24, § 2961 (2011) Maine Health Security Act: Contingent fees.** 1. LIMITATION. In an action for professional negligence, the total contingent fee for the plaintiff's attorney or attorneys shall not exceed the following amounts, exclusive of litigation expenses: A. Thirty-three and one-third percent of the first $100,000 of the sum recovered; B. Twenty-five percent of the next $100,000 of the sum recovered; and C. Twenty percent of any amount over $200,000 of the sum recovered. 3. REVIEW. If the plaintiff prevails in the action for professional negligence, the plaintiff's attorney may petition the court to review the reasonableness of the fees permitted under subsection 1. The court may award a greater fee than that permitted by subsection 1, provided that: A. The court, considering the factors established in Maine Rules of Professional Conduct, Rule 1.5 as guides in determining the reasonableness of a fee, finds that the fees permitted by subsection 1 are inadequate to compensate the attorney reasonably for the attorney's services; and

State	Limits on Attorneys' Fees
	B. The court finds that the fee found reasonable under paragraph A does not exceed the percentages set forth in the contingent fee agreement between the attorney and plaintiff as the maximum amount of compensation the attorney may receive. An attorney may petition the court under this subsection only if, prior to the signing of a contingent fee agreement by the attorney and client, the attorney informs the client, orally and in writing, of the provisions of this section.
Maryland	**Md. Code Ann., Cts. & Jud. Proc. § 3-2A-07 (2011) Health Care Malpractice Claims: Award of Costs; Counsel fees.** (a) Action maintained in bad faith.—If the arbitration panel finds that the conduct of any party in maintaining or defending any action is in bad faith or without substantial justification, the panel may require the offending party, the attorney advising the conduct, or both, to pay to the adverse party the costs of the proceeding and reasonable expenses, including reasonable attorney's fees, incurred by the adverse party in opposing it. A determination made under this subsection shall become part of the panel award and subject to judicial review. (b) Approval of disputed legal fee.—If a legal fee is in dispute, an attorney may not charge or collect compensation for services rendered in connection with an arbitration claim unless it is approved by the arbitration panel, or by the court in the event an action to nullify a panel determination has been filed therein.
Massachusetts	**Mass. Ann. Laws, ch. 231, § 60I (2010) Pleading and Practice: Limitation on Attorney Fees.** Attorney fees for services rendered on behalf of a claimant or defendant in a medical negligence case shall be fair and reasonable. An attorney representing a claimant may charge a client a contingency fee, which shall be subject to the rules and guidelines of the supreme judicial court. No contingent fee agreement, shall be enforced, and no attorney shall recover a fee thereunder, as a result of services rendered in an action against a provider of health care for malpractice, negligence, error, omission, mistake, or the unauthorized rendering of professional services if, at the time of judgment, the court determines that the amount of the recovery paid or to be paid to the plaintiff, after deduction of the attorney's reasonable expenses and disbursements for which the plaintiff is liable and the amount of the attorney's fee, is less than the total amount of the plaintiff's unpaid past and future medical expenses included in the recovery, unless the contingent attorney's fee: (a) is twenty per cent or less of the plaintiff's recovery; (b) is reduced to twenty per cent or less of the plaintiff's recovery; or (c) is reduced to a level which permits the plaintiff to be paid his unpaid past and future medical expenses included in the recovery. An attorney shall not contract for or collect a contingent fee for representing any person seeking damages in connection with an action for malpractice, negligence, error, omission, mistake, or the unauthorized rendering of professional services against a provider of health care in excess of the following limits: (1) Forty per cent of the first one hundred and fifty thousand dollars recovered; (2) Thirty-three and one-third per cent of the next one hundred and fifty thousand dollars recovered; (3) Thirty per cent of the next two hundred thousand dollars recovered; (4) Twenty-five per cent of any amount by which the recovery exceeds five hundred thousand dollars. The limitations shall apply regardless of whether the recovery is by settlement, arbitration or judgment. Nothing herein shall preclude any attorney from contracting to represent a client for less than the above limits, nor shall anything herein preclude a court from assessing reasonable attorney's fees at any amount

Table A-5. (Continued)

State	Limits on Attorneys' Fees
	below the above limits or from determining that attorney's fees below such limits are unreasonably high in a particular case.
Michigan	**Mich. Ct. R 8.121 (2011) Contingent Fees in Claims or Actions for Personal Injury and Wrongful Death.** (A) Allowable Contingent Fee Agreements. In any claim or action for personal injury or wrongful death based upon the alleged conduct of another, in which an attorney enters into an agreement, expressed or implied, whereby the attorney's compensation is dependent or contingent in whole or in part upon successful prosecution or settlement or upon the amount of recovery, the receipt, retention, or sharing by such attorney, pursuant to agreement or otherwise, of compensation which is equal to or less than the fee stated in subrule (B) is deemed to be fair and reasonable. The receipt, retention, or sharing of compensation which is in excess of such a fee shall be deemed to be the charging of a "clearly excessive fee" in violation of MRPC 1.5(a). (B) Maximum Fee. The maximum allowable fee for the claims and actions referred to in subrule (A) is one-third of the amount recovered. (C) Computation. (1) The amount referred to in subrule (B) shall be computed on the net sum recovered after deducting from the amount recovered all disbursements properly chargeable to the enforcement of the claim or prosecution of the action. In computing the fee, the costs as taxed and any interest included in or upon the amount of a judgment shall be deemed part of the amount recovered. (2) In the case of a settlement payable in installments, the amount referred to in subrule (B) shall be computed using the present value of the future payments. (a) If an annuity contract will be used to fund the future payments, "present value" is the actual cost of purchasing the annuity contract. The attorney for the defendant must disclose to the court and the parties the amount paid for the annuity contract, after any rebates or other discounts. (b) If the defendant will make the future payments directly, "present value" is the amount that an entity of the same financial standing as the defendant would pay for an annuity contract. The court may appoint an independent expert to certify the "present value" as defined in this paragraph. The court may base its findings on the expert's testimony or affidavit. (D) Agreements for Lower Fees. An attorney may enter into contingent fee arrangements calling for less compensation than that allowed by subrule(B).
Minnesota	**Minn. Stat. Ann. § 548.251 (2010) Judgments: Collateral Source Calculations.** Subd. 4. Calculation of attorney fees. If the fees for legal services provided to the plaintiff are based on a percentage of the amount of money awarded to the plaintiff, the percentage must be based on the amount of the award as adjusted under subdivision 3. Any subrogated provider of a collateral source not separately represented by counsel shall pay the same percentage of attorney fees as paid by the plaintiff and shall pay its proportionate share of the costs.
Mississippi	No statute found.
Missouri	No statute found.
Montana	No statute found.

State	Limits on Attorneys' Fees
Nebraska	**Neb. Rev. Stat. Ann. § 44-2834 (2010) Nebraska Hospital Medical Liability Act: Cause of action; attorney's fees; court costs; loss of earnings; when payable.** (1) In all cases against a health care provider for malpractice or professional negligence, upon motion of either party the court shall review the attorney's fees incurred by that party and allow such compensation as the court shall deem reasonable. (2) In all cases against health care providers for malpractice or professional negligence, the court may, upon application by the prevailing party, in its discretion and in an amount determined in its discretion tax as costs payable to the prevailing party the reasonable costs of preparation and trial including reasonable attorney's fees and the reasonable loss of earnings by the prevailing party occasioned by the trial if the court finds that the losing party did not have a reasonable chance of recovery or a reasonable chance of a successful defense. (3) A patient shall have the right to agree with his attorney to pay for the attorney's services on a mutually satisfactory per diem basis. Such election shall be exercised in written form at the time of employment or by written agreement thereafter entered into with his attorney.
Nevada	**Nev. Rev. Stat. Ann. § 7.095 (2010) Limitations on contingent fees for representation of persons in certain actions against providers of health care.** 1. An attorney shall not contract for or collect a fee contingent on the amount of recovery for representing a person seeking damages in connection with an action for injury or death against a provider of health care based upon professional negligence in excess of: (a) 40% of the first $50,000 recovered; (b) 33⅓ % of the next $50,000 recovered; (c) 25% of the next $500,000 recovered; and (d) 15% of the amount of recovery that exceeds $600,000. 2. The limitations set forth in subsection 1 apply to all forms of recovery, including, without limitation, settlement, arbitration and judgment.
New Hampshire	**N.H. Rev. Stat. Ann. § 508:4-e (2011) Attorneys' Fees for Services.** I. Contingent fee agreements between attorney and client shall be governed by Rules of Professional Conduct, Rule 1.5 as it may be amended by the supreme court from time to time and by any other rules regarding fees which are adopted or amended by the court. II. No attorney shall enter into such a contingent fee arrangement with his or her client without first advising the client of his or her right and affording the client an opportunity to retain the attorney under an arrangement whereby the attorney would be compensated on the basis of the reasonable value of his or her services. III. All fees and costs for actions, resulting in settlement or judgment of $200,000 or more, shall be subject to approval by the court. **N.H. Rev. Stat. Ann. § 507-C:8 (2011) Actions for Medical Injury: Contingent Fees.** I. In any action for medical injury, no attorney representing any party to such action shall contract for, charge or collect on a contingent fee basis any fee for his services to such party in excess of the following limits: (a) Fifty percent of the first $1,000 recovered; (b) Forty percent of the next $2,000 recovered; (c) Thirty-three and one-third percent of the next $97,000 recovered; (d) Twenty percent of all in excess of $100,000 recovered;

Table A-5. (Continued)

State	Limits on Attorneys' Fees
	(e) Where the amount recovered is for the benefit of an infant or incompetent and the action is settled without trial, the foregoing limits shall apply, except that the fee in any amount recovered up to $50,000 shall not exceed twenty five percent. This provision § 507-C:8 declared unconstitutional See Carson v. Mauerer, 424 A.2d 825 (N.H. 1980).
New Jersey	**N.J. Ct. R. § 1:21-7 (2011) Contingent Fees.** (b) An attorney shall not enter into a contingent fee arrangement without first having advised the client of the right and afforded the client an opportunity to retain the attorney under an arrangement for compensation on the basis of the reasonable value of the services. (c) In any matter where a client's claim for damages is based upon the alleged tortuous conduct of another, including products liability claims and claims among family members that are subject to Part V of these Rules but excluding statutorily based discrimination and employment claims, and the client is not a subrogee, an attorney shall not contract for, charge, or collect a contingent fee in excess of the following limits: (1) 33⅓ % on the first $500,000 recovered; (2) 30% on the next $500,000 recovered; (3) 25% on the next $500,000 recovered; (4) 20% on the next $500,000 recovered; and (5) on all amounts recovered in excess of the above by application for reasonable fee in accordance with the provisions of paragraph (f) hereof; and (6) where the amount recovered is for the benefit of a client who was a minor or mentally incapacitated when the contingent fee arrangement was made, the foregoing limits shall apply, except that the fee on any amount recovered by settlement without trial shall not exceed 25%. (e) Paragraph (c) of this rule is intended to fix maximum permissible fees and does not preclude an attorney from entering into a contingent fee arrangement providing for, or from charging or collecting a contingent fee below such limits. In all cases contingent fees charged or collected must conform to RPC 1.5(a).
New Mexico	No statute found.
New York	**N.Y. Jud. Law § 474-a (2011) Attorneys and Counselors: Contingent fees for attorneys in claims or actions for medical, dental or podiatric malpractice.** 2. Notwithstanding any inconsistent judicial rule, a contingent fee in a medical, dental or podiatric malpractice action shall not exceed the amount of compensation provided for in the following schedule: 30 % of the first $250,000 of the sum recovered; 25 % of the next $250,000 of the sum recovered; 20 % of the next $500,000 of the sum recovered; 15 % of the next $250,000 of the sum recovered; 10 % of any amount over $1,250,000 of the sum recovered.
North Carolina	No statute found.
North Dakota	No statute found.
Ohio	**Ohio Rev. Code Ann. § 2323.43 (2011) Medical Malpractice Actions: Limits on compensatory damages representing noneconomic loss.** (F) (1) If pursuant to a contingency fee agreement between an attorney and a plaintiff in a civil action upon a medical claim, dental claim, optometric claim, or chiropractic claim, the amount of the attorney's fees exceed the applicable

State	Limits on Attorneys' Fees
	amount of the limits on compensatory damages for noneconomic loss as provided in division (A)(2) or (3) of this section, the attorney shall make an application in the probate court of the county in which the civil action was commenced or in which the settlement was entered. The application shall contain a statement of facts, including the amount to be allocated to the settlement of the claim, the amount of the settlement or judgment that represents the compensatory damages for economic loss and noneconomic loss, the relevant provision in the contingency fee agreement, and the dollar amount of the attorney's fees under the contingency fee agreement. The application shall include the proposed distribution of the amount of the judgment or settlement.
Oklahoma	**Okla. Stat. tit. 5, § 7 (2010) Attorneys and Counselors: Contingent fee—Limitation on amount—Compromise or settlement—Effect on lien—Certain contracts void.** It shall be lawful for an attorney to contract for a percentage or portion of the proceeds of a client's cause of action or claim not to exceed 50% of the net amount of such judgment as may be recovered, or such compromise as may be made, whether the same arises ex contractu or ex delicto, and no compromise or settlement entered into by a client without such attorney's consent shall affect or abrogate the lien provided for in this chapter. Provided that all such contracts in personal injury or wrongful death cases including, but not restricted to, cases in which jurisdiction is in the Industrial Commission, shall be void and unenforceable (1) if secured as a result of the intervention of any laymen, association, or corporation for compensation, or promise of compensation, or anticipation of gift, compensation or hope of reward, or (2) where any laymen, association or corporation has a direct or indirect interest in, or growing out of, any judgment arising out of such claim recovery or compensation from, or settlement of any such claim.
Oregon	**Or. Rev. Stat. § 31.735 (2010) Tort Actions Damages: Distribution of punitive damages; notice to Department of Justice; order of application.** (1) Upon the entry of a verdict including an award of punitive damages, the Department of Justice shall become a judgment creditor as to the punitive damages portion of the award to which the Criminal Injuries Compensation Account is entitled pursuant to paragraph (b) of this subsection, and the punitive damage portion of an award shall be allocated as follows: (a) Forty percent shall be paid to the prevailing party. The attorney for the prevailing partyshall be paid out of the amount allocated under this paragraph, in the amount agreed upon between the attorney and the prevailing party. However, in no event may more than twenty percent of the amount awarded as punitive damages be paid to the attorney for the prevailing party.
Pennsylvania	Limits declared unconstitutional in Heller v. Frankston, 475 A.2d 1291 (Pa. 1984).
Rhode Island	No statute found.
South Carolina	No statute found.
South Dakota	No statute found.
Tennessee	**Tenn. Code Ann. § 29-26-120 (2011) Medical Malpractice: Attorneys' fees.** Compensation for reasonable attorneys' fees in the event an employment contract exists between the claimant and claimant's attorney on a contingent fee arrangement shall be awarded to the claimant's attorney in a malpractice action in an amount to be determined by the court on the basis of time and effort devoted to the litigation by the claimant's attorney, complexity of the claim and

Table A-5. (Continued)

State	Limits on Attorneys' Fees
	other pertinent matters in connection therewith, not to exceed 33 % of all damages awarded to the claimant.
Texas	No statute found.
Utah	**Utah Code Ann. § 78B-3-411 (2011) Utah Health Care Malpractice Act: Limitation on attorney's contingency fee in malpractice action.** (1) In any malpractice action against a health care provider as defined in Section 78B-3-403, an attorney may not collect a contingent fee for representing a client seeking damages in connection with or arising out of personal injury or wrongful death caused by the negligence of another which exceeds 33- 1/3% of the amount recovered. (2) This limitation applies regardless of whether the recovery is by settlement, arbitration, judgment, or whether appeal is involved.
Vermont	No statute found.
Virginia	No statute found.
Washington	No statute found.
West Virginia	No statute found.
Wisconsin	**Wis. Stat. § 655.013. (2010) Health Care Liability And Injured Patients And Families Compensation: Attorney fees.** (1) With respect to any act of malpractice after July 24, 1975, for which a contingency fee arrangement has been entered into before June 14, 1986, the compensation determined on a contingency basis and payable to all attorneys acting for one or more plaintiffs or claimants is subject to the following unless a new contingency fee arrangement is entered into that complies with subs. (1m) and (1t): (a) The determination shall not reflect amounts previously paid for medical expenses by the health care provider or the providers insurer. (b) The determination shall not reflect payments for future medical expense in excess of 25,000. (1m) Except as provided in sub. (1t), with respect to any act of malpractice for which a contingency fee arrangement is entered into on and after June 14, 1986, in addition to compensation for the reasonable costs of prosecution of the claim, the compensation determined on a contingency basis and payable to all attorneys acting for one or more plain-tiffs or claimants is subject to the following limitations: (a) Except as provided in par. (b), 33⅓ % of the first 1,000,000 recovered. (b) 25% of the first 1,000,000 recovered if liability is stipulated within 180 days after the date of filing of the original complaint and not later than 60 days before the first day of trial. (c) 20% of any amount in excess of 1,000,000 recovered. (1t) A court may approve attorney fees in excess of the limitations under sub. (1m) upon a showing of exceptional circumstances, including an appeal. (2) An attorney shall offer to charge any client in a malpractice proceeding or action on a per diem or per hour basis. Any such agreement shall be made at the time of the employment of the attorney. An attorneys fee on a per diem or per hour basis is not subject to the limitations under sub. (1) or (1m).
Wyoming	**Wyo. Contingent Fees Rule 5 (2011) Court review.** (a) It is recognized that contingent fees vary in amount depending upon those factors which are described in paragraph (f) of this rule and that a common contingent fee in casualty and wrongful death cases is 33 % of amounts recovered prior to appeal and 45-50% of amounts recovered on appeal.

State	Limits on Attorneys' Fees
	Contingent fees which do not exceed the following schedule will be presumed to be reasonable and not excessive where the total recovery does not exceed one million dollars ($1,000,000): (1) 33⅓ % of the recovery if the claim is settled prior to or within sixty (60) days after suit is filed; (2) 40% of the recovery if the claim is settled more than sixty (60) days after filing suit or if a judgment is entered upon a verdict. (b) For those amounts of a recovery in excess of one million dollars ($1,000,000) a contingent fee of 30% of such excess sum over one million dollars ($1,000,000) shall be presumed reasonable and not excessive. (c) The provisions of this rule are not intended to abridge the freedom of the attorneys and clients to contract for different percentages.

Source: LexisNexis State Statutes database.

Notes: The statutory language included is from the current version of the state's code which may not reflect very recent legislative enactments yet to be codified.

Table A-6 sets forth the statute of limitations for medical malpractice actions and product liability actions in the 50 states. Generally, for each state, this table identifies first, the medical malpractice statute of limitations, and second, the product liability statute of limitations provision. Where no product-liability specific statute could be identified, we included the general statute of limitations on an action to recover damages for personal injury or the "catch-all" statute of limitations; e.g., the D.C. Code § 12-301 provides "for which a limitation is not otherwise specifically provided—3 years" and Delaware's statute of limitations governing "personal injuries" would govern an action for product liability. (*See* Del. Code Ann titl. 10, § 8119.)

Table A-6. Statute of Limitations for Medical Malpractice and Product Liability Actions

State	Statute of Limitation
Alabama	**Ala. Code § 6-5-482 (2011) Medical Liability Actions: Statute of limitations.** (a) All actions against physicians, surgeons, dentists, medical institutions, or other health care providers for liability, error, mistake, or failure to cure, whether based on contract or tort, must be commenced within two years next after the act, or omission, or failure giving rise to the claim, and not afterwards; provided, that if the cause of action is not discovered and could not reasonably have been discovered within such period, then the action may be commenced within six months from the date of such discovery or the date of discovery of facts which would reasonably lead to such discovery, whichever is earlier; provided further, that in no event may the action be commenced more than four years after such act; except, that an error, mistake, act, omission, or failure to cure giving rise to a claim which occurred before September 23, 1975, shall not in any event be barred until the expiration of one year from such date. **Ala. Code § 6-5-502 (2011) Statute of limitations.** (a) All product liability actions against an original seller must be commenced within the following time limits and not otherwise: (1) Except as specifically provided in subsections (b), (c), and (e) of this section, within one year of the time the personal injury, death, or property damage occurs; and (2) Except as specifically provided in subsections (b), (c), and (e) of this section, each element of a product liability action shall be deemed to accrue at the time the personal injury, death, or property damage occurs;

Table A-6. (Continued)

State	Statute of Limitation
	(b) Where the personal injury, including personal injury resulting in death, or property damage (i) either is latent or by its nature is not discoverable in the exercise of reasonable diligence at the time of its occurrence, and (ii) is the result of ingestion of or exposure to some toxic or harmful or injury-producing substance, element or particle, including radiation, over a period of time as opposed to resulting from a sudden and fortuitous trauma, then, in that event, the product liability action claiming damages for such personal injury, or property damage must be commenced within one year from the date such personal injury or property damage is or in the exercise of reasonable diligence should have been discovered by the plaintiff or the plaintiff's decedent, and in such cases each of the elements of the product liability action shall be deemed to accrue at the time the personal injury is or in the exercise of reasonable diligence should have been discovered by the plaintiff or the plaintiff's decedent; and (c) Notwithstanding the provisions of subsections (a) and (b) of this section, a product liability action against an original seller must be brought within 10 years after the manufac-tured product is first put to use by any person or business entity who did not acquire the manufactured product for either resale or other distribution in its unused condition or for incorporation as a component part in a manufactured product which is to be sold or otherwise distributed in its unused condition. (d) The original seller may by express written agreement only waive or extend the period of time provided for in subsection (c) of this section; and (e) (1) Notwithstanding the provisions of subsection (c) of this section, if a plaintiff or plaintiff's decedent is entitled to maintain a product liability action because of the failure of an original seller to alter, repair, recall, inspect, or issue warnings or instructions about the manufactured product, or otherwise to take any action or precautions with regard to the safety of the manufactured product for the benefit of users or consumers after the manufactured product was sold or otherwise distributed by an original seller, and, if any federal or state governmental agency shall impose a requirement so to alter, repair, recall, inspect, or issue warnings or instructions about the manufactured product or otherwise to take any actions or precautions with regard to the safety of the manufactured product for the benefit of users or consumers after the manufactured product was sold or otherwise distributed by an original seller, then, if these two events have occurred, a product liability action for damages on account of such failure for personal injury, death, or property damage must be commenced within one year of the time the personal injury, death, or property damage resulting from such failure occurs; (2) In product liability actions predicated upon the failure to act and the governmental action, set forth in subdivision (1) of this subsection, where the personal injury, including personal injury resulting in death, or property damage (i) either is latent or by its nature is not discoverable in the exercise of reasonable diligence at the time of its occurrence, and (ii) is the result of the ingestion of or exposure to some toxic or harmful or injury-producing substance, element, or particle, including radiation, over a period of time as opposed to resulting from a sudden and fortuitous trauma, then in that event, the product liability action claiming damages for such personal injury or property damage must be commenced within one year from the date such personal injury or property damage is or in the exercise of reasonable diligence should have been discovered by the plaintiff or the plaintiff's decedent and in such cases each of the elements of the product liability action shall be deemed to accrue at the time the personal injury or property damage is or in the exercise of reasonable diligence should have been discovered by the plaintiff or plaintiff's decedent; and (3) Notwithstanding the provisions of subdivisions (1) and (2) of this subsection, a product liability action against an original seller must be brought within 10 years after the date of the imposition of such requirement by such governmental agency.
Alaska	**Alaska Stat. § 09.10.070 (2011) Actions for torts, for injury to personal property, for certain statutory liabilities, and against peace officers and coroners to be brought in two years.**

State	Statute of Limitation
	(a) Except as otherwise provided by law, a person may not bring an action (1) for libel, slander, assault, battery, seduction, or false imprisonment, (2) for personal injury or death, or injury to the rights of another not arising on contract and not specifically provided otherwise; (3) for taking, detaining, or injuring personal property, including an action for its specific recovery; (4) upon a statute for a forfeiture or penalty to the state; or (5) upon a liability created by statute, other than a penalty or forfeiture; unless the action is commenced within two years of the accrual of the cause of action. **Alaska Stat. § 09.10.055 (2011) Statute of repose of 10 years.** (a) Notwithstanding the disability of minority described under AS 09.10.140(a), a person may not bring an action for personal injury, death, or property damage unless commenced within 10 years of the earlier of the date of *** (2) the last act alleged to have caused the personal injury, death, or property damage. (b) This section does not apply if (1) the personal injury, death, or property damage resulted from (A) prolonged exposure to hazardous waste; (B) an intentional act or gross negligence; (C) fraud or misrepresentation; (D) breach of an express warranty or guarantee; (E) a defective product; in this subparagraph, "product" means an object that has intrinsic value, is capable of delivery as an assembled whole or as a component part, and is introduced into trade or commerce; or (F) breach of trust or fiduciary duty; (2) the facts that would give notice of a potential cause of action are intentionally concealed; (3) a shorter period of time for bringing the action is imposed under another provision of law; (4) the provisions of this section are waived by contract; or (5) the facts that would constitute accrual of a cause of action of a minor are not discoverable in the exercise of reasonable care by the minor's parent or guardian. (c) The limitation imposed under (a) of this section is tolled during any period in which thereexists the undiscovered presence of a foreign body that has no therapeutic or diagnostic purpose or effect in the body of the injured person and the action is based on the presence of the foreign body.
Arizona	**Ariz. Rev. Stat. § 12-542 (2011) Personal Actions: Injury to person; injury when death ensues; injury to property; conversion of property; forcible entry and forcible detainer; two year limitation.** Except as provided in section 12-551 there shall be commenced and prosecuted within two years after the cause of action accrues, and not afterward, the following actions: 1. For injuries done to the person of another including causes of action for medical malpractice as defined in section 12-561. 2. For injuries done to the person of another when death ensues from such injuries, which action shall be considered as accruing at the death of the party injured. **Ariz. Rev. Stat. § 12-551 (2011) Product liability.** A product liability action as defined in section 12-681 shall be commenced and prosecuted within the period prescribed in section 12-542, except that no product liability action may be commenced and prosecuted if the cause of action accrues more than twelve years after the product was first sold for use or consumption, unless the cause of action is based upon the negligence of the manufacturer or seller or a breach of an express warranty provided by the manufacturer or seller. **Ariz. Rev. Stat. § 12-681 (2011) Definitions.** 5. "Product liability action" means any action brought against a manufacturer or seller of a product for damages for bodily injury, death or property damage caused by or resulting from the manufacture, construction, design, formula, installation, preparation, assembly, testing, packaging, labeling, sale, use or consumption of any product, the failure to warn or protect against a danger or hazard in the use or misuse of the product or the failure to provide proper instructions for the use or consumption of any product.

Table A-6. (Continued)

State	Statute of Limitation
Arkansas	**Ark. Code Ann. § 16-114-203 (2010) Actions for Medical Injury: Statute of limitations.** (a) Except as otherwise provided in this section, all actions for medical injury shall be commenced within two (2) years after the cause of action accrues. (b) The date of the accrual of the cause of action shall be the date of the wrongful act complained of and no other time. However, where the action is based upon the discovery of a foreign object in the body of the injured person which is not discovered and could not reasonably have been discovered within such two-year period, the action may be commenced within one (1) year from the date of discovery or the date the foreign object reasonably should have been discovered, whichever is earlier. (c) (1) If an individual is nine (9) years of age or younger at the time of the act, omission, or failure complained of, the minor or person claiming on behalf of the minor shall have until the later of the minor's eleventh birthday or two (2) years from the act, omission, or failure in which to commence an action. (2) However, if no medical injury is known and could not reasonably have been discovered prior to the minor's eleventh birthday, then the minor or his representative shall have until two (2) years after the medical injury is known or reasonably could have been discovered, or until the minor's nineteenth birthday, whichever is earlier, in which to commence an action. **Ark. Code Ann. § 16-116-103 (2010) Limitation on actions.** All product liability actions shall be commenced within three (3) years after the date on which the death, injury, or damage complained of occurs.
California	**Cal. Civ. Proc. Code § 340.5 (2010) Professional neglig-ence of health care provider; Tolling of time limitation.** In an action for injury or death against a health care provider based upon such person's alleged professional negligence, the time for the commencement of action shall be three years after the date of injury or one year after the plaintiff discovers, or through the use of reasonable diligence should have discovered, the injury, whichever occurs first. In no event shall the time for commencement of legal action exceed three years unless tolled for any of the following: (1) upon proof of fraud, (2) intentional concealment, or (3) the presence of a foreign body, which has no therapeutic or diagnostic purpose or effect, in the person of the injured person. Actions by a minor shall be commenced within three years from the date of the alleged wrongful act except that actions by a minor under the full age of six years shall be commenced within three years or prior to his eighth birthday whichever provides a longer period. Such time limitation shall be tolled for minors for any period during which parent or guardian and defendant's insurer or health care provider have committed fraud or collusion in the failure to bring an action on behalf of the injured minor for professional negligence. ***See also*** **Cal. Civ. Proc. Code § 340.4 (2010) Statute of limitations for action by minor for personal injuries sustained before or during birth.** **Cal. Civ. Proc. Code § 335.1 (2011) Assault and battery; Personal injury; Wrongful death.** Within two years: An action for assault, battery, or injury to, or for the death of, an individual caused by the wrongful act or neglect of another.
Colorado	**Colo. Rev. Stat. § 13-80-102 (2010) General limitation of actions - two years.** (1) The following civil actions, regardless of the theory upon which suit is brought, or against whom suit is brought, shall be commenced within two years after the cause of action accrues, and not thereafter: (a) Tort actions, including but not limited to actions for negligence, trespass, malicious abuse of process, malicious prosecution, outrageous conduct, interference with relationships, and tortuous breach of contract; except that this paragraph (a) does not apply to any tort action arising out of the use or operation of a motor vehicle as set forth in section 13-80-101 (1) (n);

State	Statute of Limitation
	(b) All actions for strict liability, absolute liability, or failure to instruct or warn; (c) All actions, regardless of the theory asserted, against any veterinarian; (d) All actions for wrongful death. **Colo. Rev. Stat. § 13-80-102.5 (2010) Limitation of actions - medical or health care.** (1) Except as otherwise provided in this section, no action alleging negligence, breach of contract, lack of informed consent, or other action arising in tort or contract to recover damages from any health care institution, as defined in paragraph (a) of subsection (2) of this section, or any health care professional, as defined in paragraph (b) of subsection (2) of this section, shall be maintained unless such action is instituted within two years after the date that such action accrues pursuantto section 13-80-108 (1), but in no event shall an action be brought more than three years after the act or omission which gave rise to the action. (2) For the purposes of this section: (a) "Health care institution" means any hospital, health care facility, dispensary, clinic, or other institution which is licensed or certified as such under the laws of this state. (b) "Health care professional" means any physician, nurse, dentist, chiropractor, pharmacist, optometrist, psychologist, podiatrist, physical therapist, or other health care practitioner who is licensed to perform such profession under the laws of this state. (3) The limitation of actions provided in subsection (1) of this section shall not apply under the following circumstances: (a) If the act or omission which gave rise to the cause of action was knowingly concealed by the person committing such act or omission, in which case the action may be maintained if instituted within two years after the person bringing the action discovered, or in the exercise of reasonable diligence and concern should have discovered, the act or omission; or (b) If the act or omission consisted of leaving an unautho-rized foreign object in the body of the patient, in which case the action may be maintained if instituted within two years after the person bringing the action discovered, or in the exercise of reasonable diligence and concern should have discovered, the act or omission; or (c) If both the physical injury and its cause are not known or could not have been known by the exercise of reasonable diligence; or (d) If the action is brought by or on behalf of: (I) A minor under eight years of age who was under six years of age on the date of the occurrence of the act or omission for which the action is brought, in which case the action may be maintained at any time prior to his attaining eight years of age; or (II) A person otherwise under disability as defined in section 13-81-101, in which case the action may be maintained within the time period as provided in section 13-81-103. **Colo. Rev. Stat. § 13-80-106 (2010) Limitation of actions against manufacturers or sellers of products.** (1) Notwithstanding any other statutory provisions to the contrary, all actions except those governed by section 4-2-725, C.R.S., brought against a manufacturer or seller of a product, regardless of the substantive legal theory or theories upon which the action is brought, for or on account of personal injury, death, or property damage caused by or resulting from the manufacture, construction, design, formula, installation, preparation, assembly, testing, packaging, labeling, or sale of any product, or the failure to warn or protect against a danger or hazard in the use, misuse, or unintended use of any product, or the failure to provide proper instructions for the use of any product shall be brought within two years after the claim for relief arises and not thereafter. (2) If any person entitled to bring any action mentioned in this section is under the age of eighteen years, mentally incompetent, imprisoned, or absent from the United States at the time the cause of action accrues and is without spouse or natural or legal guardian, such person may bring said action within the time limit specified in this section after the disab-ility is removed. If such person has a legal representative, such person's representative shall bring the action within the period of limitation imposed by this section.

Table A-6. (Continued)

State	Statute of Limitation
Connecticut	**Conn. Gen. Stat. § 52-584 (2010) Limitation of action for injury to person or property caused by negligence, misconduct or malpractice.** No action to recover damages for injury to the person, or to real or personal property, caused by negligence, or by reckless or wanton misconduct, or by malpractice of a physician, surgeon, dentist, podiatrist, chiropractor, hospital or sanatorium, shall be brought but within two years from the date when the injury is first sustained or discovered or in the exercise of reasonable care should have been discovered, and except that no such action may be brought more than three years from the date of the act or omission complained of, except that a counterclaim may be interposed in any such action any time before the pleadings in such action are finally closed. **Conn. Gen. Stat. § 52-577a (2010) Limitation of action based on product liability claim.** (a) No product liability claim, as defined in section 52-572m, shall be brought but within three years from the date when the injury, death or property damage is first sustained or discovered or in the exercise of reasonable care should have been discovered, except that, subject to the provisions of subsections (c), (d) and (e) of this section, no such action may be brought against any party nor may any party be impleaded pursuant to subsection (b) of this section later than ten years from the date that the party last parted with possession or control of the product. (d) The ten-year limitation provided for in subsection (a) of this section shall be extended pursuant to the terms of any express written warranty that the product can be used for a period longer than ten years, and shall not preclude any action against a product seller who intentionally misrepresents a product or fraudulently conceals information about it, provided the misrepresentation or fraudulent concealment was the proximate cause of harm of the claimant.
Delaware	**Del. Code Ann. tit. 10, § 8128 (2011) Health care malpractice action limitations.** No action for the recovery of damages upon a claim based upon alleged health care malpractice, whether in the nature of a tort action or breach of contract action, shall be brought after the expiration of the time period for bringing such action set forth in § 6856 of Title 18. **Del. Code Ann. tit. 18, § 6856 (2011) Health Care Medical Negligence Insurance and Litigation: General limitations.** No action for the recovery of damages upon a claim against a health care provider for personal injury, including personal injury which results in death, arising out of medical negligence shall be brought after the expiration of 2 years from the date upon which such injury occurred; provided, however, that:
	(1) Solely in the event of personal injury the occurrence of which, during such period of 2 years, was unknown to and could not in the exercise of reasonable diligence have been discovered by the injured person, such action may be brought prior to the expiration of 3 years from the date upon which such injury occurred, and not thereafter; and (2) A minor under the age of 6 years shall have until the latter of time for bringing such an action as provided for hereinabove or until the minor's 6th birthday in which to bring an action. (3) a. Notwithstanding any provision to the contrary, a cause of action based on the sexual abuse of a child patient by a health care provider may be brought at any time following the commission of the act or acts that constituted the sexual abuse. A civil cause of action for sexual abuse of a child patient by a health care provider shall be based upon sexual acts which would constitute a criminal offense under the Delaware Code. **Del. Code Ann. tit. 10, § 8119 (2011) Personal injuries.** No action for the recovery of damages upon a claim for alleged personal injuries shall be brought after the expiration of 2 years from the date upon which it is claimed that

State	Statute of Limitation
	such alleged injuries were sustained; subject, however, to the provisions of § 8127 of this title.
District of Columbia	**D.C. Code § 12-301 (2011) Limitation of time for bringing actions.**Except as otherwise specifically provided by law, actions for the following purposes may not be brought after the expiration of the period specified below from the time the right to maintain the action accrues: (8) for which a limitation is not otherwise specially prescribed—3 years.
Florida	**Fla. Stat. Ann. § 95.11 (2011) Limitations other than for the recovery of real property.** Actions other than for recovery of real property shall be commenced as follows: (4) Within two years. (a) An action for professional malpractice, other than medical malpractice, whether founded on contract or tort; provided that the period of limitations shall run from the time the cause of action is discovered or should have been discovered with the exercise of due diligence. However, the limitation of actions herein for professional malpractice shall be limited to persons in privity with the professional. (b) An action for medical malpractice shall be commenced within 2 years from the time the incident giving rise to the action occurred or within 2 years from the time the incident is discovered, or should have been discovered with the exercise of due diligence; however, in no event shall the action be commenced later than 4 years from the date of the incident or occurrence out of which the cause of action accrued, except that this 4-year period shall not bar an action brought on behalf of a minor on or before the child's eighth birthday. An "action for medical malpractice" is defined as a claim in tort or in contract for damages because of the death, injury, or monetary loss to any person arising out of any medical, dental, or surgical diagnosis, treatment, or care by any provider of health care. The limitation of actions within this subsection shall be limited to the health care provider and persons in privity with the provider of health care. In those actions covered by this paragraph in which it can be shown that fraud, concealment, or intentional misrepres-entation of fact prevented the discovery of the injury the period of limitations is extended forward 2 years from the time that the injury is discovered or should have been disco-vered with the exercise of due diligence, but in no event to exceed 7 years from the date the incident giving rise to the injury occurred, except that this 7-year period shall not bar an action brought on behalf of a minor on or before the child's eighth birthday. This paragraph shall not apply to actions for which ss. 766.301-766.316 provide the exclusive remedy. **Fla. Stat. Ann. § 95.11 (2011) Limitations other than for the recovery of real property.** (3) Within four years. (a) An action founded on negligence (e) An action for injury to a person founded on the design, manufacture, distribution, or sale of personal property that is not permanently incorporated in an improvement to real property, including fixtures. **Fla. Stat. Ann. § 95.031 (2011) Computation of time.** (b) An action for products liability under s. 95.11(3) must be begun within the period prescribed in this chapter, with the period running from the date that the facts giving rise to the cause of action were discovered, or should have been discovered with the exercise of due diligence, rather than running from any other date prescribed elsewhere in s. 95.11(3), except as provided within this subsection. Under no circumstances may a claimant commence an action for products liability, including a wrongful death action or any other claim arising from personal injury or property damage caused by a product, to recover for harm allegedly caused by a product with an expected useful life of 10 years or less, if the harm was caused by exposure to or use of the product more than 12 years after delivery of the product to its first purchaser or lessee who was not engaged in the business of selling or leasing the product or of using the product as a component in the manufacture of another product. All products, except those included

Table A-6. (Continued)

State	Statute of Limitation
	within subparagraph 1. Or subparagraph 2., are conclusively presumed to have an expected useful life of 10 years or less.
Georgia	**Ga. Code Ann. § 9-3-71 (2011) Limitations for Malpractice Actions: General limitation.** (a) Except as otherwise provided in this article, an action for medical malpractice shall be brought within two years after the date on which an injury or death arising from a negligent or wrongful act or omission occurred. (b) Notwithstanding subsection (a) of this Code section, in no event may an action for medical malpractice be brought more than five years after the date on which the negligent or wrongful act or omission occurred. (c) Subsection (a) of this Code section is intended to create a two-year statute of limitations. Subsection (b) of this Code section is intended to create a five-year statute of ultimate repose and abrogation. ***See also*** **Ga. Code Ann. § 9-3-72 (2011) Limitations for Malpractice Actions: Foreign objects left in body; Ga. Code Ann. § 9-3-73 (2011). Limitations for Malpractice Actions: Certain disabilities and exceptions applicable.** **Ga. Code Ann. § 9-3--33 (2011) Injuries to the person; injuries to reputation; loss of consortium; exception.** Actions for injuries to the person shall be brought within two years after the right of action accrues, except for injuries to the reputation, which shall be brought within one year after the right of action accrues, and except for actions for injuries to the person involving loss of consortium, which shall be brought within four years after the right of action accrues.
Hawaii	**Haw. Rev. Stat. Ann. § 657-7 (2011) Damage to persons or property.** Actions for the recovery of compensation for damage or injury to persons or property shall be instituted within two years after the cause of action accrued, and not after, except as provided in section 657-13. **Haw. Rev. Stat. Ann. § 657-7.3 (2011) Medical torts; limitation of actions; time.** No action for injury or death against a chiropractor, clinical laboratory technologist or technician, dentist, naturopathic physician, nurse, nursing home administrator, dispensing optician, optometrist, osteopath, physician or surgeon, physical therapist, podiatrist, psychologist, or veterinarian duly licensed or registered under the laws of the State, or a licensed hospital as the employer of any such person, based upon such person's alleged professional negligence, or for rendering professional services without consent, or for error or omission in such person's practice, shall be brought more than two years after the plaintiff discovers, or through the use of reasonable diligence should have discovered, the injury, but in any event not more than six years after the date of the alleged act or omission causing the injury or death. This six-year time limitation shall be tolled for any period during which the person has failed to disclose any act, error, or omission upon which the action is based and which is known to the person. Actions by a minor shall be commenced within six years from the date of the alleged wrongful act except the actions by a minor under the age of ten years shall be commenced within six years or by the minor's tenth birthday, whichever provides a longer period. Such time limitation shall be tolled for any minor for any period during which the parent, guardian, insurer, or health care provider has committed fraud or gross negligence, or has been a party to a collusion in the failure to bring action on behalf of the injured minor for a medical tort. The time limitation shall also be tolled for any period during which the minor's injury or illness alleged to have arisen, in whole or in part, from the alleged wrongful act or omission could not have been discovered through the use of reasonable diligence.
Idaho	**Idaho Code Ann. § 5-219 (2011) Actions against officers, for penalties, on bonds, and for professional malpractice or for personal injuries.**

State	Statute of Limitation
	Within two (2) years: 4. An action to recover damages for professional malpractice, or for an injury to the person, or for the death of one caused by the wrongful act or neglect of another, including any such action arising from breach of an implied warranty or implied covenant; provided, however, when the action is for damages arising out of the placement and inadvertent, accidental or unintentional leaving of any foreign object in the body of any person by reason of the professional malpractice of any hospital, physician or other person or institution practicing any of the healing arts or when the fact of damage has, for the purpose of escaping responsibility therefor, been fraudulently and knowingly concealed from the injured party by an alleged wrongdoer standing at the time of the wrongful act, neglect or breach in a professional or commercial relationship with the injured party, the same shall be deemed to accrue when the injured party knows or in the exercise of reasonable care should have been put on inquiry regarding the condition or matter complained of; but in all other actions, whether arising from professional malpractice or otherwise, the cause of action shall be deemed to have accrued as of the time of the occurrence, act or omission complained of, and the limitation period shall not be extended by reason of any continuing consequences or damages resulting therefrom or any continuing professional or commercial relationship between the injured party and the alleged wrongdoer, and, provided further, that an action within the foregoing foreign object or fraudulent concealment exceptions must be commenced within one (1) year following the date of accrual as aforesaid or two (2) years following the occurrence, act or omission complained of, whichever is later. The term "professional malpractice" as used herein refers to wrongful acts or omissions in the performance of professional services by any person, firm, association, entity or corporation licensed to perform such services under the law of the state of Idaho. This subsection shall not affect the application of section 5-243, Idaho Code, except as to actions arising from professional malpractice. **Idaho Code Ann. § 6-1403 (2011) Length of time product sellers are subject to liability.** (2) Statute of repose. (a) Generally. In claims that involve harm caused more than ten (10) years after time of delivery, a presumption arises that the harm was caused after the useful safe life had expired. This presumption may only be rebutted by clear and convincing evidence. (b) Limitations on statute of repose. 1. If a product seller expressly warrants that its product can be utilized safely for a period longer than ten (10) years, the period of repose, after which the presumption created in subsection (2)(a) hereof arises, shall be extended according to that warranty or promise. 2. The ten (10) year period of repose established in subsection (2)(a) hereof does not apply if the product seller intentionally misrepresents facts about its product, or fraudulently conceals information about it, and that conduct was a substantial cause of the claimant's harm. 3. Nothing contained in subsection (2) of this section shall affect the right of any person found liable under this chapter to seek and obtain contribution or indemnity from any other person who is responsible for harm under this chapter. 4. The ten (10) year period of repose established in subsection (2)(a) hereof shall not apply if the harm was caused by prolonged exposure to a defective product, or if the injury-causing aspect of the product that existed at the time of delivery was not discoverable by an ordinary reasonably prudent person until more than ten (10) years after the time of delivery, or if the harm, caused within ten (10) years after the time of delivery, did not manifest itself until after that time. (3) Statute of limitation. No claim under this chapter may be brought more than two (2) years from the time the cause of action accrued as defined in section 5-219, Idaho Code
Illinois	**735 Ill. Comp. Stat. Ann. 5/13-212 (2011) Personal Actions: Physician or hospital.** (a) Except as provided in Section 13-215 of this Act, no action for damages for injury or death against any physician, dentist, registered nurse or hospital duly licensed under

Table A-6. (Continued)

State	Statute of Limitation
	the laws of this State, whether based upon tort, or breach of contract, or otherwise, arising out of patient care shall be brought more than 2 years after the date on which the claimant knew, or through the use of reasonable diligence should have known, or received notice in writing of the existence of the injury or death for which damages are sought in the action, whichever of such date occurs first, but in no event shall such action be brought more than 4 years after the date on which occurred the act or omission or occurrence alleged in such action to have been the cause of such injury or death. (b) Except as provided in Section 13-215 of this Act, no action for damages for injury or death against any physician, dentist, registered nurse or hospital duly licensed under the laws of this State, whether based upon tort, or breach of contract, or otherwise, arising out of patient care shall be brought more than 8 years after the date on which occurred the act or omission or occurrence alleged in such action to have been the cause of such injury or death where the person entitled to bring the action was, at the time the cause of action accrued, under the age of 18 years; provided, however, that in no event may the cause of action be brought after the person's 22nd birthday. If the person was under the age of 18 years when the cause of action accrued and, as a result of this amendatory Act of 1987, the action is either barred or there remains less than 3 years to bring such action, then he or she may bring the action within 3 years of July 20, 1987. (c) If the person entitled to bring an action described in this Section is, at the time the cause of action accrued, under a legal disability other than being under the age of 18 years, then the period of limitations does not begin to run until the disability is removed. **735 Ill. Comp. Stat. Ann. 5/13-213 (2011) Product liability; statute of repose.** (a) As used in this Section, the term: (3) "Product liability action" means any action based on any theory or doctrine brought against theseller of a product on account of personal injury, (including illness, disease, disability and death) or property, economic or other damage allegedly caused by or resulting from the manufacture, construction, preparation, assembly, installation, testing, makeup, characteristics, functions, design, formula, plan, recommendation, specification, prescription, advertising, sale, marketing, packaging, labeling, repair, maintenance or disposal of, or warning or instruction regarding any product. This definition excludes actions brought by State or federal regulatory agencies pursuant to statute. (b) Subject to the provisions of subsections (c) and (d) no product liability action based on the doctrine of strict liability in tort shall be commenced except within the applicable limitations period and, in any event, within 12 years from the date of first sale, lease or delivery of possession by a seller or 10 years from the date of first sale, lease or delivery of possession to its initial user, consumer, or other non-seller, whichever period expires earlier, of any product unit that is claimed to have injured or damaged the plaintiff, unless the defendant expressly has warranted or promised the product for a longer period and the action is brought within that period. (c) No product liability action based on the doctrine of strict liability in tort to recover for injury or damage claimed to have resulted from an alteration, modification or change of the product unit subsequent to the date of first sale, lease or delivery of possession of the product unit to its initial user, consumer or other non-seller shall be limited or barred by subsection (b) hereof if: (1) the action is brought against a seller making, authorizing, or furnishing materials for the accomplishment of such alteration, modification or change (or against a seller furnish-ing specifications or instructions for the accomplishment of such alteration, modification or change when the injury is claimed to have resulted from failure to provide adequate specifications or instructions), and

State	Statute of Limitation
	(2) the action commenced within the applicable limitation period and, in any event, within 10 years from the date such alteration, modification or change was made, unless defendant expressly has warranted or promised the product for a longer period and the action is brought within that period, and (3) when the injury or damage is claimed to have resulted from an alteration, modification or change of a product unit, there is proof that such alteration, modification or change had the effect of introducing into the use of the product unit, by reason of defective materials or workmanship, a hazard not existing prior to such alteration, modification or change. (d) Notwithstanding the provisions of subsection (b) and paragraph (2) of subsection (c) if the injury complained of occurs within any of the periods provided by subsection (b) and paragraph (2) of subsection (c), the plaintiff may bring an action within 2 years after the date on which the claimant knew, or through the use of reasonable diligence should have known, of the existence of the personal injury, death or property damage, but in no event shall such action be brought more than 8 years after the date on which such personal injury, death or property damage occurred. In any such case, if the person entitled to bring the action was, at the time the personal injury, death or property damage occurred, under the age of 18 years, or under a legal disability, then the period of limitations does not begin to run until the person attains the age of 18 years, or the disability is removed. (e) Replacement of a component part of a product unit with a substitute part having the same formula or design as the original part shall not be deemed a sale, lease or delivery of possession or an alteration, modification or change for the purpose of permitting commencement of a product liability action based on the doctrine of strict liability in tort to recover for injury or damage claimed to have resulted from the formula or design of such product unit or of the substitute partwhen such action would otherwise be barred according to the provisions of subsection (b) of this Section.
Indiana	**Ind. Code Ann. § 34-18-7-1 (2011) Medical Malpractice: Limitations.** (a) This section applies to all persons regardless of minority or other legal disability, except as provided in subsection (c). (b) A claim, whether in contract or tort, may not be brought against a health care provider based upon professional services or health care that was provided or that should have been provided unless the claim is filed within two (2) years after the date of the alleged act, omission, or neglect, except that a minor less than six (6) years of age has until the minor's eighth birthday to file. (c) If a patient meets the criteria stated in IC 34-18-8-6(c), the applicable limitations period is equal to the period that would otherwise apply to the patient under subsection (b) (or IC 27-12-7-1(b) before its repeal) plus one hundred eighty (180) days. **Ind. Code Ann. § 34-20-3-1 (2011) General statute of limitations.** (a) This section applies to all persons regardless of minority or legal disability. Notwithstanding IC 34-11-6-1, this section applies in any product liability action in which the theory of liability is negligence or strict liability in tort. (b) Except as provided in section 2 [IC 34-20-3-2] of this chapter, a product liability action must be commenced: (1) within two (2) years after the cause of action accrues; or (2) within ten (10) years after the delivery of the product to the initial user or consumer. However, if the cause of action accrues at least eight (8) years but less than ten (10) years after that initial delivery, the action may be commenced at any time within two (2) years after the cause of action accrues.
Iowa	**Iowa Code Ann. § 614.1 (2010) Limitations of Actions: Period.** Actions may be brought within the times herein limited, respectively, after their causes accrue, and not afterwards, except when otherwise specially declared: 9. Malpractice. a. Except as provided in paragraph "b", those founded on injuries to the person or wrongful death against any physician and surgeon, osteopathic physician and surgeon, dentist, podiatric physician, optometrist, pharmacist, chiropractor, physician assistant, or nurse, licensed under chapter 147, or a hospital licensed under chapter 135B,

Table A-6. (Continued)

State	Statute of Limitation
	arising out of patient care, within two years after the date on which the claimant knew, or through the use of reasonable diligence should have known, or received notice in writing of the existence of, the injury or death for which damages are sought in the action, whichever of the dates occurs first, but in no event shall any action be brought more than six years after the date on which occurred the act or omission or occurrence alleged in the action to have been the cause of the injury or death unless a foreign object unintentionallyleft in the body caused the injury or death. b. An action subject to paragraph "a" and brought on behalf of a minor who was under the age of eight years when the act, omission, or occurrence alleged in the action occurred shall be commenced no later than the minor's tenth birthday or as provided in paragraph "a", whichever is later. **Iowa Code Ann. § 614.1 (2010) Limitations of Actions: Period.** Actions may be brought within the times herein limited, respectively, after their causes accrue, and not afterwards, except when otherwise specially declared: 2A. With respect to products. a. Those founded on the death of a person or injuries to the person or property brought against the manufacturer, assembler, designer, supplier of specifications, seller, lessor, or distributor of a product based upon an alleged defect in the design, inspection, testing, manufacturing, formulation, marketing, packaging, warning, labeling of the product, or any other alleged defect or failure of whatever nature or kind, based on the theories of strict liability in tort, negligence, or breach of an implied warranty shall not be commenced more than fifteen years after the product was first purchased, leased, bailed, or installed for use or consumption unless expressly warranted for a longer period of time by the manufacturer, assembler, designer, supplier of specifications, seller, lessor, or distributor of the product. This subsection shall not affect the time during which a person found liable may seek and obtain contribution or indemnity from another person whose actual fault caused a product to be defective. This subsection shall not apply if the manufacturer, assembler, designer, supplier of specifications, seller, lessor, or distributor of the product intentionally misrepresents facts about the product or fraudulently conceals information about the product and that conduct was a substantial cause of the claimant's harm. b. (1) The fifteen-year limitation in paragraph "a" shall not apply to the time period in which to discover a disease that is latent and caused by exposure to a harmful material, in which event the cause of action shall be deemed to have accrued when the disease and such disease's cause have been made known to the person or at the point the person should have been aware of the disease and such disease's cause. This subsection shall not apply to cases governed by subsection 11 of this section. (2) As used in this paragraph, "harmful material" means silicone gel breast implants, which were implanted prior to July 12, 1992; and chemical substances commonly known as asbestos, dioxins, tobacco, or polychlorinated biphenyls, whether alone or as part of any product; or any substance which is determined to present an unreasonable risk of injury to health or the environment by the United States environmental protection agency pursuant to the federal Toxic Substance Control Act, 15 U.S.C. § 2601 et seq., or by this state, if that risk is regulated by the United States environmental protection agency or this state.
Kansas	**Kan. Stat. Ann. § 60-513 (2009) Personal Actions and General Provisions: Actions limited to two years.** (a) The following actions shall be brought within two years: (5) An action for wrongful death. (7) An action arising out of the rendering of or failure to render professional services by a health care provider, not arising on contract. (b) Except as provided in subsections (c) and (d), the causes of action listed in subsection (a) shall not be deemed to have accrued until the act giving rise to the cause

State	Statute of Limitation
	of action first causes substantial injury, or, if the fact of injury is not reasonably ascertainable until some time after the initial act, then the period of limitation shall not commence until the fact of injury becomes reasonably ascertainable to the injured party, (c) A cause of action arising out of the rendering of or the failure to render professional services by a health care provider shall be deemed to have accrued at the time of the occurrence of the act giving rise to the cause of action, unless the fact of injury is not reasonably ascertainable until some time after the initial act, then the period of limitation shall not commence until the fact of injury becomes reasonably ascertainable but in no event shall an action be commenced more than 10 years beyond the time of the act giving rise to the cause of action. to the injured party, but in no event shall such an action be commenced more than four years beyond the time of the act giving rise to the cause of action. **Kan. Stat. Ann. § 60-3303 (2009) Useful safe life ten-year period of repose; evidence; latent disease exception; reviving certain causes of action.** (a)(2) A product seller may be subject to liability for harm caused by a product used beyond its useful safe life to the extent that the product seller has expressly warranted the product for a longer period. (b) (1) In claims that involve harm caused more than 10 years after time of delivery, a presumption arises that the harm was caused after the useful safe life had expired. This presumption may only be rebutted by clear and convincing evidence. (2) (A) If a product seller expressly warrants that its product can be utilized safely for a period longer than 10 years, the period of repose, after which the presumption created in paragraph (1) of this subsection arises, shall be extended according to that warranty or promise. (B) The ten-year period of repose established in paragraph (1) of this subsection does not apply if the product seller intentionally misrepresents facts about its product, or fraudulently conceals information about it, and that conduct was a substantial cause of the claimant's harm. (C) Nothing contained in this subsection shall affect the right of any person liable under a product liability claim to seek and obtain indemnity from any other person who is responsible for the harm which gave rise to the product liability claim. (D) The ten-year period of repose established in paragraph (1) of this subsection shall not apply if the harm was caused by prolonged exposure to a defective product, or if the injury-causing aspect of the product that existed at the time of delivery was not discoverable by a reasonably prudent person until more than 10 years after the time of delivery, or if the harm caused within 10 years after the time of delivery, did not manifest itself until after that time. (c) Except as provided in subsections (d) and (e), nothing contained in subsections (a) and (b) above shall modify the application of K.S.A. 60-513, and amendments thereto (d) (1) In a product liability claim against the product seller, the ten-year limitation, as defined in K.S.A. 60-513, and amendments thereto, shall not apply to the time to discover a disease which is latent caused by exposure to a harmful material, in which event the action shall be deemed to have accrued when the disease and such disease's cause have been made known to the person or at the point the person should have been aware of the disease and such disease's cause.
Kentucky	**Ky. Rev. Stat. Ann. § 413.140 (2010) Actions Other Than Those Relating to Real Property: Actions to be brought within one (1) year.** (1) The following actions shall be commenced within one (1) year after the cause of action accrued: (e) An action against a physician, surgeon, dentist, or hospital licensed pursuant to KRS Chapter 216, for negligence or malpractice; (f) A civil action, arising out of any act or omission in rendering, or failing to render, professional services for others, whether brought in tort or contract, against a real estate appraiser holding a certificate or license issued under KRS Chapter 324A; 2) In respect to the action referred to in paragraph (e) of subsection (1) of this section,

Table A-6. (Continued)

State	Statute of Limitation
	the cause of action shall be deemed to accrue at the time the injury is first discovered or in the exercise of reasonable care should have been discovered; provided that such action shall be commenced within five (5) years from the date on which the alleged the cause of action shall be deemed to accrue within one (1) year from the date of the occurrence or from the date when the cause of action was, or reasonably should have been, discovered by the party injured. **Ky. Rev. Stat. Ann. § 413.140 (2010) Actions Other Than Those Relating to Real Property: Actions to be brought within one (1) year.** negligent act or omission is said to have occurred. (3) In respect to the action referred to in paragraph (f) of subsection (1) of this section, (1) The following actions shall be commenced within one (1) year after the cause of action accrued: (a) An action for an injury to the person of the plaintiff, or of her husband, his wife, child, ward, apprentice, or servant.
Louisiana	**La. Rev. Stat. Ann. § 9:5628 (2011) Actions for medical malpractice.** A. No action for damages for injury or death against any physician, chiropractor, nurse, licensed midwife practitioner, dentist, psychologist, optometrist, hospital or nursing home duly licensed under the laws of this state, or community blood center or tissue bank as defined in R.S. 40:1299.41(A), whether based upon tort, or breach of contract, or otherwise, arising out of patient care shall be brought unless filed within one year from the date of the alleged act, omission, or neglect, or within one year from the date of discovery of the alleged act, omission, or neglect; however, even as to claims filed within one year from the date of such discovery, in all events such claims shall be filed at the latest within a period of three years from the date of the alleged act, omission, or neglect. B. The provisions of this Section shall apply to all persons whether or not infirm or under disability of any kind and including minors and interdicts. C. The provisions of this Section shall apply to all healthcare providers listed herein or defined in R.S. 40:1299.41 regardless of whether the healthcare provider avails itself of the protections and provisions of R.S. 40:1299.41 et seq., by fulfilling the requirements necessary to qualify as listed in R.S. 40:1299.42 and 1299.44. **La. C.C. Art. 3492 (2011) Delictual actions.** Delictual actions are subject to a liberative prescription of one year. This prescription commences to run from the day injury or damage is sustained. It does not run against minors or interdicts in actions involving permanent disability and brought pursuant to the Louisiana Products Liability Act or state law governing product liability actions in effect at the time of the injury or damage.
Maine	**Me. Rev. Stat. tit. 24, § 2902 (2011) Statute of limitations for health care providers and health care practitioners.** Actions for professional negligence shall be commenced within 3 years after the cause of action accrues. For the purposes of this section, a cause of action accrues on the date of the act or omission giving rise to the injury. Notwithstanding the provisions of Title 14, section 853, relating to minority, actions for professional negligence by a minor shall be commenced within 6 years after the cause of action accrues or within 3 years after the minor reaches the age of majority, whichever first occurs. This section does not apply where the cause of action is based upon the leaving of a foreign object in the body, in which case the cause of action shall accrue when the plaintiff discovers or reasonably should have discovered the harm. For the purposes of this section, the term "foreign object" does not include a chemical compound, prosthetic aid or object intentionally implanted or permitted to remain in the patient's body as a part of the health care or professional services. If the provision in this section reducing the time allowed for a minor to bring a claim is found to be void or otherwise invalidated by a court of proper jurisdiction, then the statute of limitations for professional negligence shall be 2 years after the cause of

State	Statute of Limitation
	action accrues, except that no claim brought under the 3-year statute may be extinguished by the operation of this paragraph. **Me. Rev. Stat. tit. 14, § 752 (2011) Limitations of Actions: Six years.** All civil actions shall be commenced within 6 years after the cause of action accrues and not afterwards, except actions on a judgment or decree of any court of record of the United States, or of any state, or of a justice of the peace in this State, and except as otherwise specially provided.
Maryland	**Md. Code Ann., Cts. & Jud. Proc. § 5-109 (2011) Actions against health care providers.** (a) Limitations.—An action for damages for an injury arising out of the rendering of or failure to render professional services by a health care provider, as defined in § 3-2A-01 of this article, shall be filed within the earlier of: (1) Five years of the time the injury was committed; or (2) Three years of the date the injury was discovered. (b) Actions by claimants under age 11.—Except as provided in subsection (c) of this section, if the claimant was under the age of 11 years at the time the injury was committed, the time limitations prescribed in subsection (a) of this section shall commence when the claimant reaches the age of 11 years. (c) Exceptions to age limitations in certain actions.— (1) The provisions of subsection (b) of this section may not be applied to an action for damages for an injury: (i) To the reproductive system of the claimant; or (ii) Caused by a foreign object negligently left in the claimant's body. (2) In an action for damages for an injury described in this subsection, if the claimant was under the age of 16 years at the time the injury was committed, the time limitations prescribed in subsection (a) of this section shall commence when the claimant reaches the age of 16 years. **Md. Code Ann., Cts. & Jud. Proc. § 5-101 (2011) Three-year limitation in general** A civil action at law shall be filed within three years from the date it accrues unless another provision of the Code provides a different period of time within which an action shall be commenced.
Massachus-etts	**Mass. Ann. Laws, ch. 260, § 4 (2010) Limitation of Three Years; Limitation of One Year for Certain Action.** Actions of contract or tort for malpractice, error or mistake against physicians, surgeons, dentists, optometrists, hospitals and sanitoria shall be commenced only within three years after the cause of action accrues, but in no event shall any such action be commenced more than seven years after occurrence of the act or omission which is the alleged cause of the injury upon which such action is based except where the action is based upon the leaving of a foreign object in the body. **Mass. Ann. Laws, ch. 231, § 60D (2010) Limitation of Actions by Minors.** Notwithstanding the provisions of section seven of chapter two hundred and sixty, any claim by a minor against a health care provider stemming from professional services or health care rendered, whether in contract or tort, based on an alleged act, omission or neglect shall be commenced within three years from the date the cause of action accrues, except that a minor under the full age of six years shall have until his ninth birthday in which the action may be commenced, but in no event shall any such action be commenced more than seven years after occurrence of the act or omission which is the alleged cause of the injury upon which such action is based except where the action is based upon the leaving of a foreign object in the body. **Mass. Ann. Laws, ch. 260, § 2A (2010) Limitation of Three Years in Certain Cases.** Except as otherwise provided, actions of tort, actions of contract to recover for personal injuries, and actions of replevin, shall be commenced only within three years next after the cause of action accrues.
Michigan	**Mich. Comp. Laws. Serv. § 600.5838a (2011) Claim based on medical malpractice; accrual; definitions; commencement of action; burden of proof; applicability of subsection (2); limitations.**

Table A-6. (Continued)

State	Statute of Limitation
	(1) For purposes of this act, a claim based on the medical malpractice of a person or entity who is or who holds himself or herself out to be a licensed health care professional, licensed health facility or agency, or an employee or agent of a licensed health facility or agency who is engaging in or otherwise assisting in medical care and treatment, whether or not the licensed health care professional, licensed health facility or agency, or their employee or agent is engaged in the practice of the health profession in a sole proprietorship, partnership, professional corporation, or other business entity, accrues at the time of the act or omission that is the basis for the claim of medical malpractice, regardless of the time the plaintiff discovers or otherwise has knowledge of the claim. (2) Except as otherwise provided in this subsection, an action involving a claim based on medical malpractice may be commenced at any time within the applicable period prescribed in section 5805 or sections 5851 to 5856, or within 6 months after the plaintiff discovers or should have discovered the existence of the claim, whichever is later. However, except as otherwise provided in section 5851(7) or (8), the claim shall not be commenced later than 6 years after the date of the act or omission that is the basis for the claim. The burden of proving that the plaintiff, as a result of physical discomfort, appearance, condition, or otherwise, neither discovered nor should have discovered the existence of the claim at least 6 months before the expiration of the period otherwise applicable to the claim is on the plaintiff. A medical malpractice action that is not commenced within the time prescribed by this subsection is barred. This subsection does not apply, and the plaintiff is subject to the period of limitations set forth in subsection (3), under 1 of the following circumstances: (a) If discovery of the existence of the claim was prevented by the fraudulent conduct of the health care professional against whom the claim is made or a named employee or agent of the health professional against whom the claim is made, or of the health facility against whom the claim is made or a named employee or agent of a health facility against whom the claim is made. (b) There has been permanent loss of or damage to a reproductive organ resulting in the inability to procreate. (3) An action involving a claim based on medical malpractice under circumstances described in subsection (2)(a) or (b) may be commenced at any time within the applicable period prescribed in section 5805 or sections 5851 to 5856, or within 6 months after the plaintiff discovers or should have discovered the existence of the claim, whichever is later. The burden of proving that the plaintiff, as a result of physical discomfort, appearance, condition or otherwise, neither discovered nor should have discovered the existence of the claim at least 6 months before the expiration of the period otherwise applicable to the claim is on the plaintiff. A medical malpractice action that is not commenced within the time prescribed by this subsection is barred. ***See also* Mich. Comp. Laws. Serv. § 600.5851 (2011) Disabilities of infancy or insanity; tacking of successive disabilities prohibited; year of grace; removing disability of infancy; claim alleging medical malpractice accruing to person 8 years old or less or 13 years old or less.** **Mich. Comp. Laws. Serv. § 600.5805 (2011) Injuries to persons or property; limitations.** (1) A person shall not bring or maintain an action to recover damages for injuries to persons or property unless, after the claim first accrued to the plaintiff or to someone through whom the plaintiff claims, the action is commenced within the periods of time prescribed by this section. (10) The period of limitations is 3 years after the time of the death or injury for all other actions to recover damages for the death of a person, or for injury to a person or property. (13) The period of limitations is 3 years for a products liability action. However, in the case of a product that has been in use for not less than10 years, the plaintiff, in proving a prima facie case, shall be required to do so without benefit of anypresumption.

State	Statute of Limitation
Minnesota	**Minn. Stat. Ann. § 541.076 (2010) Health Care Provider Actions.** (a) For purposes of this section, "health care provider" means a physician, surgeon, dentist, occupational therapist, other health care professionals as defined in section 145.61, hospital, or treatment facility. (b) An action by a patient or former patient against a health care provider alleging malpractice, error, mistake, or failure to cure, whether based on a contract or tort, must be commenced within four years from the date the cause of action accrued. ***See also* Minn. Stat. Ann. § 541.15 (2010) Periods Of Disability Not Counted.** **Minn. Stat. Ann. § 541.05 (2010) Various Cases, Six Years.** Subd. 2. Strict liability. Unless otherwise provided by law, any action based on the strict liability of the defendant and arising from the manufacture, sale, use or consumption of a product shall be commenced within four years. **Minn. Stat. Ann. § 541.07 (2010) Two- Or Three-Year Limitations.** Except where the Uniform Commercial Code, this section, section 541.05, 541.073, 541.076, or 604.205 otherwise prescribes, the following actions shall be commenced within two years: (1) for libel, slander, assault, battery, false imprisonment, or other tort resulting in personal injury, and all actions against veterinarians as defined in chapter 156, for malpractice, error, mistake, or failure to cure, whether based on contract or tort; provided a counterclaim may be pleaded as a defense to any action for services brought by a veterinarian after the limitations period if it was the property of the party pleading it at the time it became barred and was not barred at the time the claim sued on originated, but no judgment thereof except for costs can be rendered in favor of the party so pleading it.
Mississippi	**Miss. Code Ann. § 15-1-36 (2010) Limitations applicable to malpractice action arising from medical, surgical or other professional services.** (2) For any claim accruing on or after July 1, 1998, and except as otherwise provided in this section, no claim in tort may be brought against a licensed physician, osteopath, dentist, hospital, institution for the aged or infirm, nurse, pharmacist, podiatrist, optometrist or chiropractor for injuries or wrongful death arising out of the course of medical, surgical or other professional services unless it is filed within two (2) years from the date the alleged act, omission or neglect shall or with reasonable diligence might have been first known or discovered, and, except as described in paragraphs (a) and (b) of this subsection, in no event more than seven (7) years after the alleged act, omission or neglect occurred: (a) In the event a foreign object introduced during a surgical or medical procedure has been left in a patient's body, the cause of action shall be deemed to have first accrued at, and not before, the time at which the foreign object is, or with reasonable diligence should have been, first known or discovered to be in the patient's body. (b) In the event the cause of action shall have been fraudulently concealed from the knowledge of the person entitled thereto, the cause of action shall be deemed to have first accrued at, and not before, the time at which such fraud shall be, or with reasonable diligence should have been, first known or discovered. (3) Except as otherwise provided in subsection (4) of this section, if at the time at which the cause of action shall or with reasonable diligence might have been first known or discovered, the person to whom such claim has accrued shall be six (6) years of age or younger, then such minor or the person claiming through such minor may, notwithstanding that the period of time limited pursuant to subsections (1) and (2) of this section shall have expired, commence action on such claim at any time within two (2) years next after the time at which the minor shall have reached his sixth birthday, or shall have died, whichever shall have first occurred. (4) If at the time at which the cause of action shall or with reasonable diligence might have been first known or discovered, the person to whom such claim has accrued shall be a minor without a parent or legal guardian, then such minor or the person claiming through such minor may, notwithstanding that the period of time limited pursuant to subsections (1) and (2) of this section shall have expired, commence action on such claim at any time within two (2) years next after the time at which the minor shall have

Table A-6. (Continued)

State	Statute of Limitation
	a parent or legal guardian or shall have died, whichever shall have first occurred; provided, however, that in no event shall the period of limitation begin to run prior to such minor's sixth birthday unless such minor shall have died. (5) If at the time at which the cause of action shall or with reasonable diligence might have been first known or discovered, the person to whom such claim has accrued shall be under the disability of unsoundness of mind, then such person or the person claiming through him may, notwithstan-ding that the period of time hereinbefore limited shall have expired, commence action on such claim at any time within two (2) years next after the time at which the person to whom the right shall have first accrued shall have ceased to be under the disability, or shall have died, whichever shall have first occurred. (6) When any person who shall be under the disabilities mentioned in subsections (3), (4) and (5) of this section at the time at which his right shall have first accrued, shall depart this life without having ceased to be under such disability, no time shall be allowed by reason of the disability of such person to commence action on the claim of such person beyond the period prescribed under Section 15-1-55, Mississippi Code of 1972. (7) For the purposes of subsection (3) of this section, and only for the purposes of such subsection, the disability of infancy or minority shall be removed from and after a person has reached his sixth birthday. (8) For the purposes of subsection (4) of this section, and only for the purposes of such subsection, the disability of infancy or minority shall be removed from and after a person has reached his sixth birthday or from and after such person shall have a parent or legal guardian, whichever occurs later, unless such disability is otherwise removed by law. **Miss. Code Ann. § 15-1-49 (2010) Limitations applicable to actions not otherwise specifically provided for.** (1) All actions for which no other period of limitation is prescribed shall be commenced within three (3) years next after the cause of such action accrued, and not after. (2) In actions for which no other period of limitation is prescribed and which involve latent injury or disease, the cause of action does not accrue until the plaintiff has discovered, or by reasonable diligence should have discovered, the injury. (3) The provisions of subsection (2) of this section shall apply to all pending and subsequently filed actions.
Missouri	**Mo. Rev. Stat. § 516.105 (2011) Actions against health care providers (medical malpractice).** All actions against physicians, hospitals, dentists, registered or licensed practical nurses, optometrists, podiatrists, pharmacists, chiropractors, professional physical therapists, and any other entity providing health care services and all employees of any of the foregoing acting in the course and scope of their employment, for damages for malpractice, negligence, error or mistake related to health care shall be brought within two years from the date of occurrence of the act of neglect complained of, except that: (1) In cases in which the act of neglect complained of is introducing and negligently permitting any foreign object to remain within the body of a living person, the action shall be brought within two years from the date of the discovery of such alleged negligence, or from the date on which the patient in the exercise of ordinary care should have discovered such alleged negligence, whichever date first occurs; and (2) In cases in which the act of neglect complained of is the negligent failure to inform the patient of the results of medical tests, the action for failure to inform shall be brought within two years from the date of the discovery of such alleged negligent failure to inform, or from the date on which the patient in the exercise of ordinary care should have discovered such alleged negligent failure to inform, whichever date first occurs; except that, no such action shall be brought for any negligent failure to inform about the results of medical tests performed more than two years before August 28,

State	Statute of Limitation
	1999. For purposes of this subdivision, the act of neglect based on the negligent failure to inform the patient of the results of medical tests shall not include the act of informing the patient of the results of negligently performed medical tests or the act of informing the patient of erroneous test results; and (3) In cases in which the person bringing the action is a minor less than eighteen years of age, such minor shall have until his or hertwentieth birthday to bring such action. In no event shall any action for damages for malpractice, error, or mistake be commenced after the expiration of ten years from the date of the act of neglect complained of or for two years from a minor's eighteenth birthday, whichever is later. **Mo. Rev. Stat. § 516.120 (2011) What actions within five years.** Within five years: (4) An action **** for any other injury to the person or rights of another, not arising on contract and not herein otherwise enumerated.
Montana	**Mont. Code Ann. § 27-2-205 (2010) Actions for medical malpractice.** (1) Action in tort or contract for injury or death against a physician or surgeon, dentist, registered nurse, nursing home or hospital administrator, dispensing optician, optometrist, licensed physical therapist, podiatrist, psychologist, osteopath, chiropractor, clinical laboratory bioanalyst, clinical laboratory technologist, pharmacist, veterinarian, a licensed hospital or long-term care facility, or licensed medical professional corporation, based upon alleged professional negligence or for rendering professional services without consent or for an act, error, or omission, must, except as provided in subsection (2), be commenced within 3 years after the date of injury or within 3 years after the plaintiff discovers or through the use of reasonable diligence should have discovered the injury, whichever occurs last, but in no case may an action be commenced after 5 years from the date of injury. However, this time limitation is tolled for any period during which there has been a failure to disclose any act, error, or omission upon which an action is based and that is known to the defendant or through the use of reasonable diligence subsequent to the act, error, or omission would have been known to the defendant. (2) Notwithstanding the provisions of 27-2-401, in an action for death or injury of a minor who was under the age of 4 on the date of the minor's injury, the period of limitations in subsection (1) begins to run when the minor reaches the minor's eighth birthday or dies, whichever occurs first, and the time for commencement of the action is tolled during any period during which the minor does not reside with a parent or guardian. **Mont. Code Ann. § 27-2-204 (2010) Tort actions—general and personal injury.** (1) Except as provided in 27-2-216 and 27-2-217, the period prescribed for the commencement of an action upon a liability not founded upon an instrument in writing is within 3 years. (2) The period prescribed for the commencement of an action to recover damages for the death of one caused by the wrongful act or neglect of another is within 3 years, except when the wrongful death is the result of a homicide, in which case the period is within 10 years.
Nebraska	**Neb. Rev. Stat. Ann. § 44-2828 (2010) Nebraska Hospital-Medical Liability Act: Action to recover damages; limitation of action.** Except as provided in section 25-213, any action to recover damages based on alleged malpractice or professional negligence or upon alleged breach of warranty in rendering or failing to render professional services shall be commenced within two years next after the alleged act or omission in rendering or failing to render professional services providing the basis for such action, exceptthat if the cause of action is not discovered and could not be reasonably discovered within such two-year period, the action may be commenced within one year from the date of such discovery or from the date of discovery of facts which would reasonably lead to such discovery, whichever is earlier. In no event may any action be commenced to recover damages for malpractice or professional negligence or breach of warranty in rendering or failing to render

Table A-6. (Continued)

State	Statute of Limitation
	professional services more than ten years after the date of rendering or failing to render such professional service which provides the basis for the cause of action. **Neb. Rev. Stat. Ann. § 25-222 (2010) Actions on professional negligence.** Any action to recover damages based on alleged professional negligence or upon alleged breach of warranty in rendering or failure to render professional services shallbe commenced within two years next after the alleged act or omission in rendering or failure to render professional services providing the basis for such action; Provided, if the cause of action is not discovered and could not be reasonably discovered within such two-year period, then the action may be commenced within one year from the date of such discovery or from the date of discovery of facts which would reasonably lead to such discovery, whichever is earlier; and provided further, that in no event may any action be commenced to recover damages for professional negligence or breach of warranty in rendering or failure to render professional services more than ten years after the date of rendering or failure to render such professional service which provides the basis for the cause of action. **Neb. Rev. Stat. Ann. § 25-224 (2010) Actions on product liability.** (1) All product liability actions, except one governed by subsection (5) of this section, shall be commenced within four years next after the date on which the death, injury, or damage complained of occurs. (2) (a) Notwithstanding subsection (1) of this section or any other statutory provision to the contrary, any product liability action, except one governed by section 2-725, Uniform Commercial Code or by subsection (5) of this section, shall be commenced as follows: (i) For products manufactured in Nebraska, within ten years after the date the product which allegedly caused the personal injury, death, or damage was first sold or leased for use or consumption; or (ii) For products manufactured outside Nebraska, within the time allowed by the applicable statute of repose, if any, of the state or country where the product was manufactured, but in no event less than ten years. If the state or country where the product was manufactured does not have an applicable statute of repose, then the only limitation upon the commencement of an action for product liability shall be as set forth in subsection (1) of this section. (b) If the changes made to this subsection by Laws 2001, LB 489, are declared invalid or unconstitutional, this subsection as it existed prior to September 1, 2001, shall be deemed in full force and effect and shall apply to all claims in which a final order has not been entered.
Nevada	**Nev. Rev. Stat. Ann. § 41A.097 (2010) Action for Medical or Dental** ***See also*** **Malpractice: Limitation of actions; tolling of limitation.** 1. Except as otherwise provided in subsection 3, an action for injury or death against a provider of health care may not be commenced more than 4 years after the date of injury or 2 years after the plaintiff discovers or through the use of reasonable diligence should have discovered the injury, whichever occurs first, for: (a) Injury to or the wrongful death of a person occurring before October 1, 2002, based upon alleged professional negligence of the provider of health care; (b) Injury to or the wrongful death of a person occurring before October 1, 2002, from professional services rendered without consent; or (c) Injury to or the wrongful death of a person occurring before October 1, 2002, from error or omission in practice by the provider of health care. 2. Except as otherwise provided in subsection 3, an action for injury or death against a provider of health care may not be commenced more than 3 years after the date of injury or 1 year after the plaintiff discovers or through the use of reasonable diligence should have discovered the injury, whichever occurs first, for: (a) Injury to or the wrongful death of a person occurring on or after October 1, 2002, based upon alleged professional negligence of the provider of health care;

State	Statute of Limitation
	(b) Injury to or the wrongful death of a person occurring on or after October 1, 2002, from professional services rendered without consent; or (c) Injury to or the wrongful death of a person occurring on or after October 1, 2002, from error or omission in practice by the provider of health care. 3. This time limitation is tolled for any period during which the provider of health care has concealed any act, error or omission upon which the action is based and which is known or through the use of reasonable diligence should have been known to the provider of health care. 4. For the purposes of this section, the parent, guardian or legal custodian of any minor child is responsible for exercising reasonable judgment in determining whether to prosecute any cause of action limited by subsection 1 or 2. If the parent, guardian or custodian fails to commence an action on behalf of that child within the prescribed period of limitations, the child may not bring an action based on the same alleged injury against any provider of health care upon the removal of the child's disability, except that in the case of: (a) Brain damage or birth defect, the period of limitation is extended until the child attains 10 years of age. (b) Sterility, the period of limitation is extended until 2 years after the child discovers the injury. **Nev. Rev. Stat. Ann. § 11.190 (2010) Periods of limitation.** Except as otherwise provided in NRS 125B.050; and 217.007, actions other than those for the recovery of real property, unless further limited by specific statute, may only be commenced as follows: 4. Within 2 years: (e) Except as otherwise provided in NRS 11.215, an action to recover damages for injuries to a person or for the death of a person caused by the wrongful act or neglect of another. The provisions of this paragraph relating to an action to recover damages for injuries to a person apply only to causes of action which accrue after March 20, 1951. **Nev. Rev. Stat. Ann. § 11.220 (2010) Action for relief not otherwise provided for.** An action for relief, not hereinbefore provided for, must be commenced within 4 years after the cause of action shall have accrued.
New Hampshire	**N.H. Rev. Stat Ann. § 507-C:4 (2011) Actions for Medical Injury: Statute of Limitations.** Notwithstanding any other provision of law, all actions for medical injury shall be commenced within 2 years of the act, omission or failure complained of, except that where the action is based upon discovery of a foreign object in the body of the injured person which is not discovered and could not reasonably have been discovered within such 2-year period, the action may be commenced within 2 years of the date of discovery or of the date of discovery of facts which would reasonably lead to discovery, whichever is earlier. This section applies to all persons regardless of minority or other legal disability, except that a minor under the age of 8 years at the time of the act, omission or failure complained of shall in any event have until his tenth birthday in which to commence an action. **N.H. Rev. Stat Ann. § 507-D:2 (2011) Limitation of Product Liability Actions.** Notwithstanding any other provision of law, all product liability actions must be commenced within the following time limits and not otherwise: I. Within 3 years of the time the injury is, or should, in the exercise of reasonable diligence, have been discovered by the plaintiff; and II. (a) No later than 12 years after the manufacturer of the final product parted with its possession and control or sold it, whichever occurred last; or (b) Where the defendant is a lessor, bailor or licensor of a product who is under a legal duty to inspect, maintain, repair, modify, alter or improve the product in question, no later than 12 years after the time at which the defendant ceases to have the use, possession or control of the product or ceases to be under the legal duty to inspect, maintain, repair, modify or improve it; or (c) Where the plaintiff's action is based upon a legal duty imposed by any governmental regulatory agency to alter, repair, recall,

Table A-6. (Continued)

State	Statute of Limitation
	inspect or issue warnings or instructions about the product or otherwise to take any action or precaution for the benefit of thc injured party, which legal duty arose after the defendant parted with possession and control of the product or sold the product, whichever came last, no longer than 6 years after the defendant first incurred the legal duty. This subparagraph does not shorten the time period established in subparagraphs (a) and (b) of this paragraph. III. Where the action is brought to recover indemnity or contribution for damages paid to or claimed by another, the action must be commenced within the same period established in RSA 507-D:2, I and II, plus 90 days. IV. The limitation periods established in RSA 507-D:2, I, II and III do not apply to actions based on the defendant's fraudulent misrepresentation, concealment or nondisclosure, or to any actions based upon a written contractual obligation which provides for a different period of limitation, or to actions brought under RSA 382-A:2-313, 2-314 or 2-315 which do not seek damages for or on account of injury to person or property.
New Jersey	**N.J. Rev. Stat. 2A:14-2 (2011) Actions for injury caused by wrongful act.** a. Every action at law for an injury to the person caused by the wrongful act, neglect or default of any person within this State shall be commenced within two years next after the cause of any such action shall have accrued; except that an action by or on behalf of a minor that has accrued for medical malpractice for injuries sustained at birth shall be commenced prior to the minor's 13th birthday.
New Mexico	**N.M. Stat. Ann. § 41-5-13 (2010) Limitations.** No claim for malpractice arising out of an act of malpractice which occurred subsequent to the effective date of the Medical Malpractice Act may be brought against a health care provider unless filed within three years after the date that the act of malpractice occurred except that a minor under the full age of six years shall have until his ninth birthday in which to file. This subsection [section] applies to all persons regardless of minority or other legal disability. **N.M. Stat. Ann. § 37-1-8 (2010) Actions against sureties on fiduciary bonds; injuries to person or reputation.** Actions **** for an injury to the person or reputation of any person, within three years.
New York	**N.Y. C.P.L.R. § 214-a (2011) Action for medical, dental or podiatric malpractice to be commenced within two years and six months; exceptions.** An action for medical, dental or podiatric malpractice must be commenced within two years and six months of the act, omission or failure complained of or last treatment where there is continuous treatment for the same illness, injury or condition which gave rise to the said act, omission or failure; provided, however, that where the action is based upon the discovery of a foreign object in the body of the patient, the action may be commenced within one year of the date of such discovery or of the date of discovery of facts which would reasonably lead to such discovery, whichever is earlier. For the purpose of this section the term "continuous treatment" shall not include examinations undertaken at the request of the patient for the sole purpose of ascertaining the state of the patient's condition. For the purpose of this section the term "foreign object" shall not include a chemical compound, fixation device or prosthetic aid or device. ***See also*** **N.Y. C.P.L.R. § 208 (2011) Limitations of Time: Infancy, insanity.** **N.Y. C.P.L.R. § 214 (2011) Actions to be commenced within three years: for non-payment of money collected on execution; for penalty created by statute; to recover chattel; for injury to property; for personal injury; for malpractice other than medical, dental or podiatric malpractice; to annul a marriage on the ground of fraud.** The following actions must be commenced within three years: 5. an action to recover damages for a personal injury except as provided in sections 214-b, 214-c and 215;

State	Statute of Limitation
	6. an action to recover damages for malpractice, other than medical, dental or podiatric malpractice, regardless of whether the underlying theory is based in contract or tort. **N.Y. C.P.L.R. § 214-c (2011) Certain actions to be commenced within three years of discovery.** 1. In this section: "exposure" means direct or indirect exposure by absorption, contact, ingestion, inhalation, implantation or injection. 2. Notwithstanding the provisions of section 214, the three year period within which an action to recover damages for personal injury or injury to property caused by the latent effects of exposure to any substance or combination of substances, in any form, upon or within the body or upon or within property must be commenced shall be computed from the date of discovery of the injury by the plaintiff or from the date when through the exercise of reasonable diligence such injury should have been discovered by the plaintiff, whichever is earlier. 4. Notwithstanding the provisions of subdivisions two and three of this section, where the discovery of the cause of the injury is alleged to have occurred less than five years after discovery of the injury or when with reasonable diligence such injury should have been discovered, whichever is earlier, an action may be commenced or a claim filed within one year of such discovery of the cause of the injury; provided, however, if any such action is commenced or claim filed after the period in which it would otherwise have been authorized pursuant to subdivision two or three of this section the plaintiff or claimant shall be required to allege and prove that technical, scientific or medical knowledge and information sufficient to ascertain the cause of his injury had not been discovered, identified or determined prior to the expiration of the period within which the action or claim would have been authorized and that he has otherwise satisfied the requirements of subdivisions two and three of this section. 5. This section shall not be applicable to any action for medical or dental malpractice.
North Carolina	**N.C. Gen. Stat. § 1-15 (2010) Statute runs from accrual of action.** (a) Civil actions can only be commenced within the periods prescribed in this Chapter, after the cause of action has accrued, except where in special cases a different limitation is prescribed by statute. (c) Except where otherwise provided by statute, a cause of action for malpractice arising out of the performance of or failure to perform professional services shall be deemed to accrue at the time of the occurrence of the last act of the defendant giving rise to the cause of action: Provided that whenever there is bodily injury to the person, economic or monetary loss, or a defect in or damage to property which originates under circumstances making the injury, loss, defect or damage not readily apparent to the claimant at the time of its origin, and the injury, loss, defect or damage is discovered or should reasonably be discovered by the claimant two or more years after the occurrence of the last act of the defendant giving rise to the cause of action, suit must be commenced within one year from the date discovery is made: Provided nothing herein shall be construed to reduce the statute of limitation in any such case below three years. Provided further, that in no event shall an action be commenced more than four years from the last act of the defendant giving rise to the cause of action: Provided further, that where damages are sought by reason of a foreign object, which has no therapeutic or diagnostic purpose or effect, having been left in the body, a person seeking damages for malpractice may commence an action therefor within one year after discovery thereof as hereinabove provided, but in no event may the action be commenced more than 10 years from the last act of the defendant giving rise to the cause of action. **N.C. Gen. Stat. § 1-52 (2010) Three years.** Within three years an action— (16) Unless otherwise provided by statute, for personal injury or physical damage to claimant's property, the cause of action, except in causes of actions referred to in G.S. 1-15(c), shall not accrue until bodily harm to the claimant or physical damage to his property becomes apparent or ought reasonably to have become apparent to the

Table A-6. (Continued)

State	Statute of Limitation
	claimant, whichever event first occurs. Provided that no cause of action shall accrue more than 10 years from the last act or omission of the defendant giving rise to the cause of action. **N.C. Gen. Stat. § 1-17 (2010) Limitations: Disabilities.** (b) Notwithstanding the provisions of subsection (a) of this section, an action on behalf of a minor for malpractice arising out of the performance of or failure to perform professional services shall be commenced within the limitations of time specified in G.S. 1-15(c), except that if those time limitations expire before the minor attains the full age of 19 years, the action may be brought before the minor attains the full age of 19 years. **N.C. Gen. Stat. § 1-46.1 (2010) Twelve years.** Within 12 years an action— (1) No action for the recovery of damages for personal injury, death, or damage to property based upon or arising out of any alleged defect or any failure in relation to a product shall be brought more than 12 years after the date of initial purchase for use or consumption. **N.C. Gen. Stat. § 1-53 (2010) Two years.** Within two years— (4) Actions for damages on account of the death of a person caused by the wrongful act, neglect or fault of another under G.S. 28A-18-2; the cause of action shall not accrue until the date of death. Provided that, whenever the decedent would have been barred, had he lived, from bringing an action for bodily harm because of the provisions of G.S. 1-15(c) or 1-52(16), no action for his death may be brought.
North Dakota	**N.D. Cent. Code § 28-01-16 (2011) Actions having six-year limitations.** The following actions must be commenced within six years after the claim for relief has accrued: 5. An action for criminal conversation or for any other injury to the person or rights of another not arising upon contract, when not otherwise expressly provided. **N.D. Cent. Code § 28-01-18 (2011) Actions having two-year limitations.** The following actions must be commenced within two years after the claim for relief has accrued: 3. An action for the recovery of damages resulting from malpractice; provided, however, that the limitation of an action against a physician or licensed hospital will not be extended beyond six years of the act or omission of alleged malpractice by a nondiscovery thereof unless discovery was prevented by the fraudulent conduct of the physician or licensed hospital. This limitation is subject to the provisions of section 28-01-25. 4. An action for injuries done to the person of another, when death ensues from such injuries, and the claim for relief must be deemed to have accrued at the time of the death of the party injured; provided, however, that when death ensues as the result of malpractice, the claim for relief is deemed to have accrued at the time of the discovery of the malpractice. However, the limitation will not be extended beyond six years of the act or omission of alleged malpractice by a nondiscovery thereof unless discovery was prevented by the fraudulent conduct of the physician or hospital. **N.D. Cent. Code § 28-01-25 (2011) Disabilities extend limitations on actions generally—Exceptions.** In cases alleging professional malpractice, the extension of the limitation due to infancy is limited to twelve years. **N.D. Cent. Code § 28-01.3-08 (2011) Statute of limitation and repose.** 1. Except as provided in subsections 4 and 5, there may be no recovery of damages in a products liability action unless the injury, death, or property damage occurs within ten years of the date of initial purchase for use or consumption, or within eleven years of the date of manufacture of a product. 2. This section applies to all persons, regardless of minority or other legal disability.

State	Statute of Limitation
	3. If a manufacturer, wholesaler, or retailer issues a recall of a product in any state or becomes aware of any defect in a product at any time and fails to take reasonable steps to warn users of the product defect, the provisions of subsection 1 do not bar a products liability action against the manufacturer or seller by a user of the product who is subsequently injured or damaged as a result of the defect.
Ohio	**Ohio Rev. Code Ann. § 2305.113 (2011) Limitation of actions for medical malpractice; statute of repose.** (A) Except as otherwise provided in this section, an action upon a medical, dental, optometric, or chiropractic claim shall be commenced within one year after the cause of action accrued. (B) (1) If prior to the expiration of the one-year period specified in division (A) of this section, a claimant who allegedly possesses a medical, dental, optometric, or chiropractic claim gives to the person who is the subject of that claim written notice that the claimant is considering bringing an action upon that claim, that action may be commenced against the person notified at any time within one hundred eighty days after the notice is so given. (2) An insurance company shall not consider the existence or nonexistence of a written notice described in division (B)(1) of this section in setting the liability insurance premium rates that the company may charge the company's insured person who is notified by that written notice. (C) Except as to persons within the age of minority or of unsound mind as provided by section 2305.16 of the Revised Code, and except as provided in division (D) of this section, both of the following apply: (1) No action upon a medical, dental, optometric, or chiropractic claim shall be commenced more than four years after the occurrence of the act or omission constituting the alleged basis of the medical, dental, optometric, or chiropractic claim. (2) If an action upon a medical, dental, optometric, or chiropractic claim is not commenced within four years after the occurrence of the act or omission constituting the alleged basis of the medical, dental, optometric, or chiropractic claim, then, any action upon that claim is barred. (D) (1) If a person making a medical claim, dental claim, optometric claim, or chiropractic claim, in the exercise of reasonable care and diligence, could not have discovered the injury resulting from the act or omission constituting the alleged basis of the claim within three years after the occurrence of the act or omission, but, in the exercise of reasonable care and diligence, discovers the injury resulting from that act or omission before the expiration of the four-year period specified in division (C)(1) of this section, the person may commence an action upon the claim not later than one year after the person discovers the injury resulting from that act or omission. (2) If the alleged basis of a medical claim, dental claim, optometric claim, or chiropractic claim is the occurrence of an act or omission that involves a foreign object that is left in the body of the person making the claim, the person may commence an action upon the claim not later than one year after the person discovered the foreign object or not later than one year after the person, with reasonable care and diligence, should have discovered the foreign object. **Ohio Rev. Code Ann. § 2305.10 (2011) Product liability claims and actions for bodily injury or injuring personal property; childhood sexual abuse.** (A) Except as provided in division (C) or (E) of this section, an action based on a product liability claim and an action for bodily injury or injuring personal property shall be brought within two years after the cause of action accrues. Except as provided in divisions (B)(1), (2), (3), (4), and (5) of this section, a cause of action accrues under this division when the injury or loss to person or property occurs. (B) (1) For purposes of division (A) of this section, a cause of action for bodily injury that is not described in division (B)(2), (3), (4), or (5) of this section and that is caused by exposure to hazardous or toxic chemicals, ethical drugs, or ethical medical devices accrues upon the date on which the plaintiff is informed by competent medical

Table A-6. (Continued)

State	Statute of Limitation
	authority that the plaintiff has an injury that is related to the exposure, or upon the date on which by the exercise of reasonable diligence the plaintiff should have known that the plaintiff has an injury that is related to the exposure, whichever date occurs first. (C) (1) Except as otherwise provided in divisions (C)(2), (3), (4), (5), (6), and (7) of this section or in section 2305.19 of the Revised Code, no cause of action based on a product liability claim shall accrue against the manufacturer or supplier of a product later than ten years from the date that the product was delivered to its first purchaser or first lessee who was not engaged in a business in which the product was used as a component in the production, construction, creation, assembly, or rebuilding of another product. (2) Division (C)(1) of this section does not apply if the manufacturer or supplier of a product engaged in fraud in regard to information about the product and the fraud contributed to the harm that is alleged in a product liability claim involving that product. (3) Division (C)(1) of this section does not bar an action based on a product liability claim against a manufacturer or supplier of a product who made an express, written warranty as to the safety of the product that was for a period longer than ten years and that, at the time of the accrual of the cause of action, has not expired in accordance with the terms of that warranty. (4) If the cause of action relative to a product liability claim accrues during the ten-year period described in division (C)(1) of this section but less than two years prior to the expiration of that period, an action based on the product liability claim may be commenced within two years after the cause of action accrues.
Oklahoma	**Okla. Stat. tit. 76, § 18 (2010) Torts: Limitation of action.** An action for damages for injury or death against any physician, health care provider or hospital licensed under the laws of this state, whether based in tort, breach of contract or otherwise, arising out of patient care, shall be brought within two (2) years of the date the plaintiff knew or should have known, through the exercise of reasonable diligence, of the existence of the death, injury or condition complained of; provided, however, the minority or incompetency when the cause of action arises will extend said period of limitation. ***See also* Okla. Stat. tit. 12, § 96 (2010) Persons under disability in actions other than to recover realty—** **Exceptions—Personal injury to minor arising from medical malpractice.** **Okla. Stat. tit. 12, § 95 (2010) Limitations of other actions.** A. Civil actions other than for the recovery of real property can only be brought within the following periods, after the cause of action shall have accrued, and not afterwards: 3. Within two (2) years: An action **** for injury to the rights of another, not arising on contract, and not hereinafter enumerated; an action for relief on the ground of fraud—the cause of action in such case shall not be deemed to have accrued until the discovery of the fraud.
Oregon	**Or. Rev. Stat. § 12.110 (2010) Actions for certain injuries to person not arising on contract; action for overtime or premium pay; action for professional malpractice.** (1) An action for assault, battery, false imprisonment, or for any injury to the person or rights of another, not arising on contract, and not especially enumerated in this chapter, shall be commenced within two years; provided, that in an action at law based upon fraud or deceit, the limitation shall be deemed to commence only from the discovery of the fraud or deceit. (4) An action to recover damages for injuries to the person arising from any medical, surgical or dental treatment, omission or operation shall be commenced within two years from the datewhen the injury is first discovered or in the exercise of reasonable care should have been discovered. However, notwithstanding the provisions of ORS 12.160, every such action shall be commenced within five years from the date of the treatment, omission or operation upon which the action is based or,

State	Statute of Limitation
	if there has been no action commenced within five years because of fraud, deceit or misleading representation, then within two years from the date such fraud, deceit or misleading representation is discovered or in the exercise of reasonable care should have been discovered. **Or. Rev. Stat. § 12.115 (2010) Action for negligent injury to person or property.** (1) In no event shall any action for negligent injury to person or property of another be commenced more than 10 years from the date of the act or omission complained of. (2) Nothing in this section shall be construed to extend any period of limitation otherwise established by law, including but not limited to the limitations established by ORS 12.110.
Pennsylvania	**40 Pa. Stat. § 1303.513 (2010) Medical Professional Liability: Statute of repose.** (a) GENERAL RULE.—Except as provided in subsection (b) or (c), no cause of action asserting a medical professional liability claim may be commenced after seven years from the date of the alleged tort or breach of contract. (b) INJURIES CAUSED BY FOREIGN OBJECT.—If the injury is or was caused by a foreign object unintentionally left in the individual's body, the limitation in subsection (a) shall not apply. (c) INJURIES OF MINORS.—No cause of action asserting a medical professional liability claim may be commenced by or on behalf of a minor after seven years from the date of the alleged tort or breach of contract or after the minor attains the age of 20 years, whichever is later. (d) DEATH OR SURVIVAL ACTIONS.—If the claim is brought under 42 Pa.C.S. § 8301 (relating to death action) or 8302 (relating to survival action), the action must be commenced within two years after the death in the absence of affirmative misrepresentation or fraudulent concealment of the cause of death. (e) APPLICABILITY.—No cause of action barred prior to the effective date of this section shall be revived by reason of the enactment of this section. (f) DEFINITION.—For purposes of this section, a "minor" is an individual who has not yet attained the age of 18 years. **42 Pa. Con. Stat. § 5524 (2010) Two year limitation.** The following actions and proceedings must be commenced within two years: (2) An action to recover damages for injuries to the person or for the death of an individual caused by the wrongful act or neglect or unlawful violence or negligence of another. (7) Any other action or proceeding to recover damages for injury to person or property which is founded on negligent, intentional, or otherwise tortious conduct or any other action or proceeding sounding in trespass, including deceit or fraud, except an action or proceeding subject to another limitation specified in this subchapter.
Rhode Island	**R.I. Gen. Laws § 9-1-14.1 (2011) Limitation on malpractice actions.** Notwithstanding the provisions of §§ 9-1-13 and 9-1-14, an action for medical, veterinarian, accounting, or insurance or real estate agent or broker malpractice shall be commenced within three (3) years from the time of the occurrence of the incident which gave rise to the action; provided, however, that: (1) One who is under disability by reason of age, mental incompetence, or otherwise, and on whose behalf no action is brought within the period of three (3) years from the time of the occurrence of the incident, shall bring the action within three (3) years from the removal of the disability. (2) In respect to those injuries or damages due to acts of medical, veterinarian, accounting, or insurance or real estate agent or broker malpractice which could not in the exercise of reasonable diligence be discoverable at the time of the occurrence of the incident which gave rise to the action, suit shall be commenced within three (3) years of the time that the act or acts of the malpractice should, in the exercise of reasonable diligence, have been discovered. **R.I. Gen. Laws § 9-1-13 (2011) Limitation of actions generally—Product liability.** (a) Except as otherwise specially provided, all civil actions shall be commenced within ten (10) years next after the cause of action shall accrue, and not after.

Table A-6. (Continued)

State	Statute of Limitation
South Carolina	**S.C. Code Ann. § 15-3-545 (2010) Actions for medical malpractice.** (A) In any action, other than actions controlled by subsection (B), to recover damages for injury to the person arising out of any medical, surgical, or dental treatment, omission, or operation by any licensed health care provider as defined in Article 5, Chapter 79, Title 38 acting within the scope of his profession must be commenced within three years from the date of the treatment, omission, or operation giving rise to the cause of action or three years from date of discovery or when it reasonably ought to have been discovered, not to exceed six years from date of occurrence, or as tolled by this section. (B) When the action is for damages arising out of the placement and inadvertent, accidental, or unintentional leaving of a foreign object in the body or person of any one or the negligent placement of any appliance or apparatus in or upon any such person by any licensed health care provider acting within the scope of his profession by reason of any medical, surgical, or dental treatment or operation, the action must be commenced within two years from date of discovery or when it reasonably ought to have been discovered; provided, that, in no event shall there be a limitation on the commencement of the action less than three years after the placement or leaving of the appliance or apparatus. (C) The provisions of this section apply only to causes of action which arise after June 10, 1977, and, as to causes of action which arise prior to June 10, 1977, the statute of limitations existing prior to June 10, 1977, applies. (D) Notwithstanding the provisions of Section 15-3-40, if a person entitled to bring an action against a licensed health care provider acting within the scope of his profession is under the age of majority at the date of the treatment, omission, or operation giving rise to the cause of action, the time period or periods limiting filing of the action are not tolled for a period of more than seven years on account of minority, and in any case more than one year after the disability ceases. Such time limitation is tolled for minors for any period during which parent or guardian and defendant's insurer or health care provider have committed fraud or collusion in the failure to bring an action on behalf of the injured minor. **S.C. Code Ann. § 15-3-530 (2010) Three years.** Within three years: (5) an action for assault, battery, or any injury to the person or rights of another, not arising on contract and not enum-erated by law, and those provided for in Section 15-3-545.
South Dakota	**S.D. Codified Laws § 15-2-14.1 (2011) Medical malpractice action: two-year limitation.** An action against a physician, surgeon, dentist, hospital, sanitarium, registered nurse, licensed practical nurse, chiropractor, or other practitioner of the healing arts for - malpractice, error, mistake or failure to cure, whether based upon contract or tort, can be commenced only within two years after the alleged malpractice, error, mistake or failure to cure shall have occurred, provided, a counterclaim may be pleaded as a defense to any action for services brought by a physician, surgeon, dentist, hospital, sanitarium, registered nurse, licensed practical nurse, chiropractor, or other practitioner of the healing arts after the limitation herein prescribed, notwithstanding it is barred by the provisions of this chapter, if it was the property of the party pleading it at the time it became barred and was not barred at the time the claim was sued or originated, but no judgment thereon except for costs can be rendered in favor of the party so pleading it. **S.D. Codified Laws § 15-2-12.2 (2011) Product liability action: three-year limitation.** An action against a manufacturer, lessor or seller of a product, regardless of the substantive legal theory upon which the action is brought, for or on account of personal injury, death or property damage caused by or resulting from the manufacture,

State	Statute of Limitation
	construction, design, formula, installation, inspection, preparation, assembly, testing, packaging, labeling or sale of any product or failure to warn or protect against a danger or hazard in the use, misuse or unintended use of any product, or the failure to provide proper instructions for the use of any product may be commenced only within three years of the date when the personal injury, death or property damage occurred, became known or should have become known to the injured party.
Tennessee	**Tenn. Code Ann. § 29-26-116 (2011) Medical Malpractice: Statute of limitations—Counterclaim for damages.** (a) (1) The statute of limitations in malpractice actions shall be one (1) year as set forth in § 28-3-104. (2) In the event the alleged injury is not discovered within such one (1) year period, the period of limitation shall be one (1) year from the date of such discovery. (3) In no event shall any such action be brought more than three (3) years after the date on which the negligent act or omission occurred except where there is fraudulent concea-lment on the part of the defendant, in which case the action shall be commenced within one (1) year after discovery that the cause of action exists. (4) The time limitation herein set forth shall not apply in cases where a foreign object has been negligently left in a patient's body, in which case the action shall be commenced within one (1) year after the alleged injury or wrongful act is discovered or should have been discovered. **Tenn. Code Ann. § 29-28-103 (2011) Products Liability Actions: Limitation of actions—Exception.** (a) Any action against a manufacturer or seller of a product for injury to person or property caused by its defective or unreasonably dangerous condition must be brought within the period fixed by §§ 28-3-104, 28-3-105, 28-3-202 and 47-2-725, but not with standing any exceptions to these provisions, it must be brought within six (6) years of the date of injury, in any event, the action must be brought within ten (10) years from the date on which the product was first purchased for use or consumption, or within one (1) year after the expiration of the anticipated life of the product, whichever is the shorter, except in the case of injury to minors whose action must be brought within a period of one (1) year after attaining the age of majority, whichever occurs sooner. (b) The foregoing limitation of actions shall not apply to any action resulting from exposure to asbestos or to the human implantation of silicone gel breast implants. (c) (1) Any action against a manufacturer or seller for injury to a person caused by a silicone gel breast implant must be brought within a period not to exceed twenty-five (25) years from the date such product was implanted; provided, that such action must be brought within four (4) years from the date the plaintiff knew or should have known of the injury. (2) For purposes of this subsection only, "seller" does not include a hospital or other medical facility where the procedure took place, nor does "seller" include the physician or other medical personnel involved in the procedure. (3) The provisions of this subsection only apply to causes of action not pending or decided on or before May 26, 1993. For the purposes of this subsection, a "pending case" is defined as a case actually filed by a silicone gel-filled breast implant recipient.
Texas	**Tex. Civ. Prac. & Rem. Ann. § 74.251 (2010) Statute of Limitations on Health Care Liability Claims.** (a) Notwithstanding any other law and subject to Subsection (b), no health care liability claim may be commenced unless the action is filed within two years from the occurrence of the breach or tort or from the date the medical or health care treatment that is the subject of the claim or the hospitalize-tion for which the claim is made is completed; provided that, minors under the age of 12 years shall have until their 14th birthday in which to file, or have filed on their behalf, the claim. Except as herein provided this section applies to all persons regardless of minority or other legal disability.

Table A-6. (Continued)

State	Statute of Limitation
	(b) A claimant must bring a health care liability claim not later than 10 years after the date of the act or omission that gives rise to the claim. This subsection is intended as a statute of repose so that all claims must be brought within 10 years or they are time barred. **Tex. Civ. Prac. & Rem. Code Ann. § 16.003 (2010) Two-Year Limitations Period.** (a) Except as provided by Sections 16.010, 16.0031, and 16.0045, a person must bring suit for **** personal injury, **** not later than two years after the day the cause of action accrues. (b) A person must bring suit not later than two years after the day the cause of action accrues in an action for injury resulting in death. The cause of action accrues on the death of the injured person.
Utah	**Utah Code Ann. § 78B-3-404 (2011) Statute of limitations—Exceptions—Application.** (1) A malpractice action against a health care provider shall be commenced within two years after the plaintiff or patient discovers, or through the use of reasonable diligence should have discovered the injury, whichever first occurs, but not to exceed four years after the date of the alleged act, omission, neglect, or occurrence. (2) Notwithstanding Subsection (1): (a) in an action where the allegation against the health care provider is that a foreign object has been wrongfully left within a patient's body, the claim shall be barred unless commenced within one year after the plaintiff or patient discovers, or through the use of reasonable diligence should have discovered, the existence of the foreign object wrongfully left in the patient's body, whichever first occurs; or (b) in an action where it is alleged that a patient has been prevented from discovering misconduct on the part of a health care provider because that health care provider has affirmatively acted to fraudulently conceal the alleged misconduct, the claim shall be barred unless commenced within one year after the plaintiff or patient discovers, or through the use of reasonable diligence, should have discovered the fraudulent concealment, whichever first occurs. (3) The limitations in this section shall apply to all persons, regardless of minority or other legal disability under Section 78B-2-108 or any other provision of the law. **Utah Code Ann. § 78B-6-706 (2011) Utah Product Liability Act: Statute of limitations.** A civil action under this part shall be brought within two years from the time the individual who would be the claim-ant in the action discovered, or in the exercise of due diligence should have discovered, both the harm and its cause.
Vermont	**Vt. Stat. Ann. tit. 12, § 521 (2011) Medical malpractice.** Notwithstanding section 512 of this title, and except as provided in sections 518 and 551 of this title, actions to recover damages for injuries to the person arising out of any medical or surgical treatment or operation shall be brought within three years of the date of the incident or two years from the date the injury is or reasonably should have been discovered, whichever occurs later, but not later than seven years from the date of the incident. No statute of limitations shall limit the right to recover damages for injuries to the person arising out of any medical or surgical treatment or operation where fraudulent concealment has prevented the patient's discovery of the negligence. Where the action is based upon the discovery of a foreign object in the patient's body, which is not discovered within the period of limitation under this section, the action may be commenced within two years of the date of the discovery of the foreign object. **Vt. Stat. Ann. tit. 12, § 512 (2011) Assault and battery; false imprisonment; slander and libel; injuries to person or property.** Actions for the following causes shall be commenced within three years after the cause of action accrues, and not after:

State	Statute of Limitation
	(4) Except as otherwise provided in this chapter, injuries to the person suffered by the act or default of another person, provided that the cause of action shall be deemed to accrue as of the date of the discovery of the injury.
Virginia	**Va. Code Ann. § 8.01-243 (2011) Personal action for injury to person or property generally; extension in actions for malpractice against health care provider.** A. Unless otherwise provided in this section or by other statute, every action for personal injuries, whatever the theory of recovery, and every action for damages resulting from fraud, shall be brought within two years after the cause of action accrues. C. The two-year limitations period specified in subsection A shall be extended in actions for malpractice against a health care provider as follows: 1. In cases arising out of a foreign object having no therap-eutic or diagnostic effect being left in a patient's body, for a period of one year from the date the object is discovered or reasonably should have been discovered; 2. In cases in which fraud, concealment or intentional misrepresentation prevented discovery of the injury within the two-year period, for one year from the date the injury is discovered or, by the exercise of due diligence, reasonably should have been discovered; and 3. In a claim for the negligent failure to diagnose a malignant tumor or cancer, for a period of one year from the date the diagnosis of a malignant tumor or cancer is communicated to the patient by a health care provider, provided the health care provider's underlying act or omission was on or after July 1, 2008. Claims under this section for the negligent failure to diagnose a malignant tumor or cancer, where the health care provider's underlying act or omission occurred prior to July 1, 2008, shall be governed by the statute of limitations that existed prior to July 1, 2008. However, the provisions of this subsection shall not apply to extend the limitations period beyond ten years from the date the cause of action accrues, except that the provisions of § 8.01-229 A 2 shall apply to toll the statute of limitations in actions brought by or on behalf of a person under a disability. **Va. Code Ann. § 8.01-243.1 (2011) Actions for medical malpractice; minors.** Notwithstanding the provisions of § 8.01-229 A and except as provided in subsection C of § 8.01-243, any cause of action accruing on or after July 1, 1987, on behalf of a person who was a minor at the time the cause of action accrued for personal injury or death against a health care provider pursuant to Chapter 21.1 (§ 8.01-581.1 et seq.) shall be commenced within two years of the date of the last act or omission giving rise to the cause of action except that if the minor was less than eight years of age at the time of the occurrence of the malpractice, he shall have until his tenth birthday to commence an action. Any minor who is ten years of age or older on or before July 1, 1987, shall have no less than two years from that date within which to commence such an action. **Va. Code Ann. § 8.01-249 (2011) When cause of action shall be deemed to accrue in certain personal actions.** The cause of action in the actions herein listed shall be deemed to accrue as follows: 7. In products liability actions against parties other than health care providers as defined in § 8.01-581.1 for injury to the person resulting from or arising as a result of the implantation of any prosthetic device for breast augmentation or reconstruction, when the fact of the injury and its causal connection to the implantation is first communicated to the person by a physician. **Va. Code Ann. § 8.01-243 (2011) Personal action for injury to person or property generally; extension in actions for malpractice against health care provider.** A. Unless otherwise provided in this section or by other statute, every action for personal injuries, whatever the theory of recovery, and every action for damages resulting from fraud, shall be brought within two years after the cause of action accrues. Section C. includes provisions that extend the statute of limitations for a medical malpractice action against health care provider.

Table A-6. (Continued)

State	Statute of Limitation
Washington	**Wash. Rev. Code Ann. § 4.16.080 (2011) Actions limited to three years.** The following actions shall be commenced within three years: (2) An action for taking, detaining, or injuring personal property, including an action for the specific recovery thereof, or for any other injury to the person or rights of another not hereinafter enumerated. **Wash. Rev. Code Ann. § 4.16.350 (2011) Action for injuries resulting from health care or related services—Physicians, dentists, nurses, etc.—Hospitals, clinics, nursing homes, etc.** Any civil action for damages for injury occurring as a result of health care which is provided after June 25, 1976 against: (1) A person licensed by this state to provide health care or related services, including, but not limited to, a physician, osteopathic physician, dentist, nurse, optometrist, podiatric physician and surgeon, chiropractor, physical therapist, psychologist, pharmacist, optician, physician's assistant, osteopathic physician's assistant, nurse practitioner, or physician's trained mobile intensive care paramedic, including, in the event such person is deceased, his estate or personal representative; (2) An employee or agent of a person described in subsection (1) of this section, acting in the course and scope of his employment, including, in the event such employee or agent is deceased, his estate or personal representative; or (3) An entity, whether or not incorporated, facility, or institution employing one or more persons described in subsection (1) of this section, including, but not limited to, a hospital, clinic, health maintenance organization, or nursing home; or an officer, director, employee, or agent thereof acting in the course and scope of his employment, including, in the event such officer, director, employee, or agent is deceased, his estate or personal representative; based upon alleged professional negligence shall be commenced within three years of the act or omission alleged to have caused the injury or condition, or one year of the time the patient or his representative discovered or reasonably should have discovered that the injury or condition was caused by said act or omission, whichever period expires later, except that in no event shall an action be commenced more than eight years after said act or omission: PROVIDED, That the time for commencement of an action is tolled upon proof of fraud, intentional concealment, or the presence of a foreign body not intended to have a therapeutic or diagnostic purpose or effect, until the date the patient or the patient's representative has actual knowledge of the act of fraud or concealment, or of the presence of the foreign body; the patient or the patient's representative has one year from the date of the actual knowledge in which to commence a civil action for damages. For purposes of this section, notwithstanding RCW 4.16.190, the knowledge of a custodial parent or guardian shall be imputed to a person under the age of eighteen years, and such imputed knowledge shall operate to bar the claim of such minor to the same extent that the claim of an adult would be barred under this section. Any action not commenced in accordance with this section shall be barred. For purposes of this section, with respect to care provided after June 25, 1976, and before August 1, 1986, the knowledge of a custodial parent or guardian shall be imputed as of April 29, 1987, to persons under the age of eighteen years. This section does not apply to a civil action based on intentional conduct brought against those individuals or entities specified in this section by a person for recovery of damages for injury occurring as a result of childhood sexual abuse as defined in RCW 4.16.340(5). **Wash. Rev. Code Ann. § 7.72.060 (2011) Length of time product sellers are subject to liability.** (1) Useful safe life. (a) Except as provided in subsection (1)(b) hereof, a product seller shall not be subject to liability to a claimant for harm under this chapter if the product seller proves by a preponderance of the evidence that the harm was caused after the product's "useful safe life" had expired.

State	Statute of Limitation
	"Useful safe life" begins at the time of delivery of the product and extends for the time during which the product would normally be likely to perform or be stored in a safe manner. For the purposes of this chapter, "time of delivery" means the time of delivery of a product to its first purchaser or lessee who was not engaged in the business of either selling such products or using them as component parts of another product to be sold. In the case of a product which has been remanufactured by a manufacturer, "time of delivery" means the time of delivery of the remanufactured product to its first purchaser or lessee who was not engaged in the business of either selling such products or using them as component parts of another product to be sold. (b) A product seller may be subject to liability for harm caused by a product used beyond its useful safe life, if: (i) The product seller has warranted that the product may be utilized safely for such longer period; or (ii) The product seller intentionally misrepresents facts about its product, or intentionally conceals information about it, and that conduct was a proximate cause of the claimant's harm; or (iii) The harm was caused by exposure to a defective product, which exposure first occurred within the useful safe life of the product, even though the harm did not manifest itself until after the useful safe life had expired. (2) Presumption regarding useful safe life. If the harm was caused more than twelve years after the time of delivery, a presumption arises that the harm was caused after the useful safe life had expired. This presumption may only be rebutted by a preponderance of the evidence. (3) Statute of limitation. Subject to the applicable provisions of chapter 4.16 RCW pertaining to the tolling and extension of any statute of limitation, no claim under this chapter may be brought more than three years from the time the claimant discovered or in the exercise of due diligence should have discovered the harm and its cause.
West Virginia	**W. Va. Code Ann. § 55-7B-4 (2011) Medical Professional Liability: Health care injuries; limitations of actions; exceptions.** (a) A cause of action for injury to a person alleging medical professional liability against a health care provider arises as of the date of injury, except as provided in subsection (b) of this section, and must be commenced within two years of the date of such injury, or within two years of the date when such person discovers, or with the exercise of reasonable diligence, should have discovered such injury, whichever last occurs: Provided, That in no event shall any such action be commenced more than ten years after the date of injury. (b) A cause of action for injury to a minor, brought by or on behalf of a minor who was under the age of ten years at the time of such injury, shall be commenced within two years of the date of such injury, or prior to the minor's twelfth birthday, whichever provides the longer period. (c) The periods of limitation set forth in this section shall be tolled for any period during which the health care provider or its representative has committed fraud or collusion by concealing or misrepresenting material facts about the injury. **W. Va. Code § 55-2-12 (2011) Personal actions not otherwise provided for.** Every personal action for which no limitation is otherwise prescribed shall be brought: (a) Within two years next after the right to bring the same shall have accrued, if it be for damage to property; (b) within two years next after the right to bring the same shall have accrued if it be for damages for personal injuries; and (c) within one year next after the right to bring the same shall have accrued if it be for any other matter of such nature that, in case a party die, it could not have been brought at common law by or against his personal representative.
Wisconsin	**Wis. Stat. § 893.55 (2010) Medical malpractice; limitation of actions; limitation of damages; itemization of damages.** (1m) Except as provided by subs. (2) and (3), an action to recover damages for injury arising from any treatment or operation performed by, or from any omission by, a person who is a health care provider, regardless of the theory on which the action is based, shall be commenced within the later of:

Table A-6. (Continued)

State	Statute of Limitation
	(a) Three years from the date of the injury, or(b) One year from the date the injury was discovered or, in the exercise of reasonable diligence should have been discovered, except that an action may not be commenced under this paragraph more than 5 years from the date of the act or omission. (2) If a health care provider conceals from a patient a prior act or omission of the provider which has resulted in injury to the patient, an action shall be commenced within one year from the date the patient discovers the concealment or, in the exercise of reasonable diligence, should have discovered the concealment or within the time limitation provided by sub. (1m), whichever is later. (3) When a foreign object which has no therapeutic or diagnostic purpose or effect has been left in a patients body, an action shall be commenced within one year after the patient is aware or, in the exercise of reasonable care, should have been aware of the presence of the object or within the time limitation provided by sub. (1m), whichever is later. **Wis. Stat. § 893.56 (2010) Health care providers; minors actions.** Any person under the age of 18, who is not under disability by reason of insanity, developmental disability or imprisonment, shall bring an action to recover damages for injuries to the person arising from any treatment or operation performed by, or for any omission by a health care provider within the time limitation under s. 893.55 or by the time that person reaches the age of 10 years, whichever is later. That action shall be brought by the parent, guardian or other person having custody of the minor within the time limit set forth in this section. **Wis. Stat. § 893.54 (2010) Injury to the person.** The following actions shall be commenced within 3 years or be barred: (1) An action to recover damages for injuries to the person. (2) An action brought to recover damages for death caused by the wrongful act, neglect or default of another.
Wyoming	**Wyo. Stat. Ann. § 1-3-107 (2011) Act, error or omission in rendering professional or health care services.** (a) A cause of action arising from an act, error or omission in the rendering of licensed or certified professional or health care services shall be brought within the greater of the following times: (i)Within two (2) years of the date of the alleged act, error or omission, except that a cause of action may be instituted not more than two (2) years after discovery of the alleged act, error or omission, if the claimant can establish that the alleged act, error or omission was: (A) Not reasonably discoverable within a two (2) year period; or (B) The claimant failed to discover the alleged act, error or omission within the two (2) year period despite the exercise of due diligence. (ii) For injury to the rights of a minor, by his eighth birthday or within two (2) years of the date of the alleged act, error or omission, whichever period is greater, except that a cause of action may be instituted not more than two (2) years after discovery of the alleged act, error or omission, if the claimant can establish that the alleged act, error or omission was: (A) Not reasonably discoverable within the two (2) year period; or (B) That the claimant failed to discover the alleged act, error or omission within the two (2) year period despite the exercise of due diligence. (iii) For injury to the rights of a plaintiff suffering from a legal disability other than minority, within one (1) year of the removal of the disability; (iv) If under paragraph (i) or (ii) of this subsection, the alleged act, error or omission is discovered during the second year of the two (2) year period from the date of the act, error or omission, the period for commencing a lawsuit shall be extended by six (6) months. (b) This section applies to all persons regardless of minority or other legal disability.

State	Statute of Limitation
	Wyo. Stat. Ann. § 1-3-105 (2011) Actions other than recovery of real property. (a) Civil actions other than for the recovery of real property can only be brought within the following periods after the cause of action accrues: (iv) Within four (4) years, an action for: (C) An injury to the rights of the plaintiff, not arising on contract and not herein enumerated.

Source: LexisNexis State Statutes database.

Note: The statutory language included is from the current version of the state's code which may not reflect very recent legislative enactments yet to be codified.

Many states also have various exceptions for a medical malpractice or product liability-specific statute of limitations depending on the age or status of the plaintiff, the time or manner of discovery, and the nature of the injury. For example, states commonly provide an extended statute of limitations if the plaintiff is a minor or suffering from a mental disability. Arizona, for instance, provides that "if a person ... is at the time the cause of action accrues either under eighteen years of age or of unsound mind, the period of such disability shall not be deemed a portion of the period limited for commencement of the action. Such person shall have the same time after removal of the disability which is allowed to others." (Ariz. Rev. Stat. § 12-502 (2011).) California, like many other states, extends time limitations for an action for damages sustained during birth. (*See, e.g.*, Cal. Civ. Proc. Code § 340.4 (2010).)[61] Louisiana and New York have a special time limitation for an action based blood transfusions tainted with HIV or AIDS. (*See* La. Rev. Stat. § 9:5628.1 (2011)[62] and N.Y. C.P.L.R. § 214-3 (2011).[63]) Many states, if not all, also have a statute of limitations on a specific product that is or was the subject of class action lawsuits. These include the Dalkon Shield Intrauterine Device (*see* Mass. Ann. Laws, ch. 260 § 2E (2010)) and breast implants (*see* Md. Code Ann., Cts. & Jud. Proc § 50116 (2011)). As these exceptions span a variety of areas across the 50 states, this table generally does not include these types of provisions, though the reader should be aware that many states have these special exceptions that may affect the general time limitations for certain actions.

End Notes

[1] For example, advocates of medical malpractice liability reform argue that current state tort law provides a costly and inefficient mechanism for resolving claims of health care liability and compensating injured patients, and that increasing liability insurance premiums are forcing doctors to curtail their medical practices and to engage in excessive "defensive medicine." Opponents of medical malpractice reform have argued that there is a very minimal relationship between health care costs and malpractice litigation, and that, "in reality, very few injured patients ever file a medical negligence lawsuit." *See* American Association for Justice, *Medical Negligence: A Primer*, February 2011 at 8. *See also* David M. Studdert, Michelle M. Mello, Atul A. Gawande, Tejal K. Ghandi, Allen Kachalia, Catherin Yoon, Ann Lousie Puopolo, Troyen A. Brenna, *Claims, Errors and Compensation Payments in Medical Malpractice Litigation*, 354 New Eng. J. Med. 2024 (2006). For more information on medical malpractice insurance and health reform, see CRS Report R40862, *Medical Malpractice Insurance and Health Reform*, by Baird Webel, Vivian S. Chu, and Bernadette Fernandez.

[2] Restatement (Second) of Torts, § 282.

[3] W. Page Keeton, Prosser and Keeton on Torts, § 31 (5th ed. 1984).

[4] David M. Harney, Medical Malpractice § 21.2 (3d ed. 1993).

[5] Nalder v. West Park Hospital, 254 F.3d 1168, 1176 (10th Cir. 2001).

[6] Marcia M. Boumil, et al., Medical Liability 65 (2d ed. 2003).

[7] *Id.*

[8] *See* Michael Higgins, *Homogenized Damages: Judge suggests using statistical norms to determine whether pain and suffering awards are excessive*, American Bar Association Journal (Sept. 1997) at 22.

[9] H.R. 5, § 4(a). A "health care lawsuit," defined as: any health care liability claim ... or action concerning the provision of health care goods or services or any medical product in or affecting interstate commerce, brought in a State or Federal court or pursuant to an alternative dispute resolution system *against* a health care provider, a health care organization, or the manufacturer, distributor, supplier, marketer, promoter, or seller of a medical product regardless of the theory of liability on which the claim is based, or the number of claimants, plaintiffs, defendants, or other parties, or the number of claims or causes of action, in which the claimant alleges a health care liability claim (emphasis added). H.R. 5 § 9(7). See Table A-1 for a 50-state survey on the definitions of medical malpractice action.

[10] H.R. 5, § 9(6).

[11] H.R. 5, § 4(b). Section 11 of provides that H.R. 5 would not preempt "any State law (whether effective before, on or after the date of enactment ...) that specifies a particular monetary amount of compensation or punitive damages (or the total amount of damages) that may be awarded in a health care lawsuit, *regardless of whether such monetary amount is greater or lesser* than is provided for under this Act." H.R. 5 § 11(c).

[12] H.R. 5, § 9(15).

[13] Health Affairs, Medical Malpractice and Errors: Issue Update, *Medical Liability and the Prospect of National Tort Reform*, September 7, 2010. *See also* Peter Perlman, *Don't Punish the Injured*, American Bar Association Journal (May 1986) at 34 ("By forever freezing compensation at today's levels, caps discriminate against a single class of Americans whose members are destined to suffer a lifetime of deprivation of dignity and independence.").

[14] An amendment to H.R. 5 to increase the $250,000 cap to $1,977,500 and index it to the Consumer Price Index Edward was rejected during the House Committee on the Judiciary mark up. *See also* Felsenthal, *Why a Medical Award Cap Remains Stuck at $250,000*, Wall Street Journal (Nov. 1995).

[15] In 1851, the Supreme Court wrote: "It is a well-established principle of the common law, that in actions ... for torts, a jury may inflict what are called exemplary, punitive, or vindictive damages upon a defendant, having in view the enormity of his offense rather than the measure of compensation to the plaintiff. We are aware that the propriety of this doctrine has been questioned by some writers." Day v. Woodworth, 54 U.S. (13 How.) 363, 371 (1851).

[16] W. Page Keeton, *supra* note 3, § 2.

[17] In *BMW of North American, Inc. v. Gore*, 517 U.S. 559, 616 (1996), the Supreme Court listed state statutes that provide for this restriction.

[18] H.R. 5, § 7(b)(2).

[19] Like noneconomic damages, it is possible that a state's law on punitive damages would not be affected. Section 11 of H.R. 5 provides that the bill would not preempt "any State law (whether effective before, on or after the date of enactment ...) that specifies a particular monetary amount of compensation or punitive damages (or the total amount of damages) that may be awarded in a health care lawsuit, *regardless of whether such monetary amount is greater or lesser* than is provided for under this Act" (emphasis added). H.R. 5 § 11(c)

[20] H.R. 5, § 7(a).

[21] H.R. 5, § 7(a).

[22] H.R. 5, § 9(13)

[23] H.R. 5, § 7(a).

[24] H.R. 5, § 7(b).

[25] John C. Nelson, M.D., AMA President-Elect, *AMA To Congress: Our Nation's Liability System Threatens Patients' Access to Health Care* (Oct. 2003). *See also* Steven Salbu, *Developing Rational Punitive Damage Policies: Beyond the Constitution*, 49 Fla. L. Rev. 247 (1997).

[26] Michael Rustad and Thomas Koenig, *Reconceptualizing Punitive Damages in Medical Malpractice: Targeting Amoral Corporations, Not "Moral Monsters,"* 47 Rutgers L. Rev. 975, 978, 980-981 (1995).

[27] Mark Thompson, *Applying the Brakes to Punitives—But is There Anything to Slow Down?*, American Bar Association Journal (Sept. 1997) at 68, 69.

[28] Adam Glassman, *The Imposition of Federal Caps in Medical Malpractice Liability Actions: Will They Cure the Current Crisis in Health Care?*, 37 Akron L. Rev. 417 (2004).

[29] American Association for Justice, *Medical Negligence: A primer for the Nation's Health Care Debate* at 10.

[30] Lisa M. Broman, *Punitive Damages: An Appeal for Deterrence*, 61 Neb. L. Rev. 651, 680 (1982).

[31] Tania Zamorsky, *Impact of High Court's Ruling In "Leatherman": Punitive awards reduced in four cases,* National Law Journal (Aug. 1, 2001), *citing* Cooper Industries, Inc. v. Leatherman Tool Group, Inc., 532 U.S. 424 (2001), which held that appellate courts should perform *de novo* review, rather than apply an abuse-of-discretion standard, when determining whether punitive damages are excessive in violation of the Eighth Amendment.

[32] Joseph T. Hallinan, *In Malpractice Trials, Juries Rarely Have the Last Word,* Wall Street Journal (Nov. 30, 2004).

[33] Annotation, *Propriety and Effect of "Structured Settlements" Whereby Damages are Paid in Installments Over a Period of Time, and Attorneys' Fees Arrangements in Relation Thereto*, 31 ALR 4th 95, 96.

[34] Paul J. Lesti, Structured Settlements § 21.5 (2d ed., 1993).

[35] Victor E. Schwartz, *Doctors' Delight, Attorneys' Dilemma*, Legal Times, Health-Care Law Supplement (Feb. 28, 1994) at 30.

[36] *Id.*

[37] This uniform act was promulgated in 1990; it was preceded by the 1980 Model Periodic Payment of Judgments Act. Both appear in volume 14 of the UNIFORM LAWS ANNOTATED.

[38] *Annotation, supra* note 33, at 96.

[39] A. Blackwell Stieglitz, *Defense Counsel Will Find the President's Medical Malpractice Proposals So Benign as to be Meaningless*, National Law Journal (Jan. 17, 1994) at 27.

[40] H.R. 5, § 4(d).

[41] *Report of the Tort Policy Working Group on the Causes, Extent and Policy Implications of the Current Crisis in Insurance Availability and Affordability* 64 (Feb. 1986).

[42] The Medical Care Recovery Act, 42 U.S.C. § 2651(a), provides: "In any case in which the United States is authorized or required by law to furnish or pay for hospital, medical, surgical, or dental care and treatment ... to a person who is injured or suffers a disease ... under circumstances creating a tort liability upon some third person ..., the United States shall have a right to recover ... from said third person, or that person's insurer, the reasonable value of the care and treatment ... and shall as to this right be subrogated to any right or claim that the injured or diseased person ... has against such third person to the extent of the reasonable value of the care and treatment...."

[43] Michael F. Flynn, *Private Medical Insurance and the Collateral Source Rule: A Good Bet?*, 22 U. Told. L. Rev. 39, 49 (1990).

[44] Amendment 14 to H.R. 5.

[45] *Report of the Tort Policy Working Group, supra* note 35.

[46] Barry J. Nace and Virginia C. Nelson, *Plaintiffs' Lawyers Have Already Seen Many of the Proposed Tort Reforms in the States, and Find Them Disastrous for Clients*, National Law Journal (Jan. 17, 1994) at 29.

[47] *See* National Conference of State Legislatures, *State Medical Malpractice Laws 2010*, available at http://www.ncsl.org/default.aspx?tabid=18516.

[48] H.R. 5, § 5.

[49] The Manhattan Institute, *Rethinking Contingency Fees* 28, 29 (1994).

[50] Stephen Daniels and Joanne Martin, *It's Deja Vu All Over Again: Plaintiff's Lawyers and the Evolution of Tort Law and Practice in Texas*, American Bar Foundation (Mar. 2009), http://www.americanbarfoundation.org/research/project/ 20.

[51] *See* studies cited in Association of Trial Lawyers of American, *Keys to the Courthouse: Quick Facts on the Contingent Fee System* (1994) at 4, 5.

[52] *Id.* at 6.

[53] To toll the statute of limitations means to stop its running.

[54] Colo. Rev. Stat. § 13-25-127 (2010).

[55] Haw. Rev. Stat. Ann. § 663-10.9 (2011).

[56] Iowa Code Ann. § 668.4 (2010).

[57] Idaho Code Ann. § 6-803 (2010).

[58] *See e.g.*, Ariz. Rev. Stat. § 12-568 (2010); Kan. Stat. Ann. § 7-121B (2010); Wash. Rev. Code Ann. § 7.70.70 (2011).

[59] Alaska Stat. § 09.60.080 (2011).

[60] N.D. Cent. Code § 28-26-01 (2011).

[61] The California provision states that an action "by or on behalf of a minor for personal injuries sustained before or in the course of his or her birth must be commenced within six years after the date of birth, and the time the minor is under any disability mentioned in Section 352 shall not be excluded in computing the time limited for the commencement of the action." Cal. Civ. Proc. Code § 340.4 (2010).

[62] La. Rev. Stat. Ann. § 9:5628.1 (2011) statute of limitation provision for actions for liability from the use of blood or tissue.

[63] Section 214-3 of N.Y. Civil Practice Law and Rules is the time limitation for an action to recover damages for personal injury caused by the infusion of such blood products which result in the contraction of the human immunodeficiency virus (HIV) and/or AIDS.

CHAPTER SOURCES

The following chapters have been previously published:

Chapter 1 - This is an edited, reformatted and augmented version of Congressional Research Services publication, No. R41894, from *www.crs.gov*, dated June 27, 2011.

Chapter 2 - This is an edited, reformatted and augmented version of Congressional Research Services publication, No. R41693, from *www.crs.gov*, dated May 25, 2011.

Chapter 3 - This is an edited, reformatted and augmented version of Congressional Research Services publication, No. RL31886, from *www.crs.gov*, dated October 2, 2009.

Chapter 4 - This is an edited, reformatted and augmented version of Congressional Research Services publication, No. R41661, from *www.crs.gov*, dated March 28, 2011.

INDEX

A

B

C

F

G

H

I

J

L

M

T

U

V